ENDORSEMENTS

"Martin Luther is rightly celebrated as a catalyst for the Reformation movement. By his own admission, it was the Word of God, and not he himself, who did all the work. Yet his achievements, under God, are not to be devalued on that account, and in this engaging collection of essays we are reminded of the contours of Luther's life, the central tenets of his thinking, and the wealth of his legacy both in theology and in church practice. The former monk-turned-gospel preacher would be the last to seek recognition for himself, but if these challenging studies succeed in reminding us of what God can do through one human life dedicated to his glory, they will well repay the time we spend reading them."

—DR. IAIN D. CAMPBELL
Minister
Point Free Church, Isle of Lewis, Scotland

"A quick glance at the subject and the table of contents (including the impressive array of contributors) is about all that is necessary to commend this book. If you are interested in Luther (and if you are not, you should be), and if you are looking to learn more about him, his life and ministry, the larger Reformation context, and his influence, then add *The Legacy of Luther* to your required reading list for the five-hundredth anniversary of the Reformation. This is a good time for the evangelical Protestant world to remember what the Reformation was all about. This book will help."

—DR. J. LIGON DUNCAN III
Chancellor and CEO
Reformed Theological Seminary

"Five hundred years after Luther's nailing of the Ninety-Five Theses, the message of the Reformation is needed now more than ever. Not only has the culture drifted away from the truth, but it seems that much of the church has gone with it. *The Legacy of Luther* offers a clear, bold, and much-needed call to a new Reformation. May God use it to bring renewal to both the church and the world."

—DR. MICHAEL J. KRUGER
President and Samuel C. Patterson Professor of New Testament
and Early Christianity
Reformed Theological Seminary, Charlotte, N.C.

"Martin Luther was very insistent that the Reformation was not his work nor the work of any man but a great work of God brought about by His powerful Word. Thus, Luther wouldn't have wanted us to celebrate him and his work but for us to share his biblical convictions and his commitment to Word ministry, so that God can accomplish His work today just as he did five hundred years ago. For this reason, *The Legacy of Luther* is a much-needed book. It helps us learn more about this great servant of God, but even more importantly, it reminds us of the biblical foundation of Luther's work. And most importantly, this book challenges us not just to be admirers of Luther but to follow in his footsteps. Surely, this is the great need of Luther's Germany today as it is a need of the church in all places at all times until Christ returns."

—MATTHIAS LOHMANN
Pastor, Free Evangelical Church, Munich
Chairman, Evangelium21, Germany

"Among all the servants the Lord has given his church, none has encouraged me more directly, more consistently, and with greater challenge than Martin Luther. He is one of the titanic figures on the world scene—a man without whom the history of the world as we know it could not be told. He has been for me an example of Christian faithfulness and courage in the face of trial, of steadfastness in the truth, and of a Christian man in full. Luther was a passionate follower of the Lord Jesus Christ, a happy husband and an eager father, a man whose pastor's heart should humble us all, and a man who was ready to stand, at risk of his life, on the word of God and not be moved. This new book by R.C. Sproul and Stephen Nichols is a wonderful introduction to Luther and to his theology. To know Luther the man is to know Luther the theologian. In this important book, Dr. Sproul and Dr. Nichols help us to meet Luther and to come to our own deeper commitment to the authority of Scripture and the sufficiency of Christ alone."

—DR. R. ALBERT MOHLER JR.
President and Joseph Emerson Brown Professor of Christian Theology
The Southern Baptist Theological Seminary, Louisville, Ky.

THE LEGACY OF LUTHER

THE LEGACY OF LUTHER

Edited by R.C. SPROUL *and* STEPHEN J. NICHOLS

ℝ *Reformation Trust* A DIVISION OF LIGONIER MINISTRIES, ORLANDO, FL

The Legacy of Luther

© 2016 by R.C. Sproul and Stephen J. Nichols

Published by Reformation Trust Publishing
a division of Ligonier Ministries
421 Ligonier Court, Sanford, FL 32771
Ligonier.org   ReformationTrust.com

Printed in Ann Arbor, Michigan
Sheridan Books, Inc.
September 2016
First edition

ISBN 978-1-56769-710-0 (Hardcover)
ISBN 978-1-56769-736-0 (ePub)
ISBN 978-1-56769-737-7 (Kindle)

Cover design: Brian Bobel
Interior design and typeset: Katherine Lloyd, The DESK

Scripture quotations are from the ESV® Bible (The Holy Bible, English Standard Version®), copyright © 2001 by Crossway, a publishing ministry of Good News Publishers. Used by permission. All rights reserved.

Library of Congress Cataloging-in-Publication Data
Names: Sproul, R. C. (Robert Charles), 1939-, editor.
Title: The legacy of Luther / edited by R.C. Sproul and Stephen J. Nichols ;
   foreword by John MacArthur.
Description: Orlando, FL : Reformation Trust Publishing, 2016. | Includes
   bibliographical references and index.
Identifiers: LCCN 2016013456 | ISBN 9781567697100
Subjects: LCSH: Luther, Martin, 1483-1546.
Classification: LCC BR333.3 .L44 2016 | DDC 284.1092--dc23
LC record available at https://lccn.loc.gov/2016013456

"I did nothing; the Word did everything."

—MARTIN LUTHER

CONTENTS

PART THREE: LUTHER'S LEGACY

CHRONOLOGY

1521	Placed under imperial ban, condemned as a heretic and an outlaw, May
1521–22	In exile at Wartburg Castle; translates New Testament into German
1522	Returns to Wittenberg
1524	Publishes first hymnal
1525	German Peasants' War
1525	Marries Katharina von Bora, June 13
1525	Writes *On the Bondage of the Will*
1527	Plague strikes Wittenberg; Luther's house becomes a hospital
1527	Writes "A Mighty Fortress Is Our God"
1529	Attends Marburg Colloquy, Oct. 1–4
1529	Writes Small Catechism
1530	Diet of Augsburg; Luther is unable to attend
1530	Augsburg Confession written by Philip Melanchthon
1534	Publishes complete German Bible
1537	Writes Smalcald Articles
1543	Writes *On the Jews and Their Lies*
1545	Writes *Against the Papacy at Rome, Founded by the Devil*
1546	Preaches last sermon at Wittenberg, Jan. 17
1546	Dies in Eisleben, Feb. 18; buried at Wittenberg

FOREWORD

JOHN MACARTHUR

Much of the discussion about Martin Luther these days seems to focus on his flaws rather than his faith, and that's a pity. It's quite true that some conspicuous blemishes mar the great Reformer's reputation. His most glaring faults arose from a brooding disposition. He seemed naturally prone to melancholy, impatience, a quick temper, and a sharp tongue. Even Luther's most devoted friends recognized those traits as serious shortcomings. At the Reformer's funeral, his lifelong friend and best-known colleague, Philip Melanchthon, noted in his eulogy that Luther had a reputation for "too much asperity"—then added, "I will not affirm the reverse."

There's no denying that Luther had feet of clay. In fact, to be completely candid, some of Luther's more infamous transgressions represented serious flaws. We are rightly concerned, for example, about his fondness for scatology, the sarcasm that characterizes his polemical writings, and his xenophobia—especially his anti-Semitism. It would be folly to pretend that these traits did not exist.

But Luther was, after all, a product of his times. It is a sad fact of history that parochial points of view, illiberal opinions, and harsh rhetoric were quite common features in the discourse of the early Reformation—on all sides of the debate. Sir Thomas More, for example, published a blistering critique of Luther's teaching so full of scatological invective that key parts of More's anti-Lutheran tract are unquotable. The English statesman called Luther many defamatory names, dismissing him as a liar, a "pestilential buffoon," a pig, an ape, a dolt, "a piece of scurf," and a "lousy little friar." (Ironically, More has been canonized as a saint by the Roman Catholic Church, and he is highly venerated by many of the same critics who cite Luther's own intemperate language as a way of discrediting the Reformer.)

Luther was of course influenced by some of the quirks and superstitions that infected the entire culture of sixteenth-century Europe. He and his contemporaries all stood with one foot in the Middle Ages and one foot in the Enlightenment. The vernacular of that time was frequently earthy to the point of obscenity—even in supposedly genteel settings such as courtrooms, palaces, and ecclesiastical meetings. Death was always imminent. Minds were rife with irrational fears.

Indeed, some of Luther's most disturbing imperfections were rooted in a naive, lingering attachment to certain medieval superstitions. His obsession with the devil, his fear of sorcery, and his occasional gullibility regarding tales of monsters and magic all reflect a mind swayed by the folklore of that time.

Nevertheless, it would be grossly inaccurate to categorize Martin Luther as a slave to superstition. His opposition to the Roman Catholic system began when he rejected (and openly challenged) the papal mythology regarding relics and indulgences. He especially objected to the Roman Catholic Church's practice of preying on the foolish superstitions of common people. Any objective evaluation of Luther's legacy must take all of that into account.

Luther himself was keenly aware that he was a fallen man with sinful proclivities. To his friend George Spalatin, he wrote, "I cannot deny that I am more vehement than I ought to be." He acknowledged that his temper and the sharpness of his pen sometimes carried him "beyond the decorum of modesty." But he was trying to walk a fine line. Luther firmly believed it was necessary for him to challenge the artificial refinement that squelched theological debate. He knew many men in positions of authority in the church who clearly saw and abhorred how corrupt the papacy had become, but they were too fainthearted to confront even the grossest ecclesiastical wrongdoing. In that same letter to Spalatin, Luther wrote, "I wonder where this new religion arose, in which *anything* said against an adversary is labeled abuse."

Luther's best-known intellectual adversary was Erasmus, the famous humanist, theologian, and Catholic priest. When someone complained to him about Luther's harshness, the Catholic scholar replied, "Because of the magnitude of the disorders, God gave this age a violent physician."

Luther faced his own sins honestly. He sought (and found) grace and full forgiveness in Christ alone. No one ever seriously accused Luther of unchastity, dishonesty, greed, or any other manifestation of the wanton lasciviousness to which Scripture points as the key identifying mark of false teachers (2 Peter 2:17–22). Impartial readers of the firsthand historical data will discover that Luther was a humble, generous, hospitable, respectable man of high principles, profound compassion, a tender conscience, unflinching truthfulness, and (above all) a passion for God. He was deeply beloved by those close to him, universally admired by his countrymen, and well respected (though perhaps reluctantly) even by many of his theological adversaries. Erasmus stated emphatically in a letter to Cardinal Thomas Wolsey that Luther's personal life and conduct were above reproach.

Nevertheless, Luther's more militant enemies have always emphasized and exaggerated his flaws. Some have even suggested that he may have suffered from some kind of mental illness. A simple reading of Luther's life and writings should disabuse any fair-minded person of that notion. Unfortunately, like any oft-repeated lie, the long-term, systematic defamation of Luther's character has attained the status of truth in the minds of many—especially those who can't be bothered to investigate history for themselves and have no real clue what Luther was genuinely like.

Getting to know the real Martin Luther is not terribly difficult. Few men's lives were more thoroughly documented than Martin Luther's before the development of electronic recording technology. Practically everything he said was dutifully noted and logged in journals and notebooks by Luther's regular dinner guests and students. Even offhand comments made in private conversations were taken down and collected. Those who made the notes originally intended them for their own private use. But two decades after Luther's death, a large anthology of these notes was assembled from multiple sources, edited, and published in German under the title *Tischreden,* which translates as *Table Talk.* The work fills six volumes in the Weimar edition of Luther's works.

Table Talk is a fascinating window into the mind and personality of Martin Luther. His wit, his keen insight, his boldness, and the strength of his convictions are clearly discernible. He is, as we would expect, passionate, opinionated, articulate, provocative, and zealous for the truth. Somewhat surprisingly, he is also jovial, engaging, well-versed in many subjects, and full of good-natured mischief. Unlike the younger Luther of the monastery, the Luther of *Table Talk* comes across as confident, mature, and secure in his faith. He was clearly a fascinating dinner host.

On the other hand, *Table Talk* is the source from which Luther's most objectionable remarks and opinions are generally drawn. It must be borne in mind that Luther himself had no hand in the publication of *Table Talk*. Different versions of the work were published by friends of Luther, and it is clear by comparing them that Luther's sayings have been heavily paraphrased and embellished by those who compiled the collection. It is also clear that Luther himself never intended most of these comments to be published. Though he was always a deliberate provocateur, Luther the writer was much more guarded than Luther the dinner host.

But it's not necessarily clear in the *Table Talk* entries when Luther is joking, purposely overstating his case, speaking satirically, playing devil's advocate, or just trying to get a rise out of his dinner guests. Luther's critics tend to read *Table Talk* through the same critical lens they use to appraise his more thoughtful publications. That is not fair to Luther. If our idle words were all recorded and subjected to the judgment of our adversaries, none of us would fare very well. We will one day give account for every careless thing we have said (Matt. 12:36). But we will answer to the just and merciful Judge of all the earth, not to an unfair or hostile jury of worldlings.

Despite all the publicity given to his flaws, Luther's indelible legacy will always be the example of his faith. His heroic courage, deep passion, steadfast integrity, infectious zeal, and all his other virtues are the fruit of his faith. This one man made an impact on the church and on the world that still influences all Bible-believing Christians today.

Luther would not have sought any honor for himself. By his own testimony, he owed everything to Christ. The story of his life confirms that testimony. Conversion utterly transformed Luther from an anxious, faint-hearted monk into a paragon of confident, contagious faith. The more he faced opposition from Rome, the more his biblical convictions deepened. Everything positive in Luther's life points back to his life-changing encounter with the righteousness of God and the glory of Christ in the gospel.

Of course, we can't affirm all the distinctive doctrines Luther taught. Virtually no one follows Luther's teaching slavishly today. Some of my own disagreements with his teaching are profound. But on the core principle of gospel truth—namely, the doctrine of justification by faith alone—Luther was sound and biblical. More than that, he was instrumental in recovering that biblical precept after it had long lain buried under an avalanche of Roman dogmas and papal traditions. Moreover, Luther held firmly to the authority of Scripture, the work of Christ, the power of the Holy Spirit, and the promises of God. For his firm stance in defense of all those truths, he deserves our profound gratitude and respect.

I'm therefore thrilled to see this anthology of essays honoring Luther on the five-hundredth anniversary of his nailing the Ninety-Five Theses to the door of the Castle Church in Wittenberg. It is a timely reminder that the church of our generation needs to be reformed anew. We desperately need someone like Luther to lift the banner of the gospel high, to shake worldly evangelicals out of their blind spiritual stupor, and to declare war on the devil in Christ's name.

WHY LUTHER MATTERS TODAY

R.C. SPROUL AND
STEPHEN J. NICHOLS

Two utterly fascinating Luther sites are the study at Wartburg Castle and the study in the Black Cloister in Wittenberg. The setting at the Wartburg could not be more impressive. Perched high atop a mountain, the medieval Wartburg Castle overlooks the town of Eisenach. The castle was built to impress—and it does. The particular room Luther used as his study at the Wartburg is considerably more modest. A simple chair complements an unobtrusive desk. An elephant vertebra functions as a footrest. Luther spent several months here as a "guest" after his staged kidnapping. Tourists would immediately pass this room by—were it not for the one who occupied it and for what that occupant accomplished in a few short months' time.

The effect is similar with the Augustinian Black Cloister at Wittenberg. The city of Wittenberg does not fail to impress, and the cloister, another medieval structure, commands attention. The study, however, is modest. Simply furnished and appointed, this room, too, would be passed by, were it not for what Luther accomplished in this place. Here, rather than a few months as at the Wartburg, Luther spent decades.

One could not overestimate the significance of these two studies and of the significance of the legacy of Martin Luther. If you could identify "command central" of the Reformation, you could do little better than name these two rooms, especially Luther's study in Wittenberg. What happened in these two studies changed the course of history.

Five hundred years after Luther nailed his Ninety-Five Theses to the door of the Castle Church in Wittenberg, his legacy continues. However, he did far more than write and post the Ninety-Five Theses. He lent roughly thirty years of his life to the cause of the Reformation. He wrote tract after tract, reams of letters, treatises, volumes of sermons—a virtual torrent of literature. He trained thousands of students over the length of his career as a professor and preached several thousand sermons over his career as a pastor. Men trained at Wittenberg took the Reformation with them to faraway places. His hymns continue to reverberate around the world, in languages that the German monk never knew.

The German Bible also needs to be considered. Luther worked on the New Testament while at the Wartburg. Later, at Wittenberg, there came the German translation of the Old Testament. Today, Luther's translation still leads German-speaking people to the words of eternal life.

The legacy of Martin Luther is vast and varied. This book offers an attempt to summarize that legacy. The chapters in the book form what is intended to be a "one-stop shop" for those who are interested in Martin Luther. It is written for those who may have little knowledge of him and also for those who know him fairly well.

The chapters have been grouped under three categories:

> Part One: Luther's Life
> Part Two: Luther's Thought
> Part Three: Luther's Legacy

Four chapters unpack Luther's life. The first, by Stephen J. Nichols, looks at the events leading up to the crucial moment of October 31, 1517, as well as the immediate events after the posting of the Ninety-Five Theses. Chapter two covers the initial, formative decade of the Reformation. Steven J. Lawson looks at the 1520s, a very full decade for Luther.

The Luther films of 1953 and 2003 end with the Diet of Augsburg and the Augsburg Confession. But Luther continued to live and work after that event. His wearied body grew old and he suffered much in his later life. Yet, he remained faithful. David B. Calhoun helps us not to miss these later years of Luther's life. Finally, Joel R. Beeke rounds out this section by looking at Luther the family man. Here we see Luther living his theology in plain view.

Part Two: Luther's Thought uses the five Reformation *solas* to summarize Luther's work and writings. Michael S. Horton starts with the foundational Reformation plank of *sola Scriptura* and explores Luther's doctrine of Scripture. Luther returned to the doctrine of Scripture throughout his life and writings. This chapter pulls all of this thought together in a succinct fashion. In chapter six, Guy Prentiss Waters looks at the central doctrine of justification by faith alone. *Sola fide* summarizes the heart of Luther's reforming efforts. Sadly, this doctrine is under attack today. This chapter offers not only a helpful historical look, but also looks to the present. Sinclair B. Ferguson continues to expound Luther's thoughts on salvation in chapter seven. He helps us see that we battle daily in our Christian lives, but we battle in the resources of our union with Christ. We live this life by grace. W. Robert Godfrey next focuses our attention on a topic very close to Luther, the doctrine of the church. In chapter eight, we see how the Reformation plank of *solus Christus* leads us to consider the church. Part two concludes with Gene Edward Veith's discussion of Luther's contributions to vocation. Vocation, according to Luther, is tantamount to loving and serving our neighbor. This is doctrine applied to life. In fact, Luther shows us a lived theology.

Part Three: Luther's Legacy looks at the variety of his work and contributions, as well as offering a sketch of his legacy through the centuries. Aaron Clay Denlinger looks at Luther as a biblical scholar and his work in biblical studies in chapter ten. This chapter also gives significant attention to Luther's translation of the Bible into German. Luther did not act alone. Scott M. Manetsch helps us see Luther among the other Reformers in chapter eleven. This chapter explores the friendships and the tensions Luther shared with his contemporaries and colleagues. Sean Michael Lucas leads us through the maze of the legacy of Luther in the Lutheran church. Chapter twelve starts with Luther's relationship to Philip Melanchthon and engages the various controversies after Luther's death.

Luther was almost as much of a musician as he was a theologian. He not only loved music, but left behind a legacy of hymns and started the project of Protestant hymnody. Terry Yount treats us to this aspect of Luther's legacy in chapter thirteen. Chapter fourteen turns to Luther in the pulpit. Derek W.H. Thomas shows how the sermon was central to the Reformation and how central Luther was in the development of preaching in the Reformation. In Luther's preaching, we see theological conviction and evangelistic zeal. That kind of preaching led to reformation and transformation in the sixteenth century. It can do the same for the twenty-first century.

This walk through Luther's life, thought, and legacy ends with reflections by R.C. Sproul. Here we see a pastor-theologian reflecting on the influence of a pastor-theologian. We are reminded, or perhaps we learn for the first time, how deeply pastoral Luther's concerns were. The posting of the Ninety-Five Theses was not a purely academic exercise. The theses were motivated by deeply felt pastoral concern, as were the rest of Luther's writings and efforts.

Luther was used of God five centuries ago. Of course, he would be the first to remind us that he did nothing. He stepped aside and let the Word do it all. And so we find the takeaway of these chapters and of this book. In Luther, we find the example of one who stood upon the convictions of God's Word. We see the example of one who ran everything, every single prevailing notion of his day, through the grid of God's Word. The result was a revolution, a Reformation. The result was a legacy that continues five centuries later. The moral of this story is clear. If the church today also stands confidently upon the convictions of God's Word, if the church today also runs everything through the grid of God's Word, then God may bless our work with faithfulness and bless our legacy with fruitfulness, too. I suspect Luther would have such aspirations for this tribute to him and for those who read this book.

> For as the rain and the snow come down from heaven
> > and do not return there but water the earth,
> making it bring forth and sprout,
> > giving seed to the sower and bread to the eater,
> so shall my word be that goes out from my mouth;
> > it shall not return to me empty,
> but it shall accomplish that which I purpose,
> > and shall succeed in the thing for which I sent it. (Isa. 55:10–11)

PART ONE

LUTHER'S LIFE

Chapter One

A GRACIOUS GOD
AND A NEUROTIC MONK

STEPHEN J. NICHOLS

O n January 17, 1546, Martin Luther preached what would be his last sermon from the pulpit of the Castle Church (*Schlosskirche*) in Wittenberg.
That same day, he wrote to a friend. He complained of the infirmities of
his age: "I am writing, my James, as an old man, decrepit, sluggish, tired, cold,
and now also one-eyed." He then sighs, ". . . and as a man who now that he
has died would be given the highly deserved rest (as it seems to me) he was
hoping for."[1] He would not be left in peace, however.

Luther's hometown of Eisleben faced a crisis. A dispute threatened the
civil order and even the ecclesiastical order. Worn out as he was, Luther
decided to travel to his hometown to settle the dispute. He set out from Wittenberg with his three sons and a few servants. They first made it as far as
Halle. Ice and storms made crossing the rivers a challenge. Luther imagina-
tively named the chunks of ice that floated threateningly toward their ferry,
alternating between Anabaptist opponents and Roman Catholic bishops and
popes. He might have been half-dead, but his humor was fully intact.

---

1 To Jacob Probst, January 1546, in *Luther's Works, Vol. 50: Letters III*, eds. Gottfried G. Krodel and
  Helmut T. Lehmann (Philadelphia: Fortress, 1975), 284–85. All references hereafter to *Luther's
  Works,* American edition, are abbreviated *LW.*

Halle was the home of Luther's longtime associate Dr. Justus Jonas. Since the debate at Leipzig in 1519, Jonas had been one of Luther's closest disciples. Jonas stood by him at the Diet of Worms. While Luther was in exile at Wartburg Castle, Jonas moved the Reformation forward at Wittenberg. Now, Jonas would accompany Luther on his final trip.

Luther and his enlarged traveling party made a triumphal entry into Eisleben. The hometown hero was welcomed with cheering crowds and escorted by a cavalcade. He preached that Sunday, January 31.

But the journey had taken its toll. Luther wrote to his beloved Katie of bitter winds and freezing rains, not to mention all those threatening chunks of ice. Luther was severely ill. An out-of-control fire, right outside of Luther's room, also threatened his life. His room itself was precarious. Plaster fell from the walls, which loosened a few of the stones from the wall. One stone, reported to be the size of a pillow, came rather close to falling on his head. These misadventures gave reason for Katie to grow anxious back at home. She fired off letters full of worry. So Luther wrote back, letting her know he missed her and adding, "I have a caretaker who is better than you and all the angels; he lies in the cradle and rests on a virgin's bosom, and yet, nevertheless, he sits at the right hand of God, the almighty Father."[2]

Luther wrote those words on February 7. Eleven days later, he died. Eisleben, the town of his birth, became also the town of his death. Justus Jonas preached his funeral sermon. The crowd spilled out of the church and filled the square. Luther's three sons would accompany their father's body back to Wittenberg, where more crowds would gather to pay their final respects.

Just before he died, Luther preached from his deathbed what would be his last sermon. The "sermon" consisted of simply quoting two texts, one from the Psalms and one from the Gospels. Luther cited Psalm 68:19: "Blessed be the Lord, who daily bears us up; God is our salvation." Then he cited John 3:16. Our God is indeed a God of salvation, and that salvation comes through the work of His Son. Luther could be at peace, though he was physically racked and surrounded by conflict.

Luther was not always at peace, and he didn't always think of God as the God of salvation. He initially feared God, at one point even muttering that he hated God. He was anxious throughout the early decades of his life. During these years, his life was far more struggle than rest. Prior to his "Reformation

---

2   To Mrs. Martin Luther, Halle, January 25, 1546, in *LW*, 50:302.

breakthrough" and his conversion, which likely took place in 1519, he was deeply troubled. Luther's life began in Eisleben in darkness. His life came to an end in Eisleben in the full light of the gospel. But this journey and this story are so much greater than one man. This singular story affected the whole of human history.

When Luther was born in Eisleben on November 10, 1483, there were only two options: a person either followed the ways of the Roman Catholic Church or was a pagan. When Luther died, on February 18, 1546, there was a new church in England. There was a new church in the Swiss city-states. And there was a new church in his own German lands. Two principles distinguished these churches from the church in Rome. The first principle concerned Scripture, while the second concerned the doctrine of salvation, specifically, the doctrine of justification. These two ideas express the essence of Reformation theology.

This essay tells the story of Luther's journey from darkness to light, a journey that took him from Eisleben to his heroic stand at Worms. It is a theological journey, a journey toward the Reformation planks of *sola Scriptura* and *sola fide*. It is also a literal journey, with a few key stops along the way. Six places in particular stand out during these early years of Martin Luther, from his birth in 1483 until his stand at the Diet of Worms in 1521: Eisleben, Erfurt, Rome, Wittenberg, Heidelberg, and Leipzig. Each one represents a milestone not only in Luther's journey out of darkness, but also in the history of the Reformation itself.

Eisleben: Hometown

Hans and Margarethe Luder welcomed their first child, a son, into the world on November 10, 1483. The next day, they took him to the church to be baptized. November 11 was the feast day of St. Martin of Tours, the fourth-century Roman soldier turned monk and bishop. So this young couple left the church with their baby baptized and named Martin Luder.

Hans Luder left the farmlands of his family to make what he hoped to be his fortune at the booming business of copper mining. He was what we would today call an entrepreneur. He risked what little money they had in acquiring rights for a mine and then labored relentlessly in attempts to pull profits from it. He even took on what amounted to a second job by managing another mine. His industry and tenacity paid off, gaining him a certain level of esteem in the town. Meanwhile, Margarethe managed the home. Without knowing for certain, historians believe Luther had eight siblings. Soon after Martin's birth, the family moved to Mansfeld.

As the oldest, and the primogeniture, it fell to Martin Luder to advance his family's standing. Martin would have to keep moving the family up the social and economic ladder. His parents worked hard so that he could have the education and the opportunities they had never had.

According to the custom of the time, young Martin would have attended Mass with his family. He would have been confirmed and would have partaken of his first Eucharist (the wafer only, not the cup, as was then the practice). The Luder family would have had their family shrine, centered around St. Anne, the mother of the Virgin Mary, according to tradition. Presumably, they would have been just as religious as the next family.

The Gospel accounts do not name Mary's mother. But that did not stop tradition. In the second century, an apocryphal text named the *Gospel of James*, written around 150, circulated purported details of Mary's childhood and life, identifying her mother as Anne. The church would reject this text as pure fiction. Still, that did not stop tradition. By the late medieval centuries, St. Anne had become the patron saint of miners. It was said that her womb was the source of two great jewels—Mary, and then, later, from Mary's womb, Jesus. A belief that was more superstition than theology held that honoring St. Anne would bring protection and prosperity to those who sought to bring jewels and treasure forth from mines. This was young Martin's theological and spiritual milieu.

Martin Luder's first schooling was at the town school in Mansfeld. Around his fourteenth year, he left Mansfeld for studies at Magdeburg and then headed off to Eisenach. His mother had come from Eisenach, and there were still relatives there. Martin could get the occasional family meal at one of their homes.

Eisenach would come to play a significant role later in Luther's adult life. Wartburg Castle overlooks the town of Eisenach. At the Wartburg, Luther assumed the name *Junker Jörg* while he was hiding in the aftermath of the Diet of Worms and his arranged kidnapping. That was in 1521. But back in the 1490s, Worms and his assumed persona of Knight George were a world away.

Erfurt: Becoming a Monk

During the course of his early studies, young Martin excelled, distinguishing himself from his classmates. These accomplishments opened the door for him to study at Erfurt. By the time Luther started there, the university was already more than a century old. The town, with a population hovering around twenty thousand, had industry, trade, and an extensive network of monasteries and churches. By 1502, Martin had earned his bachelor's degree. Three years later, he took his master's degree. He also took a Latinized form of his last name. He was now Martin Luther. He stayed in Erfurt, preparing for his doctorate in law.

Amid all of these academic accomplishments, Luther experienced intense struggles in his soul. No matter how much he experienced success, he could not escape the anxiety he felt. The German word for this anxiety is *Anfechtung*. It could be translated as "trial" or "affliction." Roland Bainton expresses the difficulty in grasping this word when he observes, "There is no English equivalent." *Anfechtung* refers to a deeply seated soul struggle. Bainton adds, "It may be a trial sent by God to test man, or an assault by the Devil to destroy man."[3] For Luther, we need to use the plural, *Anfechtungen*, as these crises of the soul came often. As his contemporaries did, Luther looked at spirituality and salvation as a contest between sins and merits. And it was a contest he nearly always lost.

In the summer of 1505, Luther traveled to his family's home in Mansfeld for an extended visit. On his way back to Erfurt, he got caught in a violent thunderstorm. He presumed the storm to be God's judgment on his soul. While at his family's home, he more than likely spent time before the family altar, the shrine to St. Anne. Now, in the clutches of the storm, he cried out to her, "Help me, St. Anne, and I will become a monk!" She was the only mediator he knew.

A stone to the east of Stotternheim marks the place. Luther's appeal to St. Anne is carved in the face of the granite. When Luther survived the storm and made his way back to Erfurt, he kept the words of promise. He turned his back on the law and became a monk.

Writing many years later, Luther confessed that if ever a monk could get to heaven by monkery, he was that monk. He did not leave his soul struggles behind when he entered the monastery. They followed him and, in fact, intensified. He later testified, "I tortured myself with praying, fasting, keeping vigils, and freezing—the cold alone was enough to kill me—and I inflicted upon myself such pain as I would never inflict again, even if I could."

---

3   Roland H. Bainton, *Here I Stand: A Life of Martin Luther* (New York: Abingdon, 1950), 42.

Johann von Staupitz was the vicar general of the Augustinian Order in Germany. Reports of Luther's legendary struggles in the monastery eventually made their way to Staupitz, who took an interest in the earnest and intense young monk. Staupitz was already moving away from some of the emphases of medieval Roman Catholicism, and he nurtured Luther's continued interest in reading Augustine directly.[4] Staupitz was also deeply concerned for Luther in the midst of his spiritual struggles. Recognizing Luther's academic abilities, Staupitz sent him to Wittenberg for biblical studies and theology. Luther took a BA in 1509, then returned to Erfurt to teach. Yet the distractions of academics did nothing to abate the struggles.

Rome: Holy City, Artistic Wonder, or Vanity Fair?

In 1510, Staupitz decided to send Luther on a pilgrimage to Rome. The Augustinian Order and the monasteries in Erfurt needed to renew their credentials. Staupitz thought this a fine occasion for Luther to be cured of his *Anfechtungen*. At it turns out, Staupitz miscalculated.

Rome plays a crucial role in the New Testament. Paul spent his final years there and, as we learn from tradition, was martyred there. So was Peter. The crown jewel of the New Testament is the epistle to the Romans. Rome was the capital city of a vast empire. Over the centuries, of course, Rome's stature continued to grow, as did the stature of the bishop of Rome. No longer one among many hundreds of bishops, the bishop of Rome eventually borrowed a title from the Caesars: *pontifex maximus*, the supreme priest.

The pope during Luther's visit, Julius II, was a patron of the arts. He commissioned the rebuilding of St. Peter's Basilica. Up to that point, the Basilica of St. John Lateran had served as the church's center, or "ecumenical mother." Pope Julius II set his sights on St. Peter's, across the Tiber. Julius also commissioned Michelangelo to begin painting the Sistine Chapel ceiling, a project that lasted from 1508 until 1512, coinciding with Luther's visit. Cardinals around Rome were also busy building palaces and cathedrals of their own. Church officials also called upon Raphael and a galaxy of other artists to adorn walls and ceilings, design buildings, and erect sculptures.

In 1510, Rome, the Holy City, was becoming the artistic wonder of the whole of the Western world. It was also a city of high debauchery. One historian describes the city this way: "Overall the life of Roman high society,

---

4 Bernard Lohse, *Martin Luther's Theology: Its Historical and Systematic Development* (Minneapolis: Fortress, 1999), 28.

both lay and clerical, was marked by a spirit of worldliness, moral laxity, and ostentatious luxury, in an unending round of banquets, parties, and hunts."[5] And, in 1510, Luther made his journey here.

Rome was roughly eight hundred miles directly south of Erfurt. Luther would have stopped at monasteries along the way. These monasteries were strategically placed to house pilgrims as they made their way from various places across Europe to the Holy See. Luther would have visited many shrines along the way, and he would have spent most of the hours of the pilgrimage in prayerful contemplation and meditation—all in preparation for this visit to the Holy City. He would have traversed the Alps through Germany, through the Swiss city-states and on to Italy. When he reached Rome, he would have gone through the ancient Aurelian Walls and across the Piazza del Popolo, Rome's northern public square. By the time Luther made his way down to the Basilica of St. John Lateran, he would have seen enough to make his stomach turn. Prostitutes, public lewdness, and hawkers of all sorts of wares would have pestered him along the cobbled city streets.[6]

One of the focal points for pilgrims to Rome was the *scala sancta*. Here, Luther's disillusionment reached its apex. These twenty-eight marble steps are believed to be the very steps that led up to the praetorium of Pontius Pilate in Jerusalem—the very steps Jesus walked on the way to His trial. Emperor Constantine had them removed and relocated to Rome, a gift to his rather pious mother, Helen. Today, they are housed in their own building across the street from St. John Lateran. In 1510, there would have been a table set up at the base of the steps where priests collected coins and handed out indulgences. Pilgrims, after they had turned over a few coins, would climb the steps on their knees, praying the rosary as they shuffled up and down. Luther waited his turn and then joined the stream of penitent pilgrims.

When Luther reached the top, no spiritual awakening greeted him. No waves of peace rolled gently over his soul. All he could say was, "Who knows whether it is so?"[7] Years later, he had a much more scathing review of Rome: "This city has become a harlot." He went on to say that he would not have believed it had he not seen it. Needless to say, Staupitz did not receive a

---

5 Agostino Borromeo, "Rome," in *The Oxford Encyclopedia of the Reformation* (Oxford, England: Oxford University Press, 1996), 3:448.

6 One can not help draw an allusion to Christian's walk through "Vanity Fair" in Bunyan's *The Pilgrim's Progress*, though what Luther actually saw was far worse than what Bunyan imagined.

7 Bainton, *Here I Stand,* 51.

favorable report, and his young charge was slipping even further away. The neurotic monk was becoming even worse.

Wittenberg: Fountainhead of the Reformation

In desperation, Staupitz sent Luther back to Wittenberg for more studies. He entered the Black Cloister of the Augustinian Order in 1511. He completed his doctoral studies. To qualify for his doctorate, he had to master the preeminent theological text of the day, Peter Lombard's *Sentences*. This text had a profound and far-reaching impact on Luther, but the impact did not come through Lombard's teachings or conclusions. Instead, the impact came through the figure Lombard quoted: Augustine. B.B. Warfield would later say that the Reformation was nothing short of the recovery of Augustine's doctrine of salvation.[8] Once Luther earned his doctorate, he took his place on the theology faculty at the University of Wittenberg.

Thanks to his exposure to Augustine, Luther took one step forward and two steps back in his understanding of sin. He learned that our problem is not *sins* in the plural. This quantifying of sin gets to the heart of the eclipse of the gospel in later medieval Roman Catholicism. If sin is quantified, then we look to merits or graces as the remedy. Baptism atones for original sin, or the sin of Adam that was imputed to us. What remains is our actual sins. Again, the quantity of sins is the issue. And so, the other sacraments, in addition to the sacrament of baptism, come into play. Through penance, it is possible to undo the effects of our sins.

Indulgences arose through the evolution of the doctrine and practice of penance. These documents allowed for the skipping of a few steps in the process of being restored to the good graces of the church (and thus, of God). Penance for sin entails going to confession and receiving absolution (pending, of course, the completion of the tasks prescribed by the priest). Having done the penance, one could then attend Mass and receive the grace of the Eucharist. Or, alternatively, one could skip all these steps through the simple purchase of an indulgence.

Indulgences first appeared during the Crusades. According to the Roman Catholic Church, going on a crusade was certainly a work worthy of the forgiveness of sins. But some noble families did not want to risk losing their sons in the process. Consequently, they could pay someone to go on a

---

8 Benjamin B. Warfield, "Studies in Tertullian and Augustine" in *The Works of Benjamin B. Warfield* (Grand Rapids, Mich.: Baker, 1930), 4:130, 131, 285, 411.

crusade in the son's place—they could purchase an indulgence. The practice of buying indulgences evolved over the centuries until it reached its nadir in the sixteenth century, on the eve of Luther's stand against the Roman Catholic Church.

The idea of the quantity of sins led to a similar notion of the quantity of grace, or graces. In this view, some people have more graces than they need; they are deemed *saints* by the Roman church. Their grace, their works of supererogation (works above and beyond), are stored in a treasure chest in heaven. Of course, Mary is "full of grace" and, consequently, stands at the head of this line of saints. This expression "full of grace" (from the Vulgate's translation of Luke 1:28) had come to mean that Mary possessed a great quantity of grace that could be applied to those who prayed to her or applied to the penitent who sought her out.

The pope holds the keys to this treasury of graces, and the sacraments—all controlled by the church—are the means by which those graces reach the people. All of these graces come to the penitent ultimately because of what Christ accomplished on the cross. The question is, how do those graces get mediated to the sinner? The medieval Roman answer was loud and clear: those graces only come through the church. Grace is not immediate; that is, it does not come without a mediator. Grace can only come through the church. Again, the pope holds the keys. It is at this point that Luther enters the discussion.

What Luther learned about sin from Augustine upset this entire superstructure. He learned that we are sinners at the root (*radix*, from which we derive the English word "radical," is the Latin word).[9] That's one step forward. We are sinners, and God is holy. Luther saw all this poignantly. He was a sinner through and through, and he knew this to be true. God is holy and righteous through and through, which he also knew to be true. A sinner could never please a holy God. Luther writes, adding some color as only he can:

> For this reason it is plain insanity to say that a man of his own powers can love God above all things and can perform the works of the law according to the substance of the act, even if not according to the intentions of Him who gave the commandment, because he is not in a state of grace. O fools. O pig-theologians.[10]

---

9 Lohse, *Martin Luther's Theology*, 70–72.
10 *LW, Vol. 25: Lectures on Romans*, ed. Jaroslav Pelikan (St. Louis: Concordia, 1972), 261.

Not even the most assiduous monk of all time can do anything to please God. This realization led Luther to this pronouncement:

> I did not love, yes, I hated the righteous God who punishes sinners, and secretly, if not blasphemously, certainly murmuring greatly, I was angry with God, and said, "As if, indeed, it is not enough, that miserable sinners, eternally lost through original sin, are crushed by every kind of calamity by the law of the Decalogue, without having God add pain to pain by the gospel and also by the gospel threatening us with his righteousness and wrath!" Thus I raged with a fierce and troubled conscience.[11]

The years between 1511 and 1517 were likely the hardest years of what was a hard-lived life. Luther had his routines. He would lecture at the university. Frederick the Wise, elector of Saxony, had not only built up the city and the Castle Church, but had also used his considerable wealth to establish Wittenberg's place among the constellation of European universities. No expense was spared, scholars were rewarded, and the university grew in stature.

Frederick marveled at his professor of theology. Luther was a scintillating lecturer, capable of both incisive thinking and good humor. If you have ever read Erasmus' satire on the church at this time, *In Praise of Folly*, you know that there was much fodder for comedic moments. Luther's wit, coupled with these opportune times, meant that his students would be well entertained. Humor, especially sarcasm, tends to reveal realities that are more tragic than comedic. So it was in this case. Luther was troubled because these were dark times.

As the summer of 1517 came to an end and students filed back into the classrooms for fall semester lectures, Frederick announced his plans to reveal the latest relics he had acquired for the Castle Church. Through the remarkable invention of the printing press, he published a catalog of these relics. November 1, 1517—All Saints' Day—was set aside as the day to unveil these new relics to the public.

Luther was troubled. He was even more troubled by what had recently come from Rome. After Julius II's death in 1513, Leo X ascended the papal throne. Leo expanded on the quest to make Rome the artistic center of the

---

11 Martin Luther, "Preface to the Complete Edition of Luther's Latin Writings," *LW, Vol. 34: Career of the Reformer IV* (St. Louis: Concordia, 1960), 336–37. This text was written in 1545 by Luther as he recalled his conversion.

Western world. The writer Alexander Dumas famously quipped that under Leo X, "Christianity assumed a pagan character."[12] Leo inherited debt from his predecessor and plunged the church even further into the red through his lavish and extravagant tastes. Among those who received his patronage were the artists Michelangelo, Raphael, Leonardo da Vinci, Correggio, Titian, Andrea del Sarto, Fra Bartolomeo, Giulio Romano, and Ariosto, and the author of *The Prince,* Niccolo Machiavelli. With an exhausted treasury, Leo needed a way to raise funds.

The solution was a deal with Albert, archbishop of Magdeburg. Albert wanted to obtain the archbishopric of Mainz. It was unlawful under canon law to hold two bishoprics, however, so Albert needed a papal dispensation. And to pay for the expenses related to his elevation at Mainz, Albert had had to take out a loan. Leo granted permission, in exchange for half of the money Albert raised to pay back his loan.

To raise the money, Albert recruited the Dominican friar Johann Tetzel to carry out an unprecedented sale of indulgences. As he traveled through the German lands, Tetzel's retinue would announce his impending arrival with much fanfare, and upon arriving in a town, he would preach on the pains of hell and the dangers of purgatory in the town square. Those who heard his message of judgment were well primed to purchase the offered indulgences to help offset their just-highlighted wicked deeds.

Before long, Tetzel set up shop across the Elbe River from Wittenberg. Frederick (not wanting competition with his relics and the associated indulgence sales) would not allow Tetzel to enter his territory, but Luther's parishioners were crossing the river and purchasing indulgences all the same.[13] This created a pastoral crisis for Luther. His parishioners had a piece of paper that meant they no longer had to go to confession in order to go to Mass. Luther, their parish priest, was compelled to administer the sacrament to them because of that piece of paper. He knew they were eating "unworthily." He also knew there was little he could do about it. That little piece of paper they held had the pope's seal.

These two fronts—the relics at Wittenberg and Tetzel's indulgence sale—bore down hard on Luther. As a scholar, he took up his primary weapon, the pen, and wrote a series of theses that called for a debate within the church to discuss these practices. By the time he was done, his list numbered ninety-five.

---

12 Alexander Dumas, *The Cenci* (New York: P.F. Collier & Son, 1910), 362.
13 Bainton, *Here I Stand,* 76.

On October 31, 1517, All Hallow's Eve, or the eve before All Saints' Day, Luther posted the Ninety-Five Theses on the Castle Church door in Wittenberg. The first salvo was fired. The theses that highlighted the financial aspects of the indulgence sale hit a ready audience. Bainton tells us, "This polemic would evoke a deep *Ja wohl* among the Germans, who for some time had been suffering from a sense of grievance against the venality of the Italian *curia*." Bainton adds, though, that "the financial aspect was the least in Luther's eyes."

Thesis 92 probably best expresses the aspect of indulgences that was the most virulent in Luther's eyes. He declared, "Away, then, with all those prophets who say to the people of Christ, 'Peace, peace,' and there is no peace!"[14] Sucking money from German peasants was one thing; giving them a false gospel was another altogether.

Luther prefaced the Ninety-Five Theses with these words, revealing his motivation: "Out of love for the truth and the desire to bring it to light." He then turned his attention immediately to the idea of penance. The first thesis declares, "When our Lord and Master Jesus Christ said 'Repent,' he intended that the entire life of believers should be repentance." In the second thesis, he says "repentance" cannot mean "penance."[15]

The importance of this distinction is tied to Luther's newfound access to the New Testament's original language. The year before Luther posted his theses, Erasmus had published his Greek New Testament. It was actually a parallel text, with the Latin Vulgate in one column and the Greek text in another. This was an unprecedented publishing event. And it led Luther right back to the source of all theology, right back to the original text. When Luther examined the Greek text, he noticed something striking at Matthew 4:17. The Latin Vulgate translated the Greek word meaning "repent" as *poenitentiam agite*, or "do penance." Luther knew this to be a mistranslation. Penance is about an outward act, or multiple outward acts. Repentance is a whole-souled heart change that results in outward acts of obedience. This mistranslation of the Vulgate set up a domino chain that fell in a tragically wrong direction. Instead of falling in line as the next domino in the chain, Luther went back to the source and began building his theology from there.[16]

There is no way Luther could have calculated the impact that the nailing

---

14 *Martin Luther's Ninety-Five Theses*, ed. Stephen J. Nichols (Phillipsburg, N.J.: P&R, 2002), 47.
15 Ibid., 23.
16 Ibid., 22.

of the Ninety-Five Theses to the church door would have. He certainly did not fully appreciate the ramifications of it at the moment. But soon, those ramifications rolled in like wave upon wave. Things would need be torn down before they could be built back aright.

Luther sent a copy of the theses to Albert. Remember, Luther cared deeply about his church and he longed for an open debate. Albert then sent a copy to Rome. Luther wanted a debate. But he got far more. Within months, controversy swirled.

Heidelberg: The Cross Alone

Nestled along the Rhine River, Heidelberg was the site for the General Chapter, or assembly, of the Augustinian Order in May 1518. Staupitz, the general vicar (or head) of the order, seized this moment for Luther to speak to the crisis caused by the Ninety-Five Theses. Luther responded by drafting a new set of theses, the Twenty-Eight Theses for the Heidelberg Disputation.[17] Though far less known than the theses nailed to the church door, these theses are the most important text during this period of Luther's development. At one point in his life, Luther would declare, "*Crux sola est nostra theologia*," meaning, "The cross alone is our theology." That singular expression crystalizes what Luther was aiming at in the Twenty-Eight Theses at Heidelberg.[18]

Before enumerating the theses, Luther wrote a short introductory paragraph as a preface. The preface is essential for understanding the work as a whole. Luther starts off by noting that he distrusts "completely our own wisdom," and so he relies on and draws from "St. Paul, the especially chosen vessel and instrument of Christ, and also from St. Augustine, his most trustworthy interpreter."[19]

The Latin expression *ad fontes*, "to the sources," served as the Renaissance battle cry. It meant going back to the originals, or the fountainheads. This can be seen in the revival of Greco-Roman architecture and art. It can be seen in the desire to read Plato and Aristotle directly, instead of reading layers of medieval interpretations of Plato and Aristotle. In theology, it meant

---

17 After the twenty-eight "theological" theses, Luther adds a dozen more "philosophical" theses disparaging Aristotle. Technically, there were forty theses at the Heidelberg Disputation.

18 See Lohse, *Martin Luther's Theology*, 39.

19 Martin Luther, "Heidelberg Disputation," in *Martin Luther's Basic Theological Writings*, ed. Timothy F. Lull (Minneapolis: Fortress, 1989), 30. For the full text and a current scholarly discussion of the Heidelberg Theses, see also *The Annotated Luther, Volume 1: The Roots of Reform*, ed. Timothy J. Wengert (Minneapolis: Fortress, 2015), 67–120.

reading the Bible, and Augustine too, rather than reading layers of commentary on the primary sources. *Ad fontes* of the Renaissance is mirrored in the counterpart *sola Scriptura* of the Reformation. Luther's short preface declares the sources of his teaching—Paul and Augustine. He also admits—and we need to see this—that the hearers and readers of the Twenty-Eight Theses will have to determine how "well or poorly" Luther deduced them from Paul and Augustine. Luther's source, however, was the fountainhead. It was the "source" that led him to see how wrong the practice of penance became back in October 1517. The more Luther looked to the sources, the more wrong he saw in the church of his day.

After the short paragraph preface comes the Twenty-Eight Theses. They compare and contrast what Luther calls a "theologian of glory" and a "theologian of the cross." Typically, we associate glory, especially the glory of God, with good things. In this case, however, Luther sees a theologian of glory as a bad thing. A theologian of glory is the same as the false prophet who declares peace in thesis 92 of the Ninety-Five Theses. In Heidelberg thesis 21, Luther writes, "A theologian of glory calls evil good and good evil." In using the term *glory*, Luther is talking about the inane idea that humanity itself has its own glory, or that humanity has the ability to please God and to perform righteousness. This idea leads the theologian of glory to disdain God's grace. Divine grace is the good thing that a theologian of glory calls evil. In short, the theologian of glory exults in human ability and in works-righteousness.

Standing in contrast to the theologian of glory is the theologian of the cross. The theologian of the cross starts with us—more specifically, with our misery. Thesis 18 reads, "It is certain that man must utterly despair of his own ability before he is prepared to receive the grace of Christ." Consequently, thesis 25 informs us, "He is not righteous who does much, but he who, without work, believes much in Christ."

The theologian of glory actually does far worse than call grace evil. The theologian of glory, the one who trusts in human ability and trusts in the accumulation of merits and works, actually despises Christ.

Then, in the last of the Twenty-Eight Theses, Martin Luther writes what very well may be the most beautiful sentence he ever wrote: "The love of God does not find, but creates, that which is pleasing to it." The love of God will never find anything pleasing to it in us, because we are all sinners who are unrighteous and utterly distasteful to the Holy God. And so, God makes us righteous. He (re)creates us.

One of the young monks sitting in the audience listening to Luther present and debate the Twenty-Eight Theses was Martin Bucer (1491–1551). Historian David F. Wright observes, "This experience was [Bucer's] evangelical conversion."[20] Bucer went on to be the leader of the Reformation at Strasbourg. Young Calvin desired to study there, but was stopped at Geneva for a season. When Geneva expelled Calvin, he finally got his wish and spent the years from 1538 to 1541 with Bucer. The effects of the Twenty-Eight Theses were far-reaching.

They were also near-reaching, and they led to yet another disputation for Luther at Augsburg with Cardinal Thomas Cajetan in October 1518. Cajetan demanded that Luther recant. In the middle of the night, Luther fled on horseback, returning to the safe protection of Frederick the Wise at Wittenberg.[21]

Sometime during this period, Luther was converted. The actual date of his conversion is disputed. Some place it before the posting of the Ninety-Five Theses; some put it before the Heidelberg Disputation. It is highly likely, however, that Luther's conversion came in 1519. In reading the whole of the Ninety-Five Theses, it is clear that Luther still held on to a number of formative Roman Catholic doctrines. At that point, he was not in favor of jettisoning the whole of it; he sought instead to correct and purify it from the corruptions that he saw as creeping in during the 1200s through the early 1500s. The corruption culminated in the indulgence sale of Tetzel and Albert and the relic exhibit at Wittenberg. There is also Luther's own testimony that his "breakthrough" came while he was lecturing through the Psalms a second time. Those lectures were given in the early months of 1519. Many years later, in 1545, Luther reflected on his conversion, and offered up an extraordinary account of this event, one that hinges on understanding the difference between the active and the passive. So, Luther tells us:

> Meanwhile, I had already during that year returned to interpret the Psalter anew. I had confidence in the fact that I was more skilful, after I had lectured in the university on St. Paul's epistles to the Romans, to the Galatians, and the one to the Hebrews. I had indeed been captivated with an extraordinary ardor for understanding Paul in the Epistle to the Romans. But up till then it was not the cold blood about

20 David F. Wright, "Martin Bucer," in *Biographical Dictionary of Evangelicals*, ed. Timothy Larsen (Downers Grove, Ill.: InterVarsity Press, 2003), 91.
21 Bainton, *Here I Stand*, 93–97.

the heart, but a single word in Chapter 1, "In it the righteousness of God is revealed" that had stood in my way. For I hated that word "righteousness of God," which, according to the use and custom of all the teachers, I had been taught to understand philosophically regarding the formal or active righteousness, as they call it, with which God is righteous and punishes the unrighteous sinner.

Though I lived as a monk without reproach, I felt that I was a sinner before God with an extremely disturbed conscience. I could not believe that he was placated by my satisfaction. I did not love, yes, I hated the righteous God who punishes sinners, and secretly, if not blasphemously, certainly murmuring greatly, I was angry with God, and said, "As if, indeed, it is not enough, that miserable sinners, eternally lost through original sin, are crushed by every kind of calamity by the law of the decalogue, without having God add pain to pain by the gospel and also by the gospel threatening us with his righteousness and wrath!" Thus I raged with a fierce and troubled conscience.

Nevertheless, I beat importunately upon Paul at that place, most ardently desiring to know what St. Paul wanted. At last, by the mercy of God, meditating day and night, I gave heed to the context of the words, namely, "In it the righteousness of God is revealed, as it is written, 'He who through faith is righteous shall live.'" There I began to understand that the righteousness of God is that by which the righteous lives by a gift of God, namely by faith. And this is the meaning: the righteousness of God is revealed by the gospel, namely, the passive righteousness with which merciful God justifies us by faith, as it is written, "He who through faith is righteous shall live." Here I felt that I was altogether born again and had entered paradise itself through open gates. There a totally other face of the entire Scripture showed itself to me. Thereupon I ran through the Scripture from memory. I also found in other terms an analogy, as, the work of God, that is what God does in us, the power of God, with which he makes us wise, the strength of God, the salvation of God, the glory of God. And I extolled my sweetest word with a love as great as the hatred with which I had before hated the word "righteousness of God." Thus that place in Paul was for me truly the gate to paradise.[22]

---

22 Martin Luther, preface to *LW,* 34:336–37.

This is the gospel. This is the doctrine of justification by faith alone. The key here is that Luther is passive. Christ takes on his sin. Christ achieves righteousness, in His obedience in His life and in His death on the cross. This was Luther's discovery. Christ did it. All of it.

This monumental moment occurred in 1519. Another monumental event that occurred that year was a debate with Johann Eck at the city of Leipzig.

Leipzig: Scripture Alone

Leipzig, the foremost city in Saxony, hosted a lengthy disputation from June 27 through July 17, 1519. Rome had dispatched Johann Eck to argue its side. Eck and Luther had become aware of each other in the spring of 1517. Very quickly, Eck had moved against Luther. Eck agreed to debate Luther, but not directly. He would debate Andreas Bodenstein von Karlstadt. Though born three years after Luther, Karlstadt was a professor at Wittenberg and served as Luther's "doctor-father" or supervising professor during Luther's earning of his doctorate. Luther would very quickly outpace his master, however.

Eck and Karlstadt disputed from June 17 through July 3. Eck emerged the victor. Luther could be silent no more and set about disputing Eck from July 4 until July 17. While many topics were debated, they kept circling back to the papacy and papal authority.

Eck excelled on this point, being thoroughly committed to papal primacy as a divine right.[23] The debate then turned to the church fathers. Luther made the case that many of the early church fathers had no understanding of a primate, or a pope over the bishops. The dispute focused on Athanasius for quite a while. Eck asserted but could offer no evidence that Athanasius looked to Rome or to a pope for guidance.

Then Luther made the pronouncement, "No Christian believer can be forced [to believe an article of faith] beyond Holy Scripture."[24] That was enough for Eck. By not yielding to papal authority, Luther had aligned himself with the "Bohemian." The reference, of course, was to Jan Hus. Hus had been condemned as a heretic and martyred in 1415. Because Hus was condemned, Luther would be guilty by association.

Two things resulted from Leipzig. One was the formulation of the Reformation slogan *sola Scriptura*. The other was the beginning of the end of

---

23 Lohse, *Martin Luther's Theology*, 122.
24 Ibid., 125.

Luther's tenure as a monk in good standing in the Roman Catholic Church. Luther returned to Wittenberg and to his classroom, his pulpit, and his study.

The summer and fall of 1520 proved to be rather busy for Luther. He wrote three treatises: *To the Christian Nobility of the German Nation* (August), *On the Babylonian Captivity of the Church* (October), and *On the Freedom of a Christian* (November). He was also condemned by the church. Pope Leo X issued the papal bull *Exsurge Domine*, which called on the Lord to expel Luther, the wild boar, from the vineyard of the church for trampling underfoot the gospel. History is full of ironies, but not many more acute than Leo's words in the papal bull. Luther responded to the papal bull by burning it. That action would lead him to yet another significant town in the journey of his life.

On to Worms: Conclusion

Luther's journey from Eisleben to Erfurt to Rome to Wittenberg to Heidelberg and to Leipzig eventually led him to the town of Worms.

Worms was the location of the imperial diet set to meet on and off from the end of January through the end of May 1521. Leo, of course, ordered Luther to come to Rome. Frederick the Wise simply refused to send him. Luther was a German citizen and he would face his accusers on German soil.

Luther arrived at Worms on April 16 to cheering crowds, excluding the papal authorities. On April 17, Luther appeared before the diet. In front of Luther was a large table, upon which was spread out a collection of his writings. The presiding officials demanded only two things: Luther's confession that he was the author of these books and his recantation of their contents. Luther was caught off guard. He had been promised safe passage and he expected a debate. Now, he realized he would get neither. He hesitated and asked for a day to consider his reply. The night of April 17, 1521, was passed in prayer. As with the vigils he kept as a monk, Luther prayed through a struggle. But unlike those previous vigils, this one was not followed by crushing anxiety and the throes of *Anfechtungen*. Luther instead emerged from his chamber and took the steps to his place before the diet in confidence and security and peace.

"Here I stand," he declared.

In Augustine's *Confessions*, geography plays an interesting role. Augustine leaves North Africa, wanders through various cities, including Rome, and ends up at Milan, where he is converted. He then returns home to Hippo

Regius in North Africa. Augustine made a literal journey. Yet, he also made a metaphorical journey, much like Adam once did. Adam was at home in the garden in Eden, and he was then expelled, wandering "east of Eden." The theological term for this separation is *alienation*. One of the Greek words for sin is *planaō*, from which we get the word *planets*, objects that wander through the solar system. The wandering is paradise lost. Then comes Christ, the second Adam and, through Him, we can return home. The theological word for this return is *reconciliation*.

Luther's journeys through each of these cities were literal, and they color in the picture of his life. They also chronicle a larger picture in that they reveal the development of Luther's theology and the development of the Reformation itself. Yet these journeys and these cities are also a metaphor. Luther leaves Eisleben and struggles, even rages, against God. He experiences alienation. At his death, he returns home. He is no longer at war, but he is at peace with God. There he not only stands; there he also rests.

Chapter Two

A MIGHTY FORTRESS IS OUR GOD: LUTHER AS A MAN OF CONFLICT (1520s)

STEVEN J. LAWSON

From the moment of his conversion in 1519, Martin Luther was thrust into the consuming fires of controversy. Luther provoked conflict whether in the pulpit or in print, in disputation or on trial, whenever he preached or whatever he wrote. As this Reformer proclaimed God's Word, he never mumbled his message or minced his words. Rather, his voice thundered the truth and his pen roared like a lion. Whenever he made bold affirmations of the truths of Scripture, Luther never equivocated or apologized. Such conviction was bound to generate conflict.

Never one to back down, Luther was convinced that wherever the truths of Scripture were under attack, it was precisely there that he had to stand the strongest. He declared: "If I profess with the loudest voice and clearest exposition every portion of the truth of God except precisely that little point which the world and the devil are at that moment attacking, I am not confessing Christ, however boldly I may be professing Christ. Where the battle rages, there the loyalty of the soldier is proved; and to be steady on all the battlefield besides, is mere flight and disgrace if he flinches at that point."[1] Throughout his ministry, Luther readily stepped forward, like a loyal soldier manning his post, to fight the good fight of faith.

With an acute self-awareness, Luther understood that God made him to contend for the faith: "I am rough, boisterous, stormy, and altogether warlike. I am born to fight against innumerable monsters and devils. I must remove stumps and stones, cut away thistles and thorns, and clear wild forests."[2] Luther was uniquely endowed with the unflinching courage to confront these difficulties. As a result, conflict followed this heroic Reformer throughout his days.

One decade in Luther's life proved to be most turbulent. The 1520s threw him headlong into the furnace of fiery trials, as he was the subject of a papal bull, stood trial for heresy, was confined in Wartburg Castle, witnessed the Peasants' Revolt, entered into public debate with Erasmus, was threatened by the Black Plague, and suffered the death of his young daughter. Yet, as a hammer beats glowing-hot steel into form, these trials shaped and strengthened Luther into the resilient leader that the Protestant movement would desperately need.

This chapter will focus on Luther as he faced the many conflicts that arose during the demanding decade of the 1520s. Despite the mounting controversies that confronted him, this theological titan emerged from the flames without the smell of smoke upon him.

Polemical Author (1520)

Once converted, Luther was consumed with an unquenchable desire to know the truth. In these early days, his doctrinal convictions were already growing deeper, especially regarding the unbiblical faith and practices of the Roman Catholic Church. From August to November 1520, Luther wrote three polemical works that confronted the doctrinal errors of Rome. These provocative works, Philip Schaff writes, were "the hardest blows ever dealt by human pen to the system of popery."[3] Their daring arguments immediately catapulted Luther to the front lines of spiritual conflict.

---

1 D. Martin Luthers Werke: kritische Gesamtausgabe (Weimarer Ausgabe), 3 Band: Briefwechsel (Weimar: Verlag Hermann Böhlaus Nachfolger, 1933), 3:81–82. The Latin and German edition of Luther's complete works, spanning 121 volumes, is known as the Weimarer Ausgabe; hereafter, it will be cited as WA.

2 Philip Schaff, History of the Christian Church, Vol. VII: History of the Reformation (Grand Rapids, Mich.: Eerdmans, 1910), 193.

3 Schaff, History of the Christian Church, 7:205.

In August, Luther authored *To the Christian Nobility of the German Nation.* In the preface, he announced, "The time for silence is past, and the time to speak has come."[4] The papacy and church councils, Luther believed, had utterly failed to make the reforms the church needed, so Luther called on the German nobility to step forward to make these changes. The pope and the priesthood, he argued, had built artificial walls around themselves in order to protect their position from necessary reform. Rome had claimed that only the pope and priests possessed the power to correctly interpret the Bible. Luther vehemently resisted this position, boldly asserting the priesthood of all believers. He wrote:

> It is pure invention that pope, bishops, priests and monks are to be called the spiritual estate, while princes, lords, artisans, and farmers are called the temporal estate.... All Christians are truly of the spiritual estate, and there is among them no difference except that of office.... Their claim that only the pope may interpret Scripture is an outrageous fancied fable.[5]

In October, Luther wrote his second polemical treatise of 1520, *On the Babylonian Captivity of the Church.* This theological work attacked the jugular vein of the Catholic Church by critiquing Rome's doctrine of the sacraments in light of the Bible. He was especially critical of the Roman doctrine of the Mass. His first critique addressed the Roman hierarchy's practice of withholding the cup from the laity and reserving it only for the clergy. Luther insisted that both the bread and the wine, as signs of the remission of sin, should be given to the laity. The people have already received the thing signified and therefore should not be denied the sign. Luther further argued against transubstantiation—the belief that the substance of the bread and wine are changed into the literal body and blood of Christ while retaining the characteristics of bread and wine—and against the continual repetition of the sacrifice of Christ in the Mass. In its unbiblical theology of the sacraments, Rome had carried the church away from the Scriptures and held her captive according to the whims of the pompous papacy. Luther daringly wrote: "What is asserted without the Scriptures or proven revelation may be held as an opinion, but need not be believed."[6]

---

4 *LW, Vol. 44: The Christian and Society I,* ed. James Atkinson, (Philadelphia: Fortress, 1966), 123.

5 Denis R. Janz, *A Reformation Reader* (Minneapolis: Augsburg Fortress, 1999), 91, 93.

6 *LW, Vol. 36: Word and Sacrament II,* ed. Abdel Ross Wentz (Philadelphia: Muhlenberg, 1959), 29.

The following month, Luther wrote a third polemic, *On the Freedom of a Christian*. This document laid out the foundational Reformation doctrine that justification is through faith alone in Christ alone. He claimed that this cornerstone truth "contains the whole of Christian life in a brief form."[7] In this work, Luther also underscored the Christian liberty of the believer in Christ, arguing that living however one prefers apart from the law of Christ is not a kind of freedom, but a kind of bondage. This small book was published with an open letter to Pope Leo X, which read:

> Even Antichrist himself, if he should come, could think of nothing to add to [the papacy's] wickedness. . . . A Christian is a perfectly free lord of all, subject to none. A Christian is a perfectly dutiful servant of all, subject to all. . . . He needs no works to make him righteous and save him, since faith alone abundantly confers all those things . . . and all sin is swallowed up by the righteousness of Christ.[8]

In June, Leo issued the papal bull *Exsurge Domine*. The bull condemned many of Luther's points in his Ninety-Five Theses and called on him to repent within sixty days of receipt upon threat of excommunication. The bull began: "Arise, O Lord, and judge Thy cause. A wild boar has invaded Thy vineyard."[9] Forty-one of Luther's beliefs were judged by Rome to be "heretical, or scandalous, or false, or offensive to pious ears, or seductive of simple minds, or repugnant to Catholic truth."[10] In September, the Catholic theologian Johann Eck posted the bull throughout Saxony.

Luther received it in October without flinching, saying: "This bull condemns Christ Himself."[11] He called it "the Bull of Antichrist" and declared it to be "a cursed, impudent, devilish bull."[12] On December 10, sixty days after he had received it, Luther took the bull in hand and marched outside the city wall of Wittenberg, followed by several hundred fellow professors and students. Under a large oak tree, he defiantly burned it, as well as various books of church law and Eck's writings.

---

7 *LW, Vol. 31: Career of the Reformer I*, ed. Harold J. Grimm (Philadelphia: Muhlenberg, 1957), 343.

8 Janz, *A Reformation Reader*, 99, 100, 104.

9 Bruce L. Shelley, *Church History in Plain Language* (Nashville, Tenn.: Thomas Nelson, 1982, 1995), 237.

10 Bainton, *Here I Stand*, 147.

11 Ibid., 160.

12 Schaff, *History of the Christian Church*, 7:247.

This audacious act created a permanent break with Rome. Historian Thomas Lindsay writes, "It is scarcely possible for us in the twentieth century to imagine the thrill that went through Germany, and indeed through all Europe, when the news spread that a poor monk had burnt the Pope's Bull."[13] Luther was now the chief antagonist against a thousand years of the dead religious tradition of Rome.

Defiant Stalwart (1521)

On January 3, 1521, the papal bull became official, and Luther was excommunicated. Frederick the Wise, elector of Saxony, demanded in February that Luther be given the opportunity to publicly defend himself, with the hope that he would be reinstated. The Holy Roman Emperor, Charles V, obliged and summoned Luther to an imperial diet in the city of Worms. In reality, this hearing before the civil and ecclesiastical powers would be a heresy trial for this dangerous Reformer.

Luther's friends and supporters warned him not to go to this meeting. They reminded him of the Bohemian professor and preacher Jan Hus, who in 1415 had declared the same truth of *sola fide*. Hus had been invited to the Council of Constance to "discuss" his teachings. Hus was granted safe passage, but when he arrived, he was asked one question: "Will you recant?" No opportunity for debate was given. When Hus refused to recant, he was strapped to a stake, wood was placed around him, and he was burned. Luther, despite these warnings, retorted, "Although I had known there were as many devils ready to spring upon me as there were tiles on the house-roofs, I would joyfully have sprung into their midst."[14]

On April 2, 1521, Luther departed Wittenberg for Worms. This Bible-steeped professor literally preached his way across Germany en route to his hearing. This preaching tour included stops at Erfurt, Eisenach, Gotha, and Frankfurt. When he arrived in Worms on April 16, he found a groundswell of public support. This previously obscure university teacher was fast becoming a champion of the people. All the while, however, the rage of Rome was escalating.

Luther entered Worms as a triumphant figure. Riding in an open carriage, he was preceded by an imperial herald and followed by men on horseback.

---

13 Thomas Lindsay, *Martin Luther: The Man Who Started the Reformation* (Ross-shire, Scotland: Christian Focus, 1997, 2004), 91.
14 *The Letters of Martin Luther*, ed. and trans. Margaret A. Currie (London: Macmillan, 1908), 98.

A crowd of thousands gathered to cheer him. At the beginning of the official proceedings on April 17, Luther was ushered into the solemn assembly. At the end of the hall, Emperor Charles V was seated on a throne-like chair. Spanish troops, decked out in their parade best, guarded the emperor. Beside the emperor was Eck, acting as the chief prosecutor for Rome. Also present was the papal nuncio, Jerome Aleander, along with electors, bishops, princes, knights, barons, archbishops, cardinals, legates, and representatives of great cities in the German lands.

In the midst of this gathering was a table with a pile of Luther's books. Some of his writings were about the Christian faith. Other works attacked the papacy, and still others attacked individuals. Luther had naively presumed that this venue would provide him with a platform to explain his doctrinal views. Instead, he was rebuked for daring to stand in opposition to the teachings of the church. Eck sharply confronted Luther:

> Martin, how can you assume that you are the only one to understand the sense of Scripture? Would you put your judgment above that of so many famous men and claim that you know more than they all? You have no right to call into question the most holy orthodox faith instituted by Christ the perfect lawgiver, proclaimed throughout the world by the apostles, sealed by the red blood of the martyrs, confirmed by the sacred councils, defined by the Church in which all our fathers believed until death and gave to us as an inheritance, and which now we are forbidden by the pope and the emperor to discuss lest there be no end of debate.[15]

Eck pressed Luther with two questions: "Are these your books? And will you recant?" The moment of crisis had come. Realizing the seriousness of the inquiry, Luther requested a day to marshal his defense. The next day, April 18, he addressed this elite council and issued his now-famous confession:

> Unless I am convinced by the testimony of the Scriptures or by clear reason (for I do not trust either in the pope or in councils alone, since it is well known that they have often erred and contradicted themselves), I am bound to the Scriptures I have quoted and my

---

15 Bainton, *Here I Stand*, 181.

conscience is captive to the Word of God. I cannot and I will not retract anything, since it is neither safe nor right to go against conscience. I cannot do otherwise. Here I stand. I can do no other. God help me. Amen.[16]

In this dogmatic stance, Luther declared an unwavering commitment to *sola Scriptura*. He maintained that the teaching of the church must not be based upon creeds, councils, or clerics. Neither must the truth be determined by common sense, human intuition, or mystical revelation. What the church teaches, Luther contended, must rest exclusively upon the testimony of Scripture alone.

Luther had laid the ax to the root of the papal tree. Charles condemned Luther as a heretic and pronounced the death penalty upon him. Luther was granted twenty-one days of safe conduct to put his affairs in order. The diet ordered that all his books be burned. The conflict surrounding Luther's life had shifted into high gear.

Bible Translator (1521–22)

As Luther traveled back to Wittenberg, he was confronted by a group of armed horsemen, who rode out of the forest and apprehended him. Unbeknownst to Luther, Frederick the Wise had arranged for Luther to be abducted for his own protection. He was taken to Wartburg Castle near Leipzig. He arrived on May 10 and hid in obscurity for the next eleven months. He further protected his anonymity by growing his hair and a beard and dressing as a knight, calling himself *Junker Jorg*, or Knight George.

On May 26, 1521, the twenty-one days of safety allotted to Luther expired. Emperor Charles V signed the Edict of Worms, formally condemning the rebellious Reformer. The emperor declared his teachings heretical. Luther was placed under the official ban of the Holy Roman Empire. Despite the threat, this time of confinement proved to be one of the most productive periods of his life. Luther spent the time profitably by translating Erasmus' recently collected Greek New Testament (1516) into German. Luther wrote:

> I shall be hiding here until Easter. In the meantime I shall finish the postil and translate the New Testament into German, an undertaking our friends request. I hear you are also working on this. Continue as

---

16 *LW, Vol. 32: Career of the Reformer II*, ed. George W. Forell (Philadelphia: Fortress, 1958), 113.

you have begun. I wish every town would have its interpreter, and that this book alone, in all languages, would live in the hands, eyes, ears, and hearts of all people. [17]

In February 1522, the Second Imperial Diet of Nuremberg declared the ban on Luther to be unenforceable and it was lifted. After eleven months in hiding, Luther was safe to leave Wartburg Castle. He returned to Wittenberg in March 1522 and discovered the city in an uproar. The people, long suppressed, were revolting against the political and ecclesiastical authorities. To subdue this rebellion, Luther mounted the pulpit and resumed his preaching duties. He also traveled throughout central Germany, preaching the rediscovered gospel of grace. But the conflict in which Luther found himself was not subsiding, but only increasing.

On September 21, 1522, Luther published his newly translated German New Testament. His countrymen quickly purchased this text, and in the first two months, five thousand copies were sold, to every class of people. This text was one of the few German books that the average person could afford to buy. So broad was the appeal of Luther's Bible throughout Saxony that it helped form the basis of the modern German language. Virtually overnight, Luther had become the most influential figure in his country.

Luther's Bible stoked the Reformation fires, causing its gospel-centered truths to spread like wildfire across the land. The impact of this German Bible spread far beyond the borders of Germany, igniting flames in the Netherlands, Sweden, Ireland, and Denmark. This new Bible had a direct influence on the man now known as the "Father of the English Bible," William Tyndale, who had fled from England to Continental Europe to meet with the influential Reformer. By the time Luther published his German New Testament, Tyndale was traveling to Wittenberg in order to learn how to best translate the Scriptures into his own native language.

As the Protestant movement expanded, Luther was asked to explain how such a powerful work had come to realization. Without hesitation, Luther responded:

I simply taught, preached, and wrote God's Word; otherwise I did nothing. And while I slept, or drank Wittenberg beer with my friends

---

17 *LW, Vol. 48: Letters I*, ed. Gottfried G. Krodel (Philadelphia: Fortress, 1963), 356.

Philip and Amsdorf, the Word so greatly weakened the papacy that no prince or emperor ever inflicted such losses upon it. I did nothing; the Word did everything.[18]

Expository Preacher (1522)

In Wittenberg, Luther's commitment to the primacy of the Word of God was clearly seen in his pulpit ministry. Affirming this high calling, Luther said, "If I could today become a king or emperor, I would not give up my office as preacher."[19] On an average Sunday, Luther preached twice, and on some Sundays, he said, "Often I preached four sermons on one day."[20] The day began with an early worship service in which Luther delivered a sermon on an epistle. At the mid-morning service, he gave another sermon on one of the Gospels. This was often followed by an afternoon message on the Old Testament.

In addition, Luther usually preached two to three times during the week. On religious holidays, he often preached twice a day. His resilient drive in the pulpit is seen in the staggering number of sermons he delivered. He preached 117 Sunday sermons in Wittenberg in 1522 and 137 sermons the next year. There were additional sermons that he delivered on the road. That is an average of two hundred formal sermons per year, or almost four per week, or a sermon about every two days.[21] In all, Luther preached about seven thousand sermons between 1510 and 1546.[22] Some 2,300 of these survive.[23]

Luther's preaching began to make inroads against the traditions of Rome. On March 6, 1523, the Diet of Nuremberg ordered Luther to stop publishing his sermons. The diet outlawed the preaching of anything but Roman Catholic doctrine. But Luther could not be stopped in his proclamation of the Word. On June 1, 1523, Luther published a description of Protestant public worship as it was celebrated in Wittenberg. Previously, the entire service, including the sermon, was in Latin, a language unknown to the common parishioner.

---

18 *LW, Vol. 51: Sermons I*, ed. Jaroslav Pelikan and Helmut T. Lehmann (Minneapolis: Fortress, 1960), 76–77.

19 Fred W. Meuser, *Luther the Preacher* (Minneapolis: Augsburg, 1983), 39.

20 *LW, Vol. 54: Table Talk*, ed. Theodore G. Tappert (Philadelphia: Fortress, 1967), 282.

21 Meuser, *Luther the Preacher*, 27.

22 Walther von Loewenich, *Luther: The Man and His Word*, trans. Lawrence W. Denef (Minneapolis: Augsburg, 1986), 353.

23 Patrick Ferry, "Martin Luther on Preaching: Promises and Problems of the Sermon as a Source of Reformation History and as an instrument of the Reformation," *CTQ* 54, no. 4 (1990): 266.

Luther insisted that the sermon be delivered in German so that it would be understood. Likewise, the congregational singing was to be in German. Luther called for German musicians and poets to develop songs to be used in church that would be understood by the congregation in their language.

In 1524, another Diet of Nuremberg convened and renewed the ban on Luther. But by this time, this towering figure was so popular that it was unlikely that he could be arrested without setting off a riot. At this time, Luther also published a songbook for the German church. He personally wrote many of the words and adapted tunes from popular music. Luther's goal was to give maximum exposure to the Word in the minds and hearts of the people who had been living in spiritual darkness.

Reformed Theologian (1524–25)

Later in 1524, a new conflict erupted around Luther. On September 1, the leading humanist of the day, Desiderius Erasmus of Rotterdam (1466–1536), published an attack on Luther's view on the bondage of the human will in spiritual matters. *The Freedom of the Will* was a frontal attack on the Reformer's belief in the total depravity of the unregenerate nature. This treatise by Erasmus declared an open war against Luther's Reformed teaching on the radical corruption of the human heart and will.

Despite the fall of Adam, Erasmus stated, sinful man still possesses some ability to exercise saving faith. He wrote, "By free choice . . . we mean a power of the human will by which a man can apply himself to the things which lead to eternal salvation, or to turn away from them."[24] This foremost thinker reasoned that fallen man is weakened by inherited sin, but his powers of choice remain operative. God and man are equal partners in salvation, he said. Each makes a contribution to the new birth: God supplies the grace and man supplies the faith.

In making this argument, Erasmus reasoned the way the semi-Pelagians did in response to Augustine a thousand years earlier. Erasmus argued, "What end do all the myriad of commandments serve if it is not possible for a man in any way to keep what is commanded?"[25] He maintained that whatever God commands fallen man to do, man must surely retain the natural ability to do.

Luther, however, offered no immediate response. His silence led many

---

24 *LW, Vol. 33: Career of the Reformer III,* ed. Philip S. Watson (Philadelphia: Fortress, 1972), 102.
25 *Luther and Erasmus: Free Will and Salvation,* ed. and trans. E. Gordon Rupp (Louisville, Ky.: Westminster John Knox, 1969), 57.

to believe that Erasmus had won the dispute without a shot fired by Luther. The great German theologian waited an entire year before publishing his reply. In December 1525, Luther issued what would be his magnum opus, *On the Bondage of the Will.* This work proved to be so significant that the great Princeton theologian Benjamin B. Warfield lauded it as "the manifesto of the Protestant Reformation."[26] J.I. Packer hailed it as "a brilliant and exhilarating performance, a masterpiece," and "the greatest piece of theological writing that ever came from Luther's pen."[27] *On the Bondage of the Will,* Packer concluded, "stands unsurpassed among Luther's writings."[28]

This brilliant tome addresses the moral inability of an unregenerate person to believe the gospel of Christ. In the preface, Luther thanked Erasmus for going to "the root of the controversy."[29] Instead of troubling him as others had done with peripheral issues "about the papacy, purgatory, indulgences, and other fooleries,"[30] Erasmus challenged Luther on the central matter: "I give you hearty praise and commendation on this further account—that you alone, in contrast with all others, have attacked the real thing, that is, the essential issue."[31] Erasmus had attacked the vital nerve of the Protestant view of salvation, and Luther rose to defend the core truth that salvation is all of grace.

The doctrine of justification by faith alone has been called the "article upon which the church stands or falls." But a deeper issue lies beneath the surface: What is the source of the faith that justifies? Put another way: Does saving faith originate within man? Does an unregenerate man, dead in sin and blinded by Satan, possess the capacity to believe upon Christ? Or, must saving faith be given by God as a gift of sovereign grace? Luther was convinced of the latter.

Luther asserted that saving faith requires that a person realize he can do nothing to save himself. An unsaved individual should know that he cannot believe apart from sovereign grace. The capacity to trust Jesus Christ, he argued, must come from God:

---

26 Quoted in R.C. Sproul, *Willing to Believe: The Controversy over Free Will* (Grand Rapids, Mich.: Baker, 2002), 87.

27 Martin Luther, *The Bondage of the Will,* trans. J.I. Packer and O.R. Johnson (Grand Rapids, Mich.: Baker Academic, 1990), 57.

28 Ibid., 41.

29 Schaff, *History of the Christian Church,* 7:247.

30 Ibid.

31 Luther, *The Bondage of the Will,* 319.

No man can be thoroughly humbled until he knows that his salvation is utterly beyond his own powers, devices, endeavors, will, and works, and depends entirely on the choice, will, and work of another, namely, of God alone. For as long as he is persuaded that he himself can do even the least thing toward his salvation, he retains some self-confidence and does not altogether despair of himself, and therefore he is not humbled before God, but presumes that there is—or at least hopes or desires that there may be—some place, time, and work for him, by which he may at length attain to salvation. But when a man has no doubt that everything depends on the will of God, then he completely despairs of himself and chooses nothing for himself, but waits for God to work; then he has come close to grace, and can be saved.[32]

Luther's view was essentially that of Augustine, who had taught a millennium earlier. He agreed with the fifth-century bishop of Hippo regarding the total corruption of man's nature. This condition, Luther insisted, necessitates the divine initiative in pursuing sinners. Unconverted man, Luther taught, cannot believe in Christ unless efficacious grace works in him and enables him to exercise faith. Luther wrote:

A man without the Spirit of God does not do evil against his will, under pressure, as though he were taken by the scruff of the neck and dragged into it, like a thief . . . being dragged off against his will to punishment; but he does it spontaneously and voluntarily. And this willingness of volition is something which he cannot in his own strength eliminate, restrain or alter. He goes on willing and desiring to do evil; and if external pressure forces him to act otherwise, nevertheless his will within remains averse to so doing and chafes under such constraint and opposition.[33]

Luther compared the human will to a horse or donkey that goes in the direction its rider determines. The devil dictates the way of the unconverted, controlling his sin-bound will. By contrast, God leads the choices of the regenerate. The will of man will submit to its master—either Satan or God. If someone is led by the evil one, Luther reasoned, that person cannot obey God.

---

32 *LW, Vol. 33: Career of the Reformer III,* ed. Philip S. Watson (Philadelphia: Fortress, 1972), 62.
33 Luther, *The Bondage of the Will,* 102.

In building his case, Luther said he had many "generals" with countless soldiers at their command, who could be led into this battle. But only two such high-ranking officers were needed to defeat the vain notion of free will. These two commanders are the Apostles John and Paul, who could easily rout the lame, weak arguments of Erasmus. Rather than defend the liberty of man's will, Luther championed God's autonomous freedom to save whomever He pleases. In mounting this defense, Luther exposed a litany of biblical texts in convincing fashion to support the truth of the sovereign grace of God in salvation.

Political Leader (1524–25)

Beginning in the summer of 1524, Luther faced one of the most difficult experiences of his life: the Peasants' War. At this time, the lower class of Germany was little more than slave labor for demanding landowners. They were overworked and cruelly treated. Consequently, an insurrection by the peasants erupted against the upper class and nobility in southwest Germany. This revolution was stirred up by the teachings of Luther and the many changes wrought by the Reformation. Luther's attacks upon the tyranny of the pope, his emphasis on Christian freedom, and his insistence upon the priesthood of all believers added fuel to this class struggle.

Many of the peasants mistook their spiritual liberty in Christ for a carnal license to rise up in revolt against their masters. Thousands of common laborers took Luther's teaching for support of their cause as they overthrew the tyrannical authorities who ruled them. In early 1525, this uprising spread throughout central Germany. Angry peasants destroyed the palaces of bishops and ransacked the castles of the nobility. They pillaged fields and farms.

This uprising forced Luther to enter the fray. On April 19, 1525, Luther released a poignant work, *Admonition to Peace*, in which he called the peasants to practice peaceful submission to the civil authorities. Citing Romans 13:1 and Matthew 26:52, Luther urged the riotous mob to cease using physical force in carrying out their uprising. But his words fell on deaf ears. Catholic priests were imprisoned, tortured, hanged, decapitated, and burned.[34] In a counterrevolt, Catholic princes murdered many Protestant ministers, hanging them along the sides of German roads. Rebellion reigned, and mayhem ruled.

---

34 Erasmus as quoted in Schaff, *History of the Christian Church*, 7:445.

The conflict reached new heights of brutality at the Battle of Franken-hausen on May 15, 1525. The battle was a bloodbath. Some five thousand peasants were slain in the streets and fields and another three hundred peasants were beheaded. In response, Luther penned another manifesto, *Against the Murderous, Thieving Hordes of Peasants,* in which he charged the peasants with doing the devil's work. He called the lower class "mad dogs" and petitioned the magistrates to "stab, kill, and strangle"[35] them. The peasants believed that Luther, their hero, had betrayed them.

Luther's words had been so fierce that he had to defend himself in a public letter titled *An Open Letter on the Harsh Book against the Peasants.* He wrote, "My little book shall stand, though the whole world should stumble at it."[36] Here, Luther used even stronger language, contending that it was useless to reason with rebels. In the heat of their passions, anarchists will only understand the fist and sword.

In all, more than one hundred thousand peasants were killed in the uprising. Many rebels were decapitated. Countless bodies were mutilated. Widows and orphans were left destitute. Castles and convents lay in ashes. Entire villages were burnt to the ground. Cattle were killed and crops destroyed. The ruthless slaughter dealt the cause of Protestantism tremendous injury, and a large portion of the blame was laid at the feet of the great German Reformer. Through this painful conflict, Luther's mettle was being severely tested.

Devoted Husband (1525)

In his domestic life, Luther had thrown off the unbiblical constraints of Rome. This included the church's teaching on celibacy. In 1525, Luther, age forty-one, chose to marry Katharina von Bora, twenty-six years old, a former nun. He stated that he married her in order to "please his father, tease the pope, and vex the devil."[37] He did so to "make the angels laugh and the devils weep."[38] For the remainder of his life, Luther enjoyed a happy and rich family life. Katie would bear him six children, three boys and three girls.

Later in his life, Luther's large family and the increasing demands of his ministry prompted Elector John the Steadfast to transfer to Luther the

---

35 Ibid., 7:446.
36 Ibid.
37 Ibid., 7:455.
38 Martin Brecht, *Martin Luther, Vol. 1: His Road to Reformation, 1483–1521,* trans. James L. Schaaf (Minneapolis: Fortress, 1985–1993), 230.

local monastery in Wittenberg. It was known as the Black Cloister. Luther took possession of the large house in 1532. This imposing structure was a three-story building with forty rooms on the first floor alone. Here, Luther lived with Katie and their children and hosted his many students for evening meals. His dinner dialogues with these guests were recorded and compiled into what became his famous *Table Talk*.

Because Luther's theological writings spread throughout Germany and into surrounding countries, preachers, students, and laymen traveled from throughout Continental Europe, England, and Scotland to meet with him. Among those inquirers who came were such a notable as Patrick Hamilton, the first Scottish preacher captivated by Reformed truth. After introducing Luther's theology to Scotland, Hamilton was martyred at St. Andrews in 1528.

Faithful Shepherd (1527)

Other adversities soon confronted Luther. In 1527, Luther experienced a trial so severe that church historian Philip Schaff described that year simply as "the disastrous year."[39] It was the time of Luther's "severest spiritual and physical trials."[40] As the leading figure of the Reformation, Luther paid a high price in the struggle for truth, and his physical condition deteriorated under the movement's mounting demands. On April 22, 1527, Luther was so overcome by dizziness in the pulpit that he stopped preaching and was forced to retire. Other physical problems followed for the Reformer, including severe heart problems, digestive ailments, and fainting spells. He also began to wear down emotionally, suffering bouts of discouragement and depression.

On July 6, another attack struck Luther. He was entertaining friends for dinner when he felt an intense buzzing in his left ear. He had to be carried to bed, where he frantically called for water or else, he believed, he would die. Luther became so chilled that he was convinced he had seen his last night. In a desperate prayer, he surrendered himself to the will of God and prepared to meet his Maker. Though Luther remained seriously ill for days, he eventually regained his strength.

In August, the Black Plague rapidly spread among the people in Wittenberg. Many died, and others fled for their lives. The University of Wittenberg moved to Jena, Germany. Frederick urged Luther to escape to spare his own

---

39 Schaff, *History of the Christian Church*, 7:503.
40 Ibid.

life. Adding to the danger, Katie was pregnant and they had a one-year-old child, Hans. Luther, however, considered it his moral duty to remain and minister to the sick.

Weighty trials rested heavily upon Luther's shoulders. Death surrounded him on every side. He watched people die in his house and in the streets. He chose to transform his spacious house into a hospital to care for those suffering from the plague. Hans became desperately ill, and Luther became so heavily burdened that he could not eat for eleven days. He was deeply concerned for Katie's safety and grew weak with despair.

In a letter to his trusted friend and coworker Philip Melanchthon, Luther acknowledged his increasing bouts of depression:

> I spent more than a week in death and in hell. My entire body was in pain, and I still tremble. Completely abandoned by Christ, I labored under the vacillations and storms of desperation and blasphemy against God. But through the prayers of the saints God began to have mercy on me and pulled my soul from the inferno below.[41]

In November, Luther wrote a theological tract titled *Whether One May Flee from a Deadly Plague.* He argued that a spiritual leader must stay with the community of believers under his care during a time of extreme duress. Certainly, the outbreak of the plague qualified as such a crisis, as extreme stress weighed heavy upon his heart and drained his body of strength. But in his weakness, Luther found new strength in God.

Hymn Writer (1527–29)

During these difficult years filled with controversy, death, and trial, Luther penned his most famous hymn, "A Mighty Fortress Is Our God." This magnificent work is based on Psalm 46, a worship song of unshakable trust in God. For years, Luther had translated and taught the Psalms, a book he deeply loved. This inspired collection of ancient worship songs was, in fact, the first book of Scripture that Luther had taught in the classroom. An exposition of selected penitential psalms was the subject of his first printed work.

In hard times, when Luther often found himself terribly discouraged and

---

41 James M. Kittelson, *Luther the Reformer: The Story of the Man and His Career* (Minneapolis: Augsburg, 1986), 211.

downcast, he would turn to Melanchthon and say, "Come, Philipp, let us sing the forty-sixth Psalm."[42] They would sing it in Luther's original version:

> A sure stronghold our God is He,
> A timely shield and weapon:
> Our help He'll be and set us free
> From every ill can happen.[43]

Concerning the singing of this favorite psalm, Luther said:

> We sing this psalm to the praise of God, because God is with us and powerfully and miraculously preserves and defends His church and His word against all fanatical spirits, against the gates of hell, against the implacable hatred of the devil, and against all the assaults of the world, the flesh and sin.[44]

Out of Luther's dark distress shined this brightest light of confidence in God. Philip Schaff marvels that this monumental hymn could issue from such deep travails, saying, "The deepest griefs and highest faith often meet."[45] This was the case with Luther, as "A Mighty Fortress Is Our God" was "born of deep tribulation and conquering faith."[46]

Protestant Leader (1528–29)

When the Black Plague at last cleared and the Reformation regained momentum, Luther's influence continued to sweep across Germany. The major cities in Germany embraced the Protestant cause. Among these metropolises were Erfurt, Magdeburg, Nuremberg, Strasbourg, and Bremen. Other German principalities followed suit: Hesse, Brandenburg, Brunswick-Luneburg, Schleswig-Holstein, Mansfeld, and Silesia.[47] An impressive monument that

---

42 Charles Haddon Spurgeon, *The Treasury of David: Spurgeon's Classic Work on the Psalms* (Grand Rapids, Mich.: Kregel, 1968), 2:380.

43 James Montgomery Boice, *Psalms* (Grand Rapids, Mich.: Baker, 1994), 2:388.

44 Spurgeon, *The Treasury of David*, 2:218.

45 Schaff, *History of the Christian Church*, 7:503.

46 Ibid., 7:502.

47 Rudolph W. Heinze, *Reform and Conflict: From the Medieval World to the Wars of Religion, AD 1350–1648*, Baker History of the Church, ed. Tim Dowley, vol. 4 (Grand Rapids, Mich.: Baker, 2005), 106.

still stands in Worms today records the cities that joined with Luther in his Protestant cause.

In March 1529, Luther published his Small Catechism, a concise theological statement written to teach sound doctrine to the laity in Germany. This catechism, Schaff writes, is Luther's "best work" and "bears the stamp of his religious genius, and is, next to his translation of the Bible, his most useful and enduring work."[48] This teaching document was created to address what he considered to be the deplorable ignorance of the people concerning biblical truth. In his estimation, German congregations were sadly untaught in even the most basic truths of Christianity. Luther lamented:

> The common people, especially in the villages, have no knowledge whatever of Christian doctrine, and, alas! Many pastors are altogether incapable and incompetent to teach. . . . Nevertheless, all maintain they are Christians, have been baptized and receive the [common] holy Sacraments. Yet they . . . cannot . . . recite the Lord's Prayer, or the Creed, or the Ten Commandments: they live like dumb brutes and irrational hogs; and yet, now that the Gospel has come, they have nicely learned to abuse all liberty like experts.[49]

The Small Catechism was designed to ground the church's people in the doctrinal teaching they desperately needed. Luther incorporated in this teaching device what would become the three basic parts of a standard Reformed catechism. These three divisions are the Decalogue, the Apostles' Creed, and the Lord's Prayer. Luther also included additional sections on the sacraments of baptism and the Lord's Supper.

This didactic work was followed in May 1529 by the Large Catechism. This was an expansion of the first document. Rather than utilizing the usual question-and-answer format, it takes the form of a series of points that exposit theology.

Even as Luther was writing these works, a doctrinal dispute was brewing between the leaders of the Reformation in Germany and the leaders in Switzerland. This dispute concerned the Lord's Supper. There was agreement that the Roman teaching on the Lord's Supper was to be rejected. Rome taught the doctrine of transubstantiation, meaning that the substance of the

---

48 Schaff, *History of the Christian Church*, 7:550.
49 *LW,* 54:50.

bread and wine become the actual body and blood of Christ while retaining the characteristics of bread and wine. Huldrych Zwingli, leader of the Swiss Reformers, taught that the Lord's Supper was simply a memorial of Christ's death. He understood the words of Christ—"This is my body"—as metaphorical, such that the bread and wine merely symbolize the body and blood of Christ.

Luther, however, pressed for more. He believed that Christ's words must be interpreted more literally, and he held that Christ's body and blood are actually present alongside the elements of the bread and wine (this view is sometimes called "consubstantiation," though Luther rejected that term). Zwingli and the other Swiss theologians argued that since the physical body of Christ is at the right hand of the Father in heaven, it could not simultaneously be present in churches throughout the Christian world.

To settle the growing division, the Landgrave Philip I of Hesse, a supporter of the Reformation, called the Marburg Colloquy. On October 1, 1529, Luther and Zwingli met to resolve their differences. To clarify his positions, Luther drew up fifteen articles of faith. Zwingli agreed with Luther on fourteen of these affirmations. The fifteenth article dealt with the Lord's Supper. These two leaders agreed on five essential points concerning this subject. But it was on the sixth point, regarding the presence of Christ in the supper, that the two Reformers could not find complete agreement. Despite this attempt at unity, Luther withheld his hand of fellowship from Zwingli. An agreement was not reached, and the Protestant movement was divided.

The breach between Luther and Zwingli could not be resolved. Historian Ludwig Häusser writes: "The passionate intolerant spirit of the monk, of unyielding ancient scholasticism which could brook no opposition, was aroused in him; the simple temperate character of the Swiss Reformer was repugnant to him, and he never overcame his distrust of him and his doctrines."[50] The breach would never be healed.

Despite this setback, Luther would find unity back at home. Emperor Charles V called the Diet of Augsburg in 1530 in an attempt to ease tensions between German Protestants. Luther was a fugitive from the empire at this time, and so was unable to attend, but he made his presence known through a variety of publications, and he was represented at the diet by Melanchthon.

---

50 Ludwig Häusser, *The Period of the Reformation: 1517 to 1648,* ed. Wilhelm Oncken, trans. G. Sturge (London: Strahan, 1873), 151.

His work was rewarded when the diet adopted Melanchthon's Augsburg Confession, which codified Luther's doctrinal reforms and earned the approval of German princes and other leaders, becoming one of the founding documents of the Lutheran movement.

A Decade of Conflict (1520s)

The 1520s proved to be a turbulent time for Martin Luther, one in which he found himself engaged in many battles. In the face of mounting struggles, Luther fought the good fight and remained unwavering in his devotion to the truth of the Bible. Through these sufferings, he grew deeper in the truth and stronger in faith.

Luther recognized that these conflicts came by divine design to make him the theologian God desired him to be. In commenting on Psalm 119, the Reformer expressed this conviction when he wrote about what he saw as the correct way to study theology. He affirmed three nonnegotiables for learning biblical doctrine: "Here you will find three rules. They are frequently proposed throughout the psalm and thus: *Oratio, meditatio, tentatio.*"[51] These three Latin words translate as "prayer," "meditation," and "trial." It is this third prerequisite that should arrest our attention. Luther calls *tentatio* "the touchstone" for learning the truth.

Luther believed that trials in the life of any believer, especially a theologian, are necessary in order to grow in the truth. He said that affliction "teaches you not only to know and understand, but also to experience how right, how true, how sweet, how lovely, how mighty, how comforting God's Word is, wisdom beyond all wisdom."[52] In other words, Luther maintained that theology is not learned only in the safety of a lecture hall, but in the flames of adversity. In fiery trials, one is humbled and broken. It is then that a leader is made most teachable. In difficult times, the illuminating work of the Holy Spirit often shines brightest. Broken hearts make for receptive minds.

Such affliction increases in intensity as the servant of God ministers the Word. Luther explained, "As soon as God's Word takes root and grows in you, the devil will harry you, and will make a real doctor of you, and by his assaults will teach you to seek and love God's Word."[53] Luther thanked the devil and

---

51 *LW*, 34:285.
52 Ibid., 34:287.
53 Ibid.

papists for "beating, oppressing and distressing" him to the point that they turned him into "a fairly good theologian."[54]

Amid his mounting conflicts, Luther stands as a towering example of the steadfast loyalty to the gospel that is required by God. Ministry is never without its difficulties. There are no easy places to serve the Lord. In perilous times, Luther demonstrated the unwavering devotion needed to persevere.

54 Ibid.

Chapter Three

FAITHFUL TO THE END: LUTHER IN HIS LATER YEARS (1530s–1546)

DAVID B. CALHOUN

Martin Luther was thirty-four years old when he wrote the Ninety-Five Theses. He was thirty-seven when he was excommunicated by the Roman Catholic Church, forty-one when he married former nun Katharina von Bora, and forty-six when the Augsburg Confession was produced in 1530. That event marks "a plausible dividing line between the younger and the older Luther," writes Mark U. Edwards.[1]

Most Luther biographies practically end the Reformer's career with the Diet of Augsburg, as do the Luther movies of 1953 and 2003. Several recent books, however, have sought to do justice to Luther's later life: *Luther: An Experiment in Biography* by H.G. Haile, *Luther's Last Battles* by Edwards, and the third volume of Martin Brecht's biography, *Martin Luther: The Preservation of the Church, 1532–1546.*[2]

---

1 Mark U. Edwards Jr., *Luther's Last Battles: Politics and Polemics 1531–46* (Minneapolis: Fortress, 2005), 10.

2 H.G. Haile, *Luther: An Experiment in Biography* (Garden City, N.Y.: Doubleday, 1980); Edwards, *Luther's Last Battles*; Martin Brecht, *Martin Luther: The Preservation of the Church, 1532–1546* (Minneapolis: Fortress, 1993).

In 1530, Luther was a middle-aged man, but he felt old. "The years are piling up," he lamented.[3] He was also experiencing serious episodes of alarming, painful illness. In March 1531, Luther wrote, "I am seriously declining in strength, especially in the head. It hinders me from writing, reading, or speaking much, and I am living like a sick man."[4] The next year, he had to give up preaching for a time because dizziness made it impossible for him to complete a sermon. He struggled at times with deep depression. "I can't banish the thought from my mind," he said, "when I wish that I had never started [the reform of the church]. So likewise when I wish I were dead rather than witness such contempt [for the Word of God and His faithful servants]."[5]

According to Roland Bainton, Martin Luther became "prematurely an irascible old man, petulant, peevish, unrestrained, and at times positively coarse."[6] But, Bainton writes, "Luther's later years are . . . by no means to be written off as the sputterings of a dying flame. . . . To the end he was preaching, lecturing, counseling, and writing."[7]

Despite advancing age, chronic illness, and debilitating depression, Luther gave himself to the preservation of the church that he had done so much to create and define. Brecht writes in the foreword to the third volume of his biography, "The subtitle of this volume indicates what was most important for the old Luther: the preservation of the church."[8] Acknowledging Luther's bitterness to his enemies, rudeness to his friends, and "serious errors both in

---

3 Heiko A. Oberman, *Luther: Man between God and the Devil* (Doubleday, 1992), 328. Oberman's book is dedicated to the memory of Roland H. Bainton "who combined the gifts of profound penetration and powerful presentation to make Martin Luther come alive for generations of students of the Reformation, on both sides of the Atlantic." My quotations from Luther are taken from *LW* or from secondary sources as footnoted. The footnotes of these secondary sources provide the location of the quotations from the various German editions of Luther's works.

4 Kittelson, *Luther the Reformer*, 241.

5 *LW*, 54:30. Occupying vol. 54 of *Luther's Works* is *Table Talk*, a collection of Luther's conversation with dinner guests at Luther's house, the former Augustinian monastery, in Wittenberg. Here Luther is at his best (and sometimes at his worst) in his honest, down-to-earth, and often humorous comments. *Table Talk* must, of course, be used with care since it comes not directly from Luther, but from friends and students who recorded his words. But, as Roland Bainton writes, "This material is not to be indiscriminately rejected. Often it is highly piquant and has the veritable ring of Luther" (*Studies on the Reformation* [Boston: Beacon, 1963], 99). Luther's *Table Talk* is especially important for this chapter since it comes from the older Luther (1531–44).

6 Bainton, *Here I Stand*, 292.

7 Ibid., 300.

8 Martin Brecht, *Martin Luther: The Preservation of the Church, 1532–1546* (Minneapolis: Fortress, 1993), xii. Brecht's first two volumes are titled *Martin Luther: His Road to Reformation, 1483–1521* (1985) and *Martin Luther: Shaping and Defining the Reformation, 1521–1532* (1990).

practice and in theory," Brecht concludes that "to the end, however, his positive contributions and deep insights remained more significant. Abruptness and resignation were not able to stifle the tender tones and the fundamental trust in God that came from his belief in justification by faith."[9]

Life at Home

Luther, under the ban of empire and church for the rest of his life, lived and worked in Electoral Saxony. In 1525, Elector Frederick the Wise was succeeded by his brother John and in 1532 by John's son, John Frederick, who looked to Luther as his mentor. Another part of Saxony was ruled by Duke George, a learned and sincere Roman Catholic, with whom Luther constantly clashed in increasingly sharp publications.

Luther lived in Wittenberg, in the former Black Cloister, with his wife and growing family. Without Katharina, the mature Luther would be incomprehensible. Their marriage of convenience had become a happy one. In 1531, after six years of marriage, Luther said, "I wouldn't give up my Katy for France or for Venice."[10] He described the epistle to the Galatians, which he dearly loved, as "my Katie von Bora."[11] "No sweeter thing than love of woman—may a man be so fortunate," Luther wrote in the margin beside Proverbs 31 in his German Bible translation. The words had been spoken to him by a lady in Eisenach when he was a schoolboy.[12]

In his Genesis commentary, Luther wrote, "With the woman who has been joined to me by God I may jest, have fun, and converse more pleasantly."[13] But for Luther, a good marriage was more than fun. It involved intellectual companionship and required mutual forgiving and forgetting. Luther and his wife were both realistic about marriage and about each other. He admitted that Katie had "some shortcomings" but that they were "outweighed by a great many virtues."[14] Luther teased her, and occasionally spoke sharply to her or about her, but she usually took it in good spirits. She could also express her candid opinion about her husband to him and to others. When Luther made a will in 1542, he was especially concerned to ensure Katie's future, because according to Saxon inheritance laws, she would have received little.

9   Brecht, *The Preservation of the Church*, xii.
10 *LW*, 54:7.
11 Ibid., 54:20.
12 Haile, *Luther*, 259.
13 Brecht, *The Preservation of the Church*, 235.
14 *LW*, 54:8.

Luther and his wife loved each other, and they made love. They had six children. Luther was nearly forty-three at the birth of their first child, Hans, and fifty-two when Margaret, their youngest, was born. He took delight in his children; they were a "most beautiful joy."[15] He wrote a charming letter to four-year-old Hans, creating for the little boy a tale about a beautiful garden with delicious fruit and little ponies with golden bridles and silver saddles, to motivate Hans to study, pray, and be good.[16] Luther could be cranky with his children at times and occasionally too severe, but he loved them deeply and was quick to learn important spiritual lessons from them.[17]

Luther was convinced that he could not carry on his work without Katie. He was notoriously inept at household finance and gave little thought to everyday matters. His practical-minded wife planted a large garden, operated her own brewery, and treated her husband's illnesses with the expertise of a physician. She cared for the steady stream of relatives, students, and visitors to their Wittenberg home, creating "a model for the Lutheran household in centuries to come."[18] Luther recognized in Katie "his principal support in this world. . . . His marriage with her was the single greatest new influence on his life and thinking after the monastery."[19] A short time before he died, he asked his gathered friends to comfort Katie, who "served me not only as a wife but as my assistant."[20]

Summarizing Doctrine

The year 1530 was difficult for Luther. The diet met in Augsburg; it was an important confrontation between the Catholic and Lutheran parties in the presence of Emperor Charles V. Luther, still an outlaw and without safe conduct, could not attend, but got as close as he could at the Castle Coburg, still safely within the borders of Electoral Saxony. For five months, he was again "in the wilderness," as he had been at the Wartburg. There was little he could do but read, think, write—and pray and worry. On the walls of the room he used as a study at the castle, Luther wrote several verses from the Psalms. One was Psalm 118:17: "I shall not die, but I shall live and recount the deeds

---

15 Brecht, *The Preservation of the Church*, 236.
16 Haile, *Luther*, 90–91.
17 See Roland H. Bainton, "Luther on Birds, Dogs and Babies," in *Studies on the Reformation*, 67–74.
18 Haile, *Luther*, 264.
19 Ibid., 262.
20 Ibid., 219.

of the Lord." He encouraged himself with the thought that "though the cause be great, he who has brought it about, who directs and guides it, is great too, yes, the Almighty Creator of heaven and earth. This is by no means our cause, so why should we keep on tormenting ourselves over it or plaguing ourselves to death?"[21]

Luther worried that Philip Melanchthon would yield too much to the Catholics at Augsburg, but in the end he was immensely pleased with the Augsburg Confession. He thought its moderate tone better than anything he could have achieved. "I know nothing to improve or change in it, nor would this be appropriate," Luther wrote, "since I cannot step so softly and quietly."[22]

Years later, in 1537, while suffering from heart trouble, Luther wrote a series of doctrinal statements at the request of Elector John Frederick, to be used in preparation for the anticipated General Council, long hoped for but now feared by Luther and the Protestants. In the preface, he announced that he was still alive and "still writing, preaching, and lecturing every day." He then stated "his personal and fully developed views about what matters could not be compromised."[23] Faith in Christ is "the first and chief article," Luther wrote. "We hold that man is justified, without the works of the law, through faith. . . . From this article no wavering is possible, even if heaven and earth pass away."[24] After Luther's death, this work received the title Smalcald Articles, and was incorporated into the 1580 Book of Concord. These articles, which summarize his theology, were in an important sense his last will and testament. He wrote that "those who live after me [will] have my testimony and confession to show where I have stood until now and where, by God's grace, I will continue to stand."[25]

In 1520, the young Luther wrote in *To the Christian Nobility of the German Nation* that Christ seeks as His representatives on earth not popes and prelates but ministers in the form of servants, the form in which he went about on earth "working, preaching, suffering, and dying."[26]

Late in 1531, Luther described his workload: "Four times a week I preach

---

21 *LW, Vol. 43: Devotional Writings II*, ed. Gustav. K. Wiencke (Philadelphia: Fortress, 1968), 173.

22 Ibid., 43:297–98.

23 *Martin Luther's Basic Theological Writings*, ed. Timothy F. Lull (Minneapolis: Fortress, 1989), xvii.

24 Martin Luther, *Word and Sacrament*, 38:11–21, quoted in Haile, *Luther: An Experiment in Biography*, 209.

25 Martin Luther, Smalcald Articles, in *The Book of Concord: The Confessions of the Evangelical Lutheran Church*, ed. and trans. Theodore G. Tappert (Philadelphia: Fortress, 1959), 289.

26 *LW*, 44:165.

in public, twice a week I lecture, and in addition I hear cases [for pastoral counseling], write letters, and am working on a book for publication."[27] Preaching, teaching, counseling, and writing—these tasks occupied Luther for the last fifteen years of his life.

A Man of the Bible

Martin Luther was above all a man of the Bible. He gave his life to studying the Bible, translating it, preaching and teaching it. In October 1532, Luther said: "For some years now, I have read through the Bible twice every year. If you picture the Bible to be a mighty tree and every word a little branch, I have shaken every one of these branches because I wanted to know what it was and what it meant."[28] And he wanted others, especially his fellow Germans, to read and study the Bible for themselves. In September 1534, the first complete Wittenberg Bible appeared, translated by Luther into living, everyday German. "He had truly listened to the common people—the language of the common man was not too lowly to be the language of God."[29]

Luther continued to work on his Bible translation—revising and perfecting it—with the help of others. Before dinner every Wednesday and Thursday, from the summer of 1539 to the beginning of 1541, he assembled a group of scholars, his "Sanhedrin" he called them, to assist him in revising his translation of the Old Testament. The last printed page on which he ever looked was the proof of the latest revision of his New Testament. "The German Bible is Luther's noblest achievement," Roland Bainton writes.[30]

Luther's preface to the Old Testament was revised to accompany his new translation of the Old Testament of 1545. Luther urged the reading of the Old Testament, because there, he wrote, are found "the very words, works, judgments, and deeds of the majesty, power, and wisdom of the most high God."[31] In 1546, Luther revised his preface to the New Testament to introduce his fresh translation. Once again, Luther insisted on what he saw as the chief doctrine of the Bible: what the gospel demands is not good works but faith in Christ.

Much of Luther's time in his last years was spent happily teaching and

---

27 *LW,* 54:22–23.
28 Ibid., 54:165.
29 Oberman, *Luther: Man between God and the Devil,* 305.
30 Bainton, *Here I Stand,* 255.
31 *Martin Luther's Basic Theological Writings,* 119.

preaching the Bible—"allowing the Scriptures of the past to become the tidings of the present."[32]

In 1535, Luther became dean of the University of Wittenberg, a position he held for the rest of his life. For the older Luther, no work is as revealing as his massive *Lectures on Genesis*, delivered from 1535 to 1545. Despite his insistence on the literal meaning of the text, Luther frequently went far beyond the actual text, leaving very few theological problems untouched. In these lectures we find, as Heiko Oberman writes, "concentrated summaries of his theology."[33] Luther was not satisfied, however, with his work. "The lectures are hastily thrown together and are imperfect," he said. "I can't do justice to such a thing while I'm busy with many tasks. To do much and to do it well don't fit together."[34] Luther told his students that "Genesis is a charming book and has wonderful stories. I can't altogether understand it, however. I'll have to be dead four years or so before I comprehend fully what creation means and what the omnipotence of God is."[35]

In the Pulpit

Luther taught the Bible at the university (preparing a generation of Lutheran preachers) and he preached it at Wittenberg and in other places in Saxony. Johannes Bugenhagen (called Pomeranus by Luther because he was born in Pomerania), the regular pastor of the Wittenberg town church, was frequently away on church business, and even when he was in town, he often had Luther preach. Luther criticized his colleague's preaching at one point, agreeing with Katie that Bugenhagen wandered too far from his subject. "Pomeranus preaches the way you women usually talk. He says whatever comes to mind. Dr. Justus Jonas is accustomed to say, 'One shouldn't hail every soldier one meets.'"[36] (Luther's *Table Talk* contains occasional disparaging comments about women, perhaps half in jest. After all, Katie was listening.)[37]

---

32 Oberman, *Luther: Man between God and the Devil,* 173.

33 Ibid., 166. "Although these lectures deserve to be used as an introduction to Luther's world of faith, they have nearly fallen into oblivion owing to the prevailing interest in the young Luther" (167). Martin Brecht writes that Luther's great lectures on Genesis "are unquestionably monumental documents of Luther's mature theology, and they also reflect his participation in the developments, problems, and conflicts of the last decade of his life" (136).

34 *LW,* 54:289.

35 Ibid., 54:409.

36 Ibid., 54:428.

37 Luther "was a stout defender of womankind in a world where slighting remarks were in vogue" (Haile, *Luther,* 270).

Luther called the people of Wittenberg "my congregation." Late in 1536, he said, "I've preached here [in the city church of Wittenberg] for twenty-four years. I've walked to church so often that it wouldn't be at all surprising if I had not only worn out my shoes on the pavement but even my feet."[38] "When I preach here [in Wittenberg]," he told a visiting pastor, "I adapt myself to the circumstances of the common people. I don't look at the doctors and masters, of whom scarcely forty are present, but at the hundred or the thousand young people and children. It's to them that I preach, to them that I devote myself, for they, too, need to understand. If the others don't want to listen they can leave. Therefore, my dear Bernard, take pains to be simple and direct."[39]

Luther's sermons of lively biblical exposition were simple and clear, with pointed and sometimes sharp application, not always happily received. Luther saw stinginess, greed, and usury—not using one's possessions in a Christian way—as serious problems in Wittenberg. He warned against immorality and drunkenness. The latter, Luther believed, was the prevailing sin among Germans (although he himself enjoyed his German beer). Luther knew that there could never be a sinless community on earth, but he expected a Christian city like Wittenberg to take more energetic action against abuses than it actually did. Despite the many pessimistic judgments he made in his later years, Luther could say, "I entertain no sorry picture of our Church, but rather that of the Church flourishing through pure and uncorrupted teaching and one increasing with excellent ministers from day to day."[40] In 1545, he wrote a poem about how the poor, small city of Wittenberg had become famous "by God's Word that streams from it and creates many souls for heaven."[41]

Luther was a good and effective preacher, but he was well aware of the difficulties of his task. "I have never been troubled by my inability to preach well," he said, "but I have often been alarmed and frightened to think that I was obliged to speak thus in God's presence about his mighty majesty and divine nature."[42] Early in 1533, Luther said, "If I were to write about the burdens of the preacher as I have experienced them and as I know them, I would scare everybody off."[43]

---

38 *LW*, 54:206.
39 Ibid., 54:235–36.
40 Bainton, *Here I Stand*, 286.
41 Quoted in Brecht, *The Preservation of the Church*, 265.
42 *LW*, 54:158.
43 Ibid., 54:73–74.

Luther knew the problems and challenges of preaching. He also knew its power, because God was in it. God says to us, "'Preach! I shall give the increase. I know the hearts of men.' This should be our comfort, even when the world laughs at our office."[44] Luther said that in his sermons he was also preaching to himself. He confessed, "I preach to others what I don't do myself."[45]

A pastor asked Luther, "Reverend Father, teach me in a brief way how to preach." Luther responded, "First, you must learn to go up to the pulpit. Second, you must know that you should stay there for a time. Third, you must learn to get down again." The pastor was put out with Luther for what appeared to be a flippant answer. But then it occurred to him that the doctor had hit the mark very well. Luther explained that "anybody who keeps this order will be a good preacher. First, he must learn to go up to the pulpit, that is, he should have a regular and a divine call. Second, he must learn to stay there for a time, that is, he should have the pure and genuine doctrine. Third, he must also learn to get down again, that is, he should preach not more than an hour."[46] Luther practiced what he preached. "I have learned this art," he said. "When I have nothing more to say I stop talking."[47]

Luther preached until the very end. He delivered his last sermon on February 15, 1546, three days before his death. The location of his grave was chosen with great care—in front of the pulpit in the Castle Church of Wittenberg, because Luther considered the pulpit his most important place of work.

Later Writings

When Luther was not preaching and teaching, he was writing. He wrote hundreds of letters during his later years—fully a third of his total correspondence—in which he offered instruction, counsel, comfort, correction, and warning.

Luther produced pastoral writings, such as the charming little book he wrote for his friend and barber Peter Beskendorf, who asked Luther for instruction on how to pray. In that book, titled *A Simple Way to Pray*, Luther "succeeds in being extremely practical and profound at the same time."[48] His short *Comfort for Women Who Have Had a Miscarriage* grew out of his

---

44 Ibid., 54:213.
45 Ibid., 54:75.
46 Ibid., 54:393.
47 Ibid., 54:292.
48 Timothy Keller, *Prayer: Experiencing Awe and Intimacy with God* (New York: Dutton, 2014), 271.

concern that mothers whose babies die before or at birth know that God is not angry with them, that His "will is always better than ours, though it may seem otherwise to us from our human point of view," and that their babies, though unbaptized, are not lost but saved by the prayers of their parents "in view of the promise that God willed to be their God. God . . . has not limited his power to the sacraments, but has made a covenant with us through his word."[49]

The older Luther was above all a practical theologian, working hard to structure the life of the church around the newly recovered doctrines of the Bible. He wrote a new constitution for the Lutheran churches. The important thing for Luther was not how the church was organized, but that the gospel be preached in it. He left much of the work of actually composing the new church orders and seeing them established to younger colleagues such as Melanchthon and Bugenhagen, for whom extensive travel was less difficult than for the aging and often-sick Luther.

The Bible, the catechism, the liturgy, and the hymnbook—the needs of the Reformed church—were all met by Luther himself. Luther emphasized congregational singing to encourage lay participation in worship and to teach, through words of hymns, true doctrine to ordinary people. His love for music—he said that music is second only to theology as a comfort to the human soul—and the hymns he wrote, with those he inspired, established his reputation as "father of the German hymn."[50]

Luther was shocked to discover while visiting the churches of Saxony in 1528 that the common people had "no knowledge whatever of Christian teaching."[51] He produced a Large Catechism for pastors and teachers and a Small Catechism for more general use. The Small Catechism became Luther's most widely used writing in the centuries after its first publication in 1529.

In 1544, Luther consecrated the first church built for Protestant worship in Germany, in Torgau on the Elbe. Luther believed that "good, modest churches with low arches are the best for preachers and for listeners, for the ultimate object of these buildings is not the bellowing and bawling of choristers but the Word of God and its proclamation."[52]

On the Councils and the Church was the most substantial writing of Martin Luther's later years. He wrote it in anticipation of a Catholic council,

---

49 *LW,* 43:247, 249.
50 Haile, *Luther,* 53.
51 Quoted in *Martin Luther's Basic Theological Writings,* 409.
52 *LW,* 54:272.

which was not in fact convoked until just before his death. *On the Councils and the Church* was "a work of profound historical and theological scholarship," Jaroslav Pelikan writes.[53] In it, Luther draws on immense historical documentation to define the role of church councils and gives a final statement of the exclusively spiritual nature of the church. He clearly explains the distinction and connection between the empirical church and the hidden, or, as it was later called by Protestants, the "invisible" church. Luther describes seven characteristics of the church: sermon, baptism, holy communion, absolution, ordination, divine worship, and suffering and persecution. For Luther, the heart of the matter is that the church is neither building nor institution nor structure but the gathered congregation, the people of God. Luther had written in the Smalcald Articles that "a seven-year-old child knows what the church is, namely holy believers and sheep who hear the voice of their Shepherd."[54]

It was only in his later years that Luther found opportunity to study church history more thoroughly. He found, to his delight, that historical sources supported the theological convictions that he had drawn directly from his reading of the Bible. He then used history, as well as the Bible, to undermine papal claims and to portray the papacy as the kingdom of the Antichrist.

Polemical Works

On the Councils and the Church is not only an important work of ecclesiology; it is a prime example of Luther's "polemical overkill."[55] In his last years, Luther produced a stream of polemics against an assortment of enemies—Roman Catholics, Erasmus, other Protestants (including renegade Lutherans, Zwinglians, and Anabaptists), Turks, and Jews. The polemics of the older Luther are more violent, abusive, and vulgar than those of the younger man. "I hate Erasmus from the bottom of my heart," he declared.[56] He railed against Protestants who disagreed with him. He found no reason to be more charitable with these "false brethren" than he was with his opponents from Rome. Huldrych Zwingli, Johannes Oecolampadius, the Anabaptists, and even at times Martin Bucer, Luther said, were instruments of the devil.

---

53 Jaroslav Pelikan, *The Melody of Theology: A Philosophical Dictionary* (Cambridge, Mass.: Harvard University Press, 1988), 157.
54 Luther, Smalcald Articles, in *The Book of Concord* (1959), 315.
55 *Martin Luther's Basic Theological Writings*, xiii.
56 *LW*, 54:84.

Luther recognized that anger was his besetting sin. He knew that at times he was "proud and arrogant—as you see in my books that I despise my adversaries. I take them for fools."[57] Luther believed, however, that his anger served a useful purpose. "Anger refreshes all my blood, sharpens my mind, and drives away temptations," he commented. He saw himself as "a coarse woodsman, who must pioneer and hew a path."[58] Luther said, "I was born to go to war and give battle to sects and devils. That is why my books are stormy and warlike. I have to root out the stumps and clumps, hack away the thorns and brambles."[59] Melanchthon agreed. In his funeral oration for his friend, He agreed with Erasmus' statement that "Because of the magnitude of the disorders, God gave this age a violent physician."[60]

Some have attempted to excuse or soften Luther's harsh polemics. Haile argues that these writings should not be dismissed "as mere emotional outburst. Few authors have had as much experience with the pen as he, and rare is the human who has so carefully searched his own soul. Luther knew what he was doing."[61] Luther's abusiveness was "a deliberate rhetorical tactic," Edwards argues. He could write a moderate, well-reasoned polemic if political circumstances made it advisable. "When Luther was harsh and abusive, it was by choice."[62] Edwards notes that Luther directed "his attacks more against the devil allegedly motivating the opponent than against the man himself."[63] The devil, of course, in Luther's view, deserved all the abuse that could be heaped upon him. Kittelson claims that Luther's harsh words were "in no way an emotional outburst from a sick, old man. Rather, like most public actions, they grew from a combination of internal convictions and external developments."[64] Gritsch says that Luther's fierce *Against Hanswurst* "displayed his masterful use of medieval abusive language and wit to expound the distinctions he made between the true church of the gospel and the false church of Rome."[65]

It is frequently said that sharp polemics were common in the sixteenth century and that Luther was simply following a well-established practice. But

57 Ibid., 54:93.
58 Edwards, *Luther's Last Battles*, 6.
59 Haile, *Luther*, 161.
60 Clyde Manschreck, *Melanchthon: The Quiet Reformer* (New York: Abingdon, 1958), 275.
61 Haile, *Luther: An Experiment in Biography*, 164.
62 Edwards, *Luther's Last Battles*, 143, 162.
63 Ibid., 152.
64 Kittelson, *Luther the Reformer*, 259.
65 Eric W. Gritsch, *Martin: God's Court Jester; Luther in Retrospect* (Philadelphia: Fortress, 1983), 82.

Luther appears to have gone beyond most other figures of his time in extreme expression. Melanchthon at times regretted Luther's violent language. Even Katie objected. Luther was harshly criticizing Caspar Schwenckfeld's book on Christ when Katie interrupted, "Ah, dear Sir, that's much too coarse!" Luther replied that people like Schwenckfeld cause him to be coarse, because "this is the way one must talk to the devil."[66] Luther's attack on Catholics in *Against Hanswurst* was, Heinrich Bullinger wrote to Martin Bucer, "unbecoming, completely immodest, entirely scurrilous, and frivolous."[67] It is difficult to read Luther's extreme language without a profound sadness that a great man and earnest Christian did not see that there was a better way to stand for the truth. Luther, rebuking Erasmus, wrote in *On the Bondage of the Will* that a true Christian delights in assertions—"I mean a constant adhering, affirming, confessing, maintaining, and an invincible persevering."[68] Yes, but how one does that is not unimportant.

Against the Papacy at Rome, Founded by the Devil, the last major polemic of Luther's life, was written at the request of his prince, John Frederick, to strengthen the resolve of the Protestants on what became the eve of religious war in Germany. "Without question it is the most intentionally violent and vulgar writing to come from Luther's pen," Edwards writes. "It was also superb for rallying the faithful on the eve of battle."[69] The heart of Luther's writing was his intense conviction that he was attacking the Antichrist. He combined logic, history, Scripture, and verbal abuse in depicting the horrifying nature of the papacy in the most vivid way he could.

In 1541, Elector John Frederick asked Luther to write an appeal for prayer against the Turks to help build morale for defeating the Turks militarily. But in his *Appeal for Prayer against the Turks*, Luther seemed more concerned with the lack of Christian commitment on the part of the German people and saw the advancing Turkish armies as a sign of God's rod of chastisement. He began:

> They say there is no helping up a man who turns down good counsel. We Germans have heard the word of God now for many years, by which God, the Father of all mercies, enlightens us and calls us from the abominable darkness and idolatry of the papacy into the light of

---

66 *LW*, 54:470.
67 Quoted in Edwards, *Luther's Last Battles*, 155.
68 *LW*, 33:19.
69 Edwards, *Luther's Last Battles*, 163.

his holy kingdom. But today it is a horrible sight to see how thankless and ungrateful we have been toward it.

Luther concluded his appeal by warning that

we Christians are not to put our hope in our cleverness, nor in our might. . . . Our solace, boldness, self-confidence, security, victory, life, joy, our honor and glory are seated up there in person at the right hand of God the Father Almighty. . . . We commit all to him. He will do all things well as he has from the beginning, does now, and always will do unto all eternity. Amen.[70]

Luther's central conviction was that the Turks "were God's punishment on a sinful Christendom that, among other sins, tolerated the papal abomination."[71] For this reason, Luther's polemics against the Turks seem more restrained than his writings against the Jews, Catholics, and even some other Protestants.

The tone of Luther's writings about the Jews shifted over time from cautious hope to bitter denunciation. Luther reminded his people that Gentiles are the pagans and the Jews are the blood relatives of Christ.[72] He described David and the writers of the New Testament as "real Jews," and stated that we Gentile Christians are in no way equal to the Jews—except for Augustine, "who is the only doctor in the church of the Gentiles who stands out above others."[73] Luther argued that if the Jews were treated kindly and were correctly taught the Holy Scripture—Old and New Testaments—then "many of them would become true Christians and would return to the faith of their fathers, the prophets and the patriarchs." When Jews converted to Christianity, Luther said, they became our brothers and sisters in Christ.

Few Jews, however, became Christians. When it was rumored that some Jews were attempting to convert Christians to Judaism, it was too much for Luther. His earlier, more accepting attitude turned into angry rejection, not because the Jews were Jews but because they were not Christians. In 1543, Luther published *On the Jews and Their Lies*, in which he urged German

---

70 *LW,* 43:219, 241.
71 Edwards, *Luther's Last Battles,* 98.
72 Ibid., 122.
73 *LW,* 54:340.

leaders to "chase all the Jews out of their land."[74] It was, Gritsch writes, "an unforgivably harsh judgment" for one who had shown so much love for the people of Israel in his work as an Old Testament scholar.[75]

Wrestling with His Legacy

In March 1545, Luther completed the preface to the Wittenberg edition of his Latin writings. At times, Luther seemed proud and pleased that he had written so many books. At other times, he expressed misgivings about them. When printers urged Luther to allow them to publish his collected works, Luther said, "I'd rather that all my books would disappear and the Holy Scriptures alone would be read." When he completed his large commentary on Galatians, he said, "I wonder who encourages this mania for writing! Who wants to buy such stout tomes? And if they're bought, who'll read them? And if they're read, who'll be edified by them?"[76]

Later, Luther said, "If my advice were taken, only the books of mine that contain doctrine would be printed, such as my *Galatians*, *Deuteronomy*, and *John*. The rest [of my books] should be read merely for the history, in order to see how it all [the Reformation] began."[77] In the preface to his Latin books, Luther described the beginnings of the Reformation, creating "an important historical personal testimony."[78]

Dealing with Political Authorities

Luther spent the last years of his life as a counselor to princes, attempting to support the religious movement he began and to prevent it from becoming entangled in political interests. He did not relish this role. In earlier years, Luther adamantly rejected armed resistance to the emperor in defense of the faith. Later, Luther shifted his position somewhat, holding that the right of military resistance to the emperor was a political and legal question and not a theological one. He attempted to quiet the consciences of those, including himself, who might worry that resistance to the emperor in defense of religion would be a violation of God's will.

---

74 Ibid., 54:426.
75 Gritsch, *Martin: God's Court Jester*, 83.
76 *LW*, 54:311.
77 Ibid., 54:440.
78 Brecht, *The Preservation of the Church*, 144.

It was not in Luther's character to compromise on matters of Scripture and theology. He was never theologically comfortable with the notion of defending the gospel with the sword. Circumstances, however, required concession and accommodation, and Luther reluctantly adjusted while attempting to remain true to his convictions.

Pessimism about the World

Luther had no great hope for much improvement in the state of the world. He said, "God does not think so much of his temporal realm as he does of his spiritual realm. . . . So I would not advise that any changes be made. We just have to patch and darn as best we can while we live, punish the abuses, and lay bandages and poultices over the sores."[79] Luther's illustration of the futility of human efforts to solve the world's problems is often quoted: "The world is like a drunken peasant. If you lift him into the saddle on one side, he will fall off on the other side. One can't help him, no matter how one tries. He wants to be the devil's."[80]

Despite his pessimistic attitude, Luther did not give way to cynicism or passivity. He worked to try to help make life in this world more tolerable. The last days of his life were spent at the negotiating table dealing with secular matters. Luther clung to the view that he set forth years earlier in *To the Christian Nobility of the German Nation*: his national program for "his beloved Germans" was one of "repentance, repair, and reform, with no prospect of a golden age until after the Second Coming."[81] Luther took comfort in his conviction that he lived in the last days when God would return and make everything right. He believed that the Diet of Augsburg in 1530 was "truly the last trump before the day of judgment."[82] Ten years later, he said, "I always hope that the day of judgment isn't far away and that we'll live to see it."[83] Even encouraging events Luther interpreted as signs of the end times. "I think the last day is not far off," he commented at table. "My reason is that a last great effort is now being made to advance the gospel. It's like a candle. Just before it burns out it makes a last great spurt, as if it would continue to burn for a long time, and then it goes out."[84]

---

79 Haile, *Luther*, 101.

80 *LW*, 54:111.

81 Oberman, *Luther: Man between God and the Devil*, 47.

82 *LW*, 54:186.

83 Ibid., 54:402.

84 Gritsch, *Martin: God's Court Jester*, 82.

Spiritual Warfare

Once, Luther, joking with his friends, told them that he was "a simple man." "You are more learned than I am in economic and political matters," he said. "I'm not interested in such things. I'm concerned about the church and must defend myself against the attacks of the devil."[85] The devil was very real to Luther—and very powerful. Luther said, "The devil is as big as the world, as wide as the world, and he extends from heaven down into hell."[86]

Luther wrote: "Reader, be commended to God, and pray for the growth of the word against Satan. Strong and evil, now also very furious and savage, he knows his time is short and the kingdom of his pope is in danger."[87] The devil often troubled Luther by saying, "Before there was glorious peace, but now you have disturbed it, and who ordered you to do so?"[88] Luther sometimes dealt with the devil by making fun of him with coarse, rude language. He also learned how to answer the devil's theological arguments. Luther told a guest who was obsessed by thoughts of his sins: "Do not argue with Satan about the law. Make him discuss grace."[89]

While facing the power of the devil and the strategies of evil men, Christians seem to be fighting a losing battle. "Neither sweat nor sword can ever advance the messianic kingdom," Luther said. Rather, it comes by "enduring, working, persevering, waiting—publicly proclaiming the Gospel, openly beseeching God to intervene."[90]

Suffering

In *To the Christian Nobility of the German Nation*, the young Luther had written that it is the suffering Christ who seeks representation on earth not only through our working and preaching but also through our suffering and dying. The older Luther knew what it was to suffer. During the last decade and a half of his life, his physical ailments and discomforts became critical and at times life-threatening. He was often in pain, sometimes in agony, from kidney stones and gallstones, stomach disorders, increasing deafness, shortness of breath, severe headaches, and heart problems. He suffered mentally

---

85 *LW*, 54:405.
86 Haile, *Luther*, 185.
87 *LW*, 34:338.
88 *LW*, 54:96.
89 Haile, *Luther*, 188.
90 Oberman, *Luther: Man between God and the Devil*, 72.

and emotionally, troubled by spiritual depression and doubt and despair for the world, and sometimes for the church. He was deeply disappointed about the progress of the Reformation movement and anxious about the dangers that political involvement might bring. Toward the end, Luther began to question his own sanity, and even had thoughts of suicide. But he was able to say, "Well. All right. If I go mad, God will remain sane and Christ my Lord will be my wisdom."[91]

In times of depression, Luther said, we must "double up our fists and pray," but he admitted that it was not always easy to do so.[92] He urged the prayers of friends. He depended on Katie's love and wisdom. Eating a fine meal and drinking good beer also helped. Music, he found, was a good way to "banish trials and thoughts," since the devil hates it so.[93] Above all, Luther turned to the Bible for help in times of trouble. Preaching from 1 Peter 5:5–11, he urged Christians to fling aside "care and fearful apprehensions . . . but not into a corner . . . for when cares cling to the heart, they cannot be flung aside in that way. Let the Christian learn to cast both his heart and his cares upon God's back, for God has a strong neck and strong shoulders; He can easily carry the load."[94]

Commenting on Ecclesiastes 6:12, Luther asked, "Why are we so vexed by thoughts, seeing that the future is not in our power for one moment? Let us, then, be satisfied with the present and commit ourselves to the hand of God, who alone knows and controls the past and the future."[95] During a time of sickness in 1542, he found help in Psalm 31, admitting that he had not really understood "My times are in thy hand" until then. "That is, my whole life, each day, hour, moment—which is the same as to say, 'My health, sickness, misfortune, happiness, life, death, joy, and sorrow are in thy hand.'"[96]

Luther suffered the loss of friends and relatives. While he was at Coburg Castle in 1530, news of his father's death shook him. He took his psalter, went to his room, and wept for two days.[97] The next year, Luther's mother died. Nothing caused Luther greater suffering than the death of his thirteen-year-old

---

91 Haile, *Luther,* 217.
92 Ibid., 302.
93 Ibid.
94 *What Luther Says,* 3:1541.
95 Ibid., 3:1542.
96 Haile, *Luther,* 300.
97 Oberman, *Luther: Man between God and the Devil,* 311.

daughter, Magdalena, on September 20, 1542.[98] The separation caused by her death troubled him beyond measure. He said, "It's strange to know that she is surely at peace and that she is well off there [with her Father in heaven], very well off, and yet to grieve so much!" To friends who sympathized with him, he said simply, "I've sent a saint to heaven."[99]

Despite his suffering, Luther kept on preaching, teaching, and writing. It could even be said that *because of* his suffering, he kept on. From Psalm 119, he derived three rules for the "correct way of studying theology"—"*oratio* [prayer], *meditatio* [meditation], *tentatio* [suffering]." It is primarily through *tentatio* in its many forms that one comes to understand "how right, how true, how sweet, how lovely, how mighty, how comforting God's Word is, wisdom beyond all wisdom."[100]

Martyrdom was important to Luther because it epitomized his idea of the church as a suffering community. In his 1539 book *On the Councils and the Church*, he explicitly identified suffering and persecution as one of the marks of the true church:

> The holy Christian people are externally recognized by the holy possession of the sacred cross. They must endure every misfortune and persecution, all kinds of trials and evil from the devil, the world, and the flesh ... by inward sadness, timidity, fear, outward poverty, contempt, illness, and weakness, in order to become like their head, Christ.[101]

On July 1, 1523, two Augustinian monks from the monastery at Eisleben, Luther's birthplace, were burned before the town hall of Brussels. When Luther received the news, he began to weep and said, "I thought that I should be the first to be martyred for the Holy Gospel; but I was not worthy of it."[102] During a serious illness a few years later, Luther became depressed because he thought that God did not consider him worthy of martyrdom. Robert Barnes, an Augustinian monk from the Cambridge monastery who had studied in Wittenberg, was burned at Smithfield on July 30, 1540, by order of King

---

98 Luther's eight-month-old daughter, Elizabeth, had died August 3, 1528.
99 *LW*, 54:432–33.
100 Brecht, *The Preservation of the Church*, 143.
101 *LW, Vol. 41: Church and Ministry III*, ed. Eric W. Gritsch (Philadelphia: Fortress, 1966), 164.
102 Oberman, *Luther: Man between God and the Devil*, 265.

Henry VIII. Luther published a German translation of Barnes' last confession of faith. In the foreword, Luther wrote: "It is a particular joy to me to hear that our good and pious companion at home and table has so graciously been called upon by God to shed his blood for the sake of His beloved Son and to become a holy martyr."[103] From his first lectures on the Bible to his last on Genesis, Luther's view of the church remained unchanged: it is a visible and suffering communion of Christians. Through his long study of the prolonged trials of the patriarchs in Genesis, Luther learned that life can be a greater and truer martyrdom than any death, however spectacular.

World-Weariness

Luther enjoyed life in Wittenberg with his wife, children, students, friends, and his dog. He was delighted with the beauty of nature around him. On January 1, he greeted the year 1538 with the words, "How good, joyful, and auspicious is the beginning of a new year for the glory of Christ, the salvation of his church, and the confusion of Satan and his adherents!"[104] In 1539, he reveled in the flowers of a spring day, "whose blooms are a parable of the resurrection of the dead. How pleasant the trees are! How delightfully green everything is beginning to be! . . . If God can take such delight in our earthly sojourn, what must it be like in the life to come?"[105]

More and more, however, Luther was plagued with discouragement—about himself, the state of the world, and even the church. In April 1533, Luther declared, "I am quite tired of living. May our Lord God come soon and quickly take me away!"[106] In 1538, he said, "I am now exhausted and full of cares, yet I am plagued with many duties."[107] A few years later, he confessed, "I'm fed up with the world, and it is fed up with me."[108]

Approaching the End

In his lectures, Luther came to the last chapters of Genesis as he came to the last weeks of his life. There, he found many precious truths to strengthen his faith. He said about Jacob's death, "Jacob dies, it is true, yet his death is tantamount to life—indeed, it is the closest thing to life." Luther spoke for Jacob in

---

103 Ibid., 269.
104 *LW*, 54:255.
105 Ibid., 54:351.
106 Ibid., 54:83.
107 Ibid., 54:281.
108 Ibid., 54:448.

the first person, "I am dying and shall lie in the sepulcher, but God lives. He who has promised the land into which he will lead you will also set me over into another, far better land. For it is his promise."[109] Luther lectured for a few more weeks on the burial of Jacob and on Joseph's death and burial. He finally ended his ten-year labor on the book of Genesis on Tuesday, November 17, 1545, with the words: "And that is the sweet book of Genesis. May our Lord God give it to others to do a better job after me. I can do no more. I am weak. Pray God for me, that he may give me a blissful end."[110]

Luther was sick and weak, but he was still feisty. In January 1546, a few weeks before he died, he began a treatise against the Louvain theologians. He was more enraged at them than befits a theologian and an old man, he explained, "but one must resist Satan's monsters even if one must blow at them with one's last breath!"[111]

On February 7, Luther was in Eisleben on his third trip to help two counts, who were brothers, reconcile their differences. While there, he wrote to his wife in a playful and bantering tone:

> To my dear wife, Katherine Luther, doctoress and self-tormentor at Wittenberg, my gracious lady,
>
> Grace and peace in the Lord! Read, dear Katie, John and the Small Catechism, of which you once said: Indeed, everything in this book is said about me. For you want to assume the cares of your God, just as if He were not almighty and were unable to create ten Dr. Martins if this old one were drowned in the Saale or suffocated in a stove or trapped on Wolf's fowling floor. Leave me in peace with your worrying! I have a better Caretaker than you and all the angels. He it is who lies in a manger and nurses at a virgin's breast, but at the same time sits at the right hand of God, the almighty Father. Therefore be at rest. Amen.[112]

Catholics and Protestants awaited news of Luther's death—the Catholics hoped for a terrible death (to prove that he was wrong) and the Protestants a triumphant one (to prove that he was right). There are many great events in

---

109 Haile, *Luther*, 321.
110 Ibid., 324.
111 Edwards, *Luther's Last Battles*, 201.
112 *What Luther Says*, 3:1545.

Luther's life, but none greater than his last few days. Two days before he died, he wrote a few lines in Latin, found next to his deathbed. They read in part, "No one should believe that he has tasted the Holy Scriptures sufficiently unless he has spent one hundred years leading churches with the prophets." This was followed by the words "We are beggars" in German, and in Latin again, "That is true."[113] With those words, Luther aptly and humbly summed up his life as a Reformer and theologian. It was not what he did, but what God did through him. He was a beggar. That is true.

Martin Luther died in the early morning hours of February 18, 1546, only a few steps from the house in Eisleben where he was born sixty-two years earlier. A crowd of people surrounded his bed and tried to comfort him, as he kept repeating, "For God so loved the world that he gave his only Son." His comfort was not in what he had done for God, not in his love for God, but in God's love for him such that He gave His only Son to die for his sins. Luther had given his life to preaching and teaching Scripture alone, Christ alone, grace alone, received by faith alone. His one great message was that "the life of a Christian is linked to the lifeline of mercy which God established in Christ. Thus, the Christian truly lives by faith alone rather than by the merit of good works aimed at pacifying God."[114] Luther's longtime friend Justus Jonas, then pastor in Halle, asked, "Reverend father, will you die steadfast in Christ and the doctrines you have preached?" "Yes," replied the clear voice for the last time.[115]

Oberman ends his biography of Luther: "According to the medieval *memento mori*, in the midst of life we are surrounded by death. Luther's faith enabled him to vigorously turn this on its head: 'In the midst of death we are surrounded by life.'"[116]

Martin Luther was buried in front of the pulpit in the Castle Church of Wittenberg on February 22, 1546. It was an appropriate place. The pulpit was the place of his life's work. He was a preacher of the Word of God.

And he was faithful to the end.

---

113 Oberman, *Luther: Man between God and the Devil*, 167.
114 Gritsch, *Martin: God's Court Jester*, 75.
115 Oberman, *Luther: Man between God and the Devil*, 3.
116 Ibid., 330.

Chapter Four

THE FAMILY MAN:
LUTHER AT HOME

JOEL R. BEEKE

I n 1525, in Wittenberg, Germany, a former monk married a former nun: Katharina von Bora (b. January 29, 1499) became the wife of Dr. Martin Luther.[1] In some ways, this act was just as significant as Luther's nailing his Ninety-Five Theses to the church door. As William Lazareth writes, "Luther's marriage remains to this day the central evangelical symbol of the Reformation's liberation and transformation of Christian daily life."[2]

Luther's writings on domestic life shook the culture of Western Christendom and led to a new view of the family that later Reformers nurtured. Martin Brecht writes, "One should not underestimate the effect of Luther's writings on marriage, for they initiated a change in society."[3] In fact, scholars believe that Luther's ethical teachings have had a greater impact on family relationships than on any other aspect of ordinary life.[4]

---

1 On Luther's life, see Martin Brecht, *Martin Luther*, trans. James L. Schaaf, 3 vols. (Minneapolis: Fortress, 1985, 1990, 1993). I wish to thank Paul M. Smalley for his invaluable research assistance on this chapter.

2 William H. Lazareth, *Luther on the Christian Home: An Application of the Social Ethics of the Reformation* (Philadelphia: Muhlenberg, 1960), vii.

3 Brecht, *Martin Luther: Shaping and Defining the Reformation, 1521–1532*, 95.

4 Michael Parsons, *Reformation Marriage: The Husband and Wife Relationship in the Theology of Luther and Calvin*, Rutherford Studies in Historical Theology (Edinburgh, Scotland: Rutherford House, 2005), 2.

Luther had inherited the medieval view of marriage as a sacrament or special means of supernatural grace dispensed by the church. This view was asserted by Pope Innocent III at the beginning of the thirteenth century and affirmed at the Council of Florence (1439). As late as 1519, Luther affirmed that marriage was a Christian sacrament.[5] However, in 1520, Luther published *On the Babylonian Captivity of the Church*, in which he proposed that only baptism and the Lord's Supper were divinely instituted sacraments with a promise of saving grace.[6] Consequently, he no longer regarded marriage as a sacrament, though he did see it as a symbol of the "mystery" (*sacramentum*) of Christ and His church (Eph. 5:31–32).[7]

Paradoxically, while medieval Christianity affirmed marriage as a sacrament, it generally degraded women and human sexuality. Jerome's *Adversus Jovinianum* had become the "basic medieval textbook for antifeminism," though Augustine tried to bring more balance to the subject in his *De Bono Conjugali*.[8] The negativity prevailed despite the fact that in practice a number of people recognized the essential equality of women to men as well as their necessary place in daily life.[9] Peter Lombard noted that the first woman was created from Adam's side, "so that it should be shown that she was created for the partnership of love, lest, if perhaps she had been made from his head, she should be perceived as set over man in domination; or if from his feet, as if subject to him in servitude."[10] However, despite moderating voices, a negative attitude toward women, sex, and marriage prevailed and grew into what B.J. van der Walt calls "a chorus of contempt,"[11] one fed by the continuing influ-

---

5   "A Sermon on the Estate of Marriage (1519)," trans. James Atkinson, in *LW*, 44:10–12.

6   "The Babylonian Captivity of the Church (1520)," trans. A.T.W. Steinhäuser, rev. Frederick C. Ahrens and Abdel R. Wentz, in *LW*, 36:18, 124.

7   *LW*, 36:92–96.

8   Christopher N.L. Brooke, *The Medieval Idea of Marriage* (Oxford, England: Oxford University Press, 1989), 61–62. On this topic, see also Frances Gies and Joseph Gies, *Marriage and the Family in the Middle Ages* (New York: Harper and Row, 1987).

9   Eileen Power, *Medieval Women*, ed. M.M. Postan (Cambridge, England: Cambridge University Press, 1975), 34.

10 Peter Lombard, *The Sentences*, trans. Giulio Silano (Toronto: Pontifical Institutes of Mediaeval Studies, 2008), 2:77 (b. 2, dist. xviii, ch. 2).

11 B.J. van der Walt, "Woman and Marriage in the Middle Ages, in Calvin, and in Our Own Time," in *John Calvin's Institutes: His Magnum Opus*, proceedings of the Second South African Congress for Calvin Research, ed. B.J. van der Walt (Potchefstroom, South Africa: Potchefstroom University for Christian Higher Education, 1986), 188.

ence of ancient pagan writers, among other things.[12] The Reformation turned the church back to a more Christian view that sought to honor God's creation of woman in His image and His institution of marriage. As a result of Luther's writing and example, Martin Brecht says, "marriage and women were valued more highly."[13]

Luther had also been raised to believe that the holy service of God mandated celibacy. In the late middle ages, the church demanded that its priests not marry, though cases of clerical concubinage and immorality were notorious throughout Europe.[14] Luther later rejected monastic celibacy and mandatory celibacy for pastors as unbiblical but remained celibate for several years after the Reformation began. He commended celibacy to those with the "grace of chastity," for it is "the finest life . . . that one could possibly have."[15] Though encouraged to marry by friends, he had no mind to do it, "since he anticipated that he would soon have to face death" at the hands of his persecutors.[16]

However, Luther increasingly saw that to be consistent with his own teaching of the freedom of Christians to marry, he would do well to enter into matrimony himself. In April 1525, he visited his parents, and they encouraged him to marry. When some of Luther's friends learned about Luther's impending marriage, they were not supportive, but Luther pushed ahead anyway. Martin Luther was wedded to Katharina von Bora on Tuesday, June 13, 1525, in the presence of five witnesses. Their wedding feast was held two weeks later so that guests could arrive from more distant places. The city gave the newlyweds twenty silver *gulden* and a barrel of beer.[17]

Marriage was an adjustment for Luther, but a blessed one. In his first year of marriage, he said he had to get used to "a pair of pigtails lying beside him." He learned patience when Katie interrupted his intense theological study.[18] Marriage was also an adjustment for Katie; she discovered that the straw in Luther's bed had not been replaced for a year, and it was rotting in his sweat.[19]

---

12 *LW*, 45:36, quoted in Scott H. Hendrix, "Luther on Marriage," in *Harvesting Martin Luther's Reflections on Theology, Ethics, and the Church*, ed. Timothy J. Wengert (Grand Rapids, Mich.: Eerdmans, 2004), 170.

13 Brecht, *Shaping and Defining the Reformation*, 95.

14 Parsons, *Reformation Marriage*, 79.

15 "Matthew 18–24, Expounded in Sermons," in *LW, Vol. 68: Sermons on the Gospel of Matthew, Chapters 19–24*, ed. Benjamin T.G. Mayes (St. Louis: Concordia, 2014), 16.

16 Brecht, *Shaping and Defining the Reformation*, 196.

17 Ibid., 197–200.

18 *LW*, 54:191.

19 Brecht, *Shaping and Defining the Reformation*, 202.

Even so, after six years of marriage, Luther said, "I wouldn't give up my Katy for France or for Venice.[20] Years later, he declared, "I shall die as one who loves and lauds marriage."[21]

Luther on Marriage and Sexuality

Luther grounded his doctrine of marriage upon Genesis 2.[22] He observed, "The lawful joining of a man and a woman is a divine ordinance and institution. . . . Marriage is a divine kind of life because it was established by God Himself."[23] Later, Luther offered this definition: "Marriage is the divinely instituted and lawful union of a man and a woman."[24]

Though Luther's definition of marriage had much in common with that of his Christian forefathers, he developed his own doctrine of marriage in contrast to the medieval exaltation of celibacy as the noblest way of life for the Christian. With Paul (1 Tim. 4:1–3), he argued that Satanic influences had led people to think of marriage as impure and a concession to human weakness, and one fruit of the Reformation was the restoration of the honor of marriage and a realistic assessment of celibacy as practical only for those with "a greater gift than ordinary folks."[25]

The Goodness and Honor of the Woman

One's view of marriage is inseparable from one's view of women. Luther's view of women is complex, for it both affirms and denies their equality in different respects.[26] He said the first woman "was not the equal of the male in glory and prestige,"[27] but she did share the same essential humanity and image of God (Gen. 1:27). Luther noted:

---

20 *LW*, 54:7.

21 Brecht, *Shaping and Defining the Reformation*, 200.

22 "Sermon on the Estate of in Marriage," *LW*, 44:7–9.

23 *LW, Vol. 1: Lectures on Genesis, Chapters 1–5*, ed. Jaroslav Pelikan (Philadelphia: Fortress), 134 (Gen. 2:22).

24 *LW, Vol. 4: Lectures on Genesis, Chapters 21–25*, ed. Jaroslav Pelikan and Walter A. Hansen (St. Louis: Concordia, 1964), 244 (Gen. 24:1–4). For Luther's views on bigamy and polygamy, see Martin Luther, *Letters of Spiritual Counsel*, ed. and trans. Theodore G. Tappert (Vancouver: Regent College Publishing, 1960), 276, 288–91; *LW, Vol. 3: Lectures on Genesis, Chapters 15–20*, ed. Jaroslav Pelikan (St. Louis: Concordia, 1961), 45–47 (Gen. 16:1–2, 4); "Table Talk," Nos. 414, 5046, 5096, in *LW*, 54:65–66, 382, 387–90.

25 *LW*, 1:135 (Gen. 2:22).

26 Parsons, *Reformation Marriage*, 188–92.

27 *LW*, 1:69 (Gen. 1:27).

Thus even today the woman is the partaker of the future life, just as Peter says that they are joint heirs of the same grace (1 Peter 3:7). In the household the wife is a partner in the management and has a common interest in the children and property, and yet there is a great difference between the sexes. The male is like the sun in heaven, the female is like the moon, the animals like the stars, over which the sun and moon have dominion.[28]

Luther elsewhere said that woman by creation was "the equal of Adam" in ability and dominion over the earth and would have remained so apart from the fall.[29] Luther believed that the fall of mankind resulted in woman's subjection to her husband (Gen. 3:16).[30] Unlike some in Christendom, Luther did not blame women for the fall, but blamed the weakness of human nature.[31] He said Eve should be "praised as a most holy woman, full of faith and love" when considered after the fall.[32]

For a man of his time and place, Luther was no misogynist. He supported evangelical efforts to defend the female gender against sexist slurs.[33] Women are not a curse, but a blessing from God. Luther said, "Imagine what it would be like without this [female] sex. The home, cities, economic life, and government would virtually disappear. Men can't do without women. Even if it were possible for men to beget and bear children, they still couldn't do without women."[34]

The Holy and Honorable State of Matrimony

Medieval perspectives on marital sex granted the necessity of sexual relations to produce children but lamented the act itself as intrinsically sinful. In the eleventh century, Cardinal Damian viewed sexual relations with horror,

---

28 Ibid.

29 Ibid., 1:115 (Gen. 2:18).

30 Ibid., 1:203 (Gen. 3:16). See Mickey L. Mattox, "Luther on Eve, Women, and the Church," in *The Pastoral Luther: Essays on Martin Luther's Practical Theology*, ed. Timothy J. Wengert (Grand Rapids, Mich.: Eerdmans, 2009), 263.

31 *LW, Vol. 2: Lectures on Genesis, Chapters 6–14*, eds. Jaroslav Pelikan and Daniel E. Poellot (St. Louis: Concordia, 1960), 30 (Gen. 6:3).

32 *LW*, 1:324–25 (Gen. 4:25).

33 Scott H. Hendrix, "Christianizing Domestic Relations: Women and Marriage in Johann Freder's *Dialogus dem Ehestand zu Ehren*," *Sixteenth Century Journal* 23, No. 2 (1992): 251–66.

34 *LW*, 54:161.

arguing that marital sex excluded people from the highest places of heaven. He said sex is righteous only if one takes no pleasure in it.[35]

By contrast, Luther stressed the goodness and honor of sexual relations between husband and wife (Heb. 13:4). He said:

> This estate should not be condemned and rejected as something foul and unclean, as the pope and his followers do. For to be married is an ordinance and institution of God, since when God created man and woman, he himself placed them in this estate in which they not only could but should live godly, honorable, pure, and chaste lives, bearing children and peopling the world, indeed, the kingdom of God.[36]

Husbands and wives should thank God for giving them their own distinct genders and placing them together "in the holy estate of marriage."[37] Even if the Lord Jesus were to come in glory "when man and woman were having marital intercourse," they would have no reason to fear, for they would be fulfilling the calling God placed upon them.[38] Sex in marriage is not sin; the "natural, ardent desire" of sexual attraction is ordained by God.[39] Satan "slanders and shames marriage but adulterers, whores, and knaves remain in highest honor."[40] Though lust, pain, and shame have marred our sexuality since the fall, we must never cease to recognize the goodness of God's creation, for the Holy Spirit is unashamed to speak of human sexuality in His most pure and holy Word.[41] In particular, Luther rejected the idea that making love to one's spouse with great passion is the equivalent of adultery.[42]

Luther was deeply concerned with the plight of priests, monks, and nuns forbidden by church law to marry, though they often lacked the supernatural gift of celibacy. Luther said they should be allowed to live as husbands or

---

35 Parsons, *Reformation Marriage*, 85, 88; Brooke, *The Medieval Idea of Marriage*, 73.

36 "Sermon at Marriage of Sigismund von Lindenau," in *LW,* 51:359.

37 Ibid., 51:360.

38 Ibid., 51:362.

39 *LW,* 54:324; To Wolfgang Reissenbusch, March 27, 1525, in *Luther: Letters of Spiritual Counsel,* ed. and trans. Theodore G. Tappert, Library of Christian Classics XVIII (Philadelphia: Westminster, 1955), 272–73.

40 To Wolfgang Reissenbusch, in *Luther: Letters of Spiritual Counsel,* 274–75.

41 *LW,* 54:31; *LW,* 1:104 (Gen. 2:16–17).

42 Jane E. Strohl, "Luther on Marriage, Sexuality, and the Family," in *The Oxford Handbook of Martin Luther's Theology,* ed. Robert Kolb, Irene Dingel, and Ľubomír Batka (Oxford, England: Oxford University Press, 2014), 374. Henceforth cited as *Oxford Handbook.*

wives with the people they loved.[43] Many priests needed a legitimate outlet for their sexual desires and a woman's help in housekeeping. Luther said that in appointing female housekeepers, the church was "putting straw and fire together and forbidding them to smoke or burn!"[44] He encouraged priests, monks, and nuns to get married despite the severe penalties that Roman authorities often imposed.[45]

Luther urged one of his young theological students: "You cannot be without a wife and remain without sin. After all, marriage is an ordinance and creation of God. Therefore it is not Satan's idea when a man desires to marry an honorable girl, for Satan hates this kind of life. So make the venture in the name of the Lord and on the strength of his blessing and institution!"[46]

The Dangers that Threaten Marriage

Luther urged people to seek God's blessing on their marriages from beginning to end. God created the first woman and brought her to Adam, so people today should "earnestly pray to God for a spouse," knowing that a wife is a gift from God (Prov. 19:14).[47] They should also pray for the grace to persevere in love for each other, realizing that the devil can tear apart a marriage through bitter hatred.[48]

Luther warned that "the devil cannot bear to see spouses living together in harmony," so he wars against marriages.[49] Spouses must not think they live in paradise; marriage must be lived out "in the midst of demons."[50] Our sinful condition also wars against marriage. Luther wrote, "Our old Adam does not like what God gives, and what [God] does not give, that he wants."[51] Luther also described what could happen if "old Adam" prevails in marriage:

> I have often seen two of you come together with great burning desire
> and love, and each wanted to gobble up the other out of love, but

---

43 "To the German Nobility Concerning the Reform of the Christian Estate (1520)," *LW*, 44:177.
44 Ibid., 44:178.
45 To Three Nuns, August 6, 1524, in *Luther: Letters of Spiritual Counsel*, 271; To Wolfgang Reissenbusch, in *Luther: Letters of Spiritual Counsel*, 274; Brecht, *Shaping and Defining the Reformation*, 100–101; *Table Talk* nos. 1346, 2925b, in *LW*, 54:141–42, 181.
46 *LW*, 54:31.
47 "Sermon on the Estate of Marriage," in *LW*, 44:8.
48 *LW*, 54:25–26.
49 *LW*, 68:14.
50 Paul Althaus, *The Ethics of Martin Luther*, trans. Robert C. Schultz (Philadelphia: Fortress, 1972), 91.
51 *LW*, 68:14.

before even half a year had passed, he was an adulterer and she, an adulteress. Others I have known to be married and at enmity with each other, yet they produced five or six children together—thus they were bound one to the other not only by marriage but also by their offspring—and still they ran away from each other.[52]

Despite the fickleness of fallen mankind, Luther said the law of creation (Gen. 2) and of Christ (Matt. 19) prohibited divorce except in cases of adultery or abandonment.[53] Luther concluded, "If you get angry and become at odds with each other, then be reconciled to each other again. . . . But there should be no divorce among you."[54] Marriage is "a divine order and institution that He does want to have torn apart, but united until death."[55] Luther counseled one husband that even though he had the right to divorce his wife, it would be better to show her mercy and patience "if she behaves uprightly in the future," for "grace goes before the law."[56]

Although marriage is an earthly, temporal institution, it is restored to its divine purpose by the heavenly grace of Christ obtained through faith and prayer. Michael Parsons explains: "The gospel confirms and establishes the creation ordinances of God. So it is by the grace of God and through the Word that he restores marriage to what it ought to be."[57] When the Luther family received news of a woman caught in adultery and her husband's violent response, Katie exclaimed, "How can people be so wicked and defile themselves with such sin!" Martin replied, "Ah, dear Katy, people don't pray."[58]

Love and Authority in Marriage

Luther also taught that the husband is the head of the household, and his wife should voluntarily submit to his authority, even if he is an unbeliever (1 Peter 3:1).[59] Inward submission based on a desire to please God is "a high and noble treasure" that makes all of a wife's works "golden" and her person

---

52 Ibid..

53 Ibid., 68:6; To John Wickmann, November 2, 1537, in *Luther: Letters of Spiritual Counsel*, 284; "Table Talk," Nos. 3967, 4499, in *LW*, 54:302, 349.

54 *LW*, 68:8.

55 Ibid., 68:12.

56 To Valentine Hausmann, January 27, 1538, in *Luther: Letters of Spiritual Counsel*, 285.

57 Parsons, *Reformation Marriage*, 120. He cites *LW*, 29:20; 17:139; 33:52; 54:177.

58 *LW*, 54:415.

59 "Sermons on the First Epistle of St. Peter (1523)," in *LW, Vol. 30: The Catholic Epistles*, ed. Jaroslav Pelikan and Walter A Hansen (St. Louis: Concordia, 1967), 87.

"magnificent" and rich in Christ.[60] The godly wife need not live in fear but can live with confidence in the reign of God over all things, knowing that He is pleased with her.[61]

Luther observed that a meek and quiet spirit is "a rare quality in a woman," and the female inclination to rule often results in "marital discord, blows, and beatings."[62] He spoke frankly about marital conflict and domestic abuse, saying, "Women are a fragile sex and under authority; therefore they can suffer miserably. . . . The rule is perfect, but life is not."[63] He admonished men not to beat their wives, for voluntary submission cannot be coerced. He warned husbands: "You will accomplish nothing with blows; they will not make a woman pious and submissive. If you beat one devil out of her, you will beat two into her, as the saying goes."[64]

He exhorted husbands to remember their wives' physical and emotional weaknesses, and to be patient and positive in their attitude toward them. He said, "One can always find more good than bad in women."[65] He also admonished husbands to "take on the form of a servant" like Christ (Phil. 2:7), but he said that they must not stand by passively when their wives defiantly trample on their authority.[66] The husband must treat his wife with thoughtful care, "for you are her husband to help, support, and protect her, not to harm her." Luther urged men to honor their Christian wives, knowing that in having such wives they possess all the blessings of Christ (1 Peter 3:7).[67] A husband must exercise authority over his wife "with love and discernment," Luther said. If his wife is angry and hurt, a harsh reply may break "the bond of marriage, namely, love," and give Satan a place in the family.[68]

Luther affirmed the spiritual equality of the different roles of men and women: "For inwardly we are all alike; there is no difference between a man and a woman. Externally, however, God wants the husband to rule and the wife to be submissive to him."[69] This reflects Luther's distinction between the

---

60 *LW,* 30:88, 90.
61 Ibid., 30:91.
62 "Lectures on Titus (1527)," in *LW, Vol. 29: Lectures on Titus, Philemon, and Hebrews,* ed. Jaroslav Pelikan (St. Louis: Concordia, 1968), 55.
63 *LW,* 29:57.
64 *LW,* 30:88.
65 *LW,* 29:57; cf. "Sermons on the First Epistle of St. Peter," in *LW,* 30:91.
66 To Stephen Roth, April 12, 1528, in *Luther: Letters of Spiritual Counsel,* 277–78.
67 "Sermons on the First Epistle of St. Peter," in *LW,* 30:92–93.
68 *LW,* 3:58 (Gen. 16:6).
69 *LW,* 30:93.

spiritual kingdom of Christ, in which all believers are equal (Gal. 3:28), and the temporal kingdom of this world, in which social life is defined by distinctions of status and authority in the order established by God.[70]

The Health of the Marital Relationship

For Luther, marriage is not just an economic and physical arrangement but a relationship of love. God intended that "the love of a man and woman" should be "the greatest and purest of all loves."[71] It is "not good" for man to be alone, God said (Gen. 2:18), because (1) men need women to increase the human race, (2) "for companionship," (3) for help in administrating the home—"the management of the household must have the ministration of the dear ladies"—and (4) as "an antidote against sin," so that people do not commit fornication.[72] Luther saw marriage as sharing life together for the glory of God: "For if the wife is honorable, virtuous, and pious, she shares in all the cares, endeavors, duties, and functions of her husband."[73]

Luther emphasized the goodness of sexual relations in marriage in contrast to the asceticism of enforced celibacy. He said an essential component of marriage is "the natural desire of sex."[74] Luther also said that wives "should enjoy their husbands' bodies."[75] He called for "moderation in intercourse" and for husbands and wives to "not grow tired of their own spouses and lose their desire for them," lamenting, "I have seen many who became disgusted with marital relations."[76] Sexual relations in marriage must be governed by the law of love, in which each party offers his or her body to serve the needs of the other (1 Cor. 7).[77]

God also designed marriage for friendship and companionship. The relationship intended by God between husband and wife is "inseparable and intimate."[78] Spouses cannot simply take for granted that they once made vows to each other or that they share a bed; they must work at becoming more united in mind and habit. Luther said: "There's more to it than a union of

---

70 Parsons, *Reformation Marriage*, 127–30. For a table on the distinctions between the spiritual kingdom and the temporal kingdom in Luther's theology, see pp. 122–23n74.

71 "Sermon on the Estate of Marriage," in *LW*, 44:8.

72 *LW*, 1:116 (Gen. 2:18).

73 Ibid., 1:137 (Gen. 2:23).

74 *LW*, 54:25.

75 *LW*, 29:54.

76 Ibid., 29:56.

77 Strohl, "Luther on Marriage, Sexuality, and the Family," in *Oxford Handbook*, 374.

78 *LW*, 1:117 (Gen. 2:18).

flesh. There must be harmony with respect to patterns of life and ways of thinking. The bonds of matrimony alone won't do it."[79]

The marriage of Martin and Katie Luther was marked by affection and joy. Though he did not pursue her out of sexual desire, Luther said, "I cherish her," which was "a strong affirmation of love that goes deeper than passion."[80] He addressed his letters to Katie, "My Dearest," and ended them, "Your Loved One," which were not conventional expressions. He said, "With the woman who has been joined to me by God I may jest [and] have fun."[81]

Luther also stressed the importance of trust in marriage to achieve true intimacy. Referring to Proverbs 31:11, he said: "Among the foremost praises of a wife is this, that her husband's heart trusts her. . . . And truly, if there is no trust, hearts will never unite closely; nor will there ever be any true love between them. But this world has nothing more beautiful than this union of hearts between spouses."[82] He said that when such trust is moderated by a realistic view of one's spouse as a fallible human being, it makes one "readier to forgive" and prevents harmony from being disturbed. The Scriptures commend love and "mutual trust" between spouses, not "suspicion and hatred."[83] Luther expressed confidence in Katie when he praised her in his will of 1542 "as a pious and faithful spouse" who "has at all times held me dear."[84]

Luther on Family Life

Luther also appreciated family life, both as a natural blessing and a means of sanctification. Ulrich Leupold writes, "In opposition to the medieval glorification of celibacy, Luther never tired of praising the married estate as a divine institution. No wonder he loved and frequently quoted the 128th Psalm!"[85] Luther said the names "father" and "mother" are the greatest honors of our sexuality, and procreation is "delightful" and "sacred."[86]

A year after Katie married Martin, she bore Hans (1526); followed by

---

79 *LW,* 54:444.

80 Hendrix, "Luther on Marriage," in *Harvesting Martin Luther's Reflections,* 179, citing *LW, Vol. 49: Letters II,* ed. Gottfried G. Krodel (Philadelphia: Fortress, 1972), 117.

81 Brecht, *The Preservation of the Church,* 235.

82 *LW,* 2:301 (Gen. 12:11–13).

83 Ibid., 2:302.

84 Brecht, *The Preservation of the Church,* 244.

85 Ulrich S. Leupold, editorial introduction to Martin Luther, "Happy Who in God's Fear Doth Stay" (1524), trans. George MacDonald, in *LW, Vol. 53: Liturgy and Hymns,* ed. Ulrich S. Leupold (Philadelphia: Fortress, 1965), 242–43.

86 *LW,* 1:118 (Gen. 2:18).

Elizabeth (1528), who died eight months later to the piercing grief of her father; Magdalene (1529); Martin (1531); Paul (1533); and Margaret (1534). The Luthers also shared their home with the children of Martin's sister, Katie's aunt, and various students and visitors.[87] It was a busy household.

The Duties of a Child toward Father and Mother

Luther taught that honoring those in authority over us, especially our parents, is our highest duty to mankind (Ex. 20:12). Keeping the rest of the Ten Commandments in future generations depends on keeping this command (Ps. 78:5–6).[88] All authority among human beings derives from the authority of parents over children.[89] Luther defined honor broadly: "It means that we obey them, have regard for what they do and what they say, esteem them highly, give way to them, and accept what they say." Honor requires "that we endure their treatment of us without complaint," unless they command us to be unfaithful to God, and to "provide them with food, clothing, and shelter when they are in need." Honor means respect joined with love, not fear and hate, but a fear of offending our parents joined with trust in them.[90] Luther believed that went far beyond mere courtesy and necessitated a humble awareness that there is a "majesty hidden" bestowed on parents by God.[91]

Honoring one's parents is difficult, for the commands of godly parents often cut across a child's corrupt will, and he is tempted to despise them, complain against them, or worse. Children need God's grace to truly honor their parents.[92] The tendency of children by nature is to respond to discipline and to being restrained from evil with "poisonous resentment."[93] Yet, honoring one's parents bears fruit in generations to come. Luther warned, "This is why so few marriages turn out well," namely, because in the first place the couple scorned their parents.[94]

---

87 Brecht, *Shaping and Defining the Reformation*, 203–4, 432; Brecht, *The Preservation of the Church*, 20–21.

88 "Treatise on Good Works" (1520), in *LW*, 44:81, 83.

89 Althaus, *The Ethics of Martin Luther*, 99.

90 "Treatise on Good Works," in *LW*, 44:81.

91 Althaus, *The Ethics of Martin Luther*, 100. On parental authority over the marriage of a son or daughter, see *Luther: Letters of Spiritual Counsel*, 263–69, 283, 286–88; "Table Talk," No. 5441, in *LW*, 54:424.

92 "Treatise on Good Works," in *LW*, 44:82.

93 "Ten Sermons on the Catechism" (1528), ed. and trans. John W. Doberstein, in *LW*, 51:146.

94 "Ten Sermons on the Catechism," in *LW*, 51:147.

Luther loved and honored his own parents. In February 1530, Luther wrote a beautiful letter of gospel hope to his dying father. Luther's parents had embraced the evangelical faith, attended Luther's wedding to Katie, and visited the family several times.[95] Luther's father died on May 29, and Luther wrote to Melanchthon, "This death has cast me into deep mourning, not only because of the ties of nature but also because it was through his sweet love to me that my Creator endowed me with all that I am and have." Luther found consolation, however, in the way his father died: "My father fell asleep softly and strong in his faith in Christ." Even so, Luther wrote that "his kindness and the memory of his pleasant conversation have caused so deep a wound in my heart that I have scarcely ever held death in such low esteem."[96]

A year later, Luther's mother, Margaret, also died. When Luther heard of her illness, he wrote a tender letter reminding her that Jesus Christ is the Savior and that He has overcome the world (John 16:33). He concluded, "All your children and my Katie pray for you. Some weep. Others say when they eat, 'Grandmother is very sick.' God's grace be with us all. Amen."[97]

The Good Works of Being a Father and Mother

Luther viewed family life as a noble, heavenly calling. As he saw it, nothing is more important in our pilgrimage to heaven than bringing up our children in the Lord, and nothing damns parents to hell so effectively as allowing their children to sin without discipline. Luther wrote that each father should "regard his child as nothing else but an eternal treasure God has commanded him to protect, and so prevent the world, the flesh, and the devil from stealing the child away and bringing him to destruction."[98]

Luther believed that the Christian home is where faith can work by love to please God. Faith is the first and most fundamental work of the Christian (John 6:28–29), for it alone gives the sinner confidence before God through Christ's death (1 John 2:1–2) and makes the heart "sweet" toward God, thus motivating all other good works.[99] Christian parenting is a prime example of the compassion for the needy that Christ said would set apart the righteous

---

95 To Father John Luther, February 15, 1530, in *Luther: Letters of Spiritual Counsel*, 29–32. On his father's faith, see "Table Talk," No. 1388, in *Luther: Letters of Spiritual Counsel*, 32–33.

96 *Luther: Letters of Spiritual Counsel*, 30.

97 To Mrs. John Luther, May 20, 1531, in *Luther: Letters of Spiritual Counsel*, 33–36.

98 "Sermon on the Estate of Marriage," in *LW*, 44:12–13.

99 "Treatise on Good Works," in *LW*, 44:23, 37.

on judgment day (Matt. 25:35–36). However, apart from faith in Christ, no work of child-rearing pleases God.[100]

Good works require practical management of resources. A husband and wife serve God in an economic partnership with each other, which Luther summarized in the aphorism, "The husband should earn and the wife save."[101] Luther said, "It is the chief praise of a woman if she takes care of the house" with "decency and discipline" (see Titus 2:5). This involves avoiding "frivolous" spending of the husband's income, cheerfully staying at home, and working in the kitchen.[102] Luther's refusal to take payment for his books and his immense generosity and hospitality to others greatly strained the household budget, but Katie's careful oversight of their finances and property helped to keep them afloat.[103]

Through faith in Christ, household work becomes holy work. Luther said the Holy Spirit is unashamed to bless a woman's household chores.[104] If a wife works in the kitchen, feeds the children, washes them, and puts them to bed as a believer trusting in Christ, then she is a saint.[105] In Christ, the ordinary becomes extraordinary: "The life of married people, if they are in the faith, deserves to be rated higher than those who are famous for miracles."[106] Indeed, in the ordinary labors of common life, men and women serve as God's coworkers.[107]

The good works of the Christian home are not limited to the home, but also serve the purposes of mission and doxology (Titus 2:5). Luther said to wives and parents, "Through faith we are justified; through good works God is glorified. . . . And God wants to use your life to convert other nations, that the kingdom of Christ may be expanded." Thus the ordinary duties of home and family, if pursued faithfully, will support the church's evangelistic mission and impact the world for the glory of God.[108]

---

100 "Treatise on Good Works," in *LW*, 44:85–87.
101 *LW*, 54:337.
102 Luther, "Lectures on Titus," in *LW*, 29:56.
103 Rudolf K. Markwald and Marilynn M. Markwald, *Katharina von Bora: A Reformation Life* (St. Louis: Concordia, 2002), 86–88.
104 *LW*, 29:56–57.
105 *LW*, 3:204 (Gen. 18:9).
106 Ibid., 3:210 (Gen. 18:11–12).
107 Lazareth, *Luther on the Christian Home*, 145.
108 *LW*, 29:57.

Bringing Up Children in the Nurture and Admonition of the Lord

Luther said parents should not merely lavish honors and possessions on their children but should "enrich their souls with the arts, with study, with sound literature," and especially "in the fear of God." If this is done diligently, fathers and mothers will find that they have "plenty of opportunity" to practice godliness and good works in their own households without running around looking for something to do.[109] Luther strongly believed in education. He required that Katie study the Bible, though she sometimes felt that she knew enough; he had his children tutored by older students, and his sons studied law, theology, and medicine.[110]

Luther used catechisms to encourage household piety. In the Small Catechism, Luther directed the head of the household to teach his family the meaning of the Lord's Supper, how to begin and end each day in prayer, and how to give thanks to God at meals.[111] He also included a list of Scripture verses relevant to different kinds of people, including husbands (Col. 3:19; 1 Peter 3:7), wives (1 Peter 3:1, 6), parents (Eph. 6:4), and children (Eph. 6:1–3).[112] Luther wanted to shift the focus of spirituality from the monastery to the home, turning each family into a house of prayer with every member instructed by the Word of Christ. In the preface to his Large Catechism, he wrote, "It is the duty of every head of household at least once a week to examine the children one after another" in their knowledge.[113] They should be required to recite the Ten Commandments, the Apostles' Creed, and the Lord's Prayer every day "when they arise in the morning, when they go their meals, and when they go to bed at night."[114]

Luther said loving one's children requires a regular use of "the rod and discipline" because of the foolishness of a child's heart (Prov. 3:11; 23:13).[115] Luther believed in corporal discipline, but a restrained and merciful use of it. Luther said: "One shouldn't whip children too hard. My father once whipped

---

109 Ibid., 29:55.

110 Brecht, *The Preservation of the Church*, 236–37, 443n12.

111 Martin Luther, The Small Catechism (1529), in *The Book of Concord: The Confessions of the Evangelical Lutheran Church*, eds. Robert Kolb and Timothy J. Wengert (Minneapolis: Fortress, 2000), 362–64.

112 Luther, "The Household Chart of Some Bible Passages," The Small Catechism, in *The Book of Concord* (2000), 365–66.

113 Martin Luther, preface to the Large Catechism (1529), in *The Book of Concord* (2000), 383.

114 Luther, Large Catechism, in *The Book of Concord* (2000), 385.

115 *LW,* 29:55.

me so severely that I ran away from him, and he was worried that he might not win me back again. I wouldn't like to strike my little Hans [almost six years old at the time] very much, lest he should become shy and hate me." Luther reminded his hearers that though God chastises His children, He is quick to rescue and raise up those who run to Him.[116] Discipline must be joined with kindness: "One must punish in such a way that the rod is accompanied by the apple."[117] He warned that a harsh and stern father "makes his children either dispirited or hopeless," and said, "Praise and punishment belong together."[118]

Luther called people to use "simple and playful methods" to "bring up young people in the fear and honor of God." Mere corporal discipline will not build heart conviction but will only result in temporary conformity. Therefore, God's people must teach children at their level, using "baby talk" that will "sink into their minds."[119] Luther concluded, "Therefore let all heads of a household remember that it is their duty, by God's injunction and command, to teach their children or have them taught the things they ought to know."[120]

Luther summed up the godly parent's legacy in his words to his one-year-old son when he put him to bed, perhaps sung as a lullaby: "Go now and be godly. No money will I leave you, but a rich God will I leave you. Only be godly."[121]

The Christian Family in a Fallen World

Luther grounded his teaching on family life upon earthy realism. He knew that Katie had her hands full. In 1532, she was nursing one child while pregnant with another.[122] Later in 1540, she was incapacitated for two or three months after a miscarriage.[123] Yet for all the burdens of motherhood, she was amazingly active. One biographer wrote, "Kate became gardener, fisher, brewer, fruit grower, cattle and horse breeder, cook, bee-keeper, provisioner, nurse, and vintner."[124] In 1542, for example, the Luthers had five cows, nine calves, one goat, two kids, eight pigs, two sows, and three piglets.[125]

---

116 *LW,* 54:157.
117 Ibid., 54:235.
118 Ibid., 54:457.
119 Luther, Large Catechism, in *The Book of Concord* (2000), 396.
120 Ibid., 476.
121 Brecht, *The Preservation of the Church,* 20.
122 *LW,* 54:162.
123 Brecht, *The Preservation of the Church,* 235.
124 Markwald and Markwald, *Katharina von Bora,* 82.
125 Brecht, *The Preservation of the Church,* 243.

As a family man, Luther said celibacy is full of temptations, but he also admitted that marriage is full of busyness and annoyances. He said, "We have become so infected with original sin that there's no kind of life which, once undertaken, isn't a matter of regret at times." Yet, he said, "It seems to me that it is the pleasantest kind of life to have a moderate household, to live with an obedient wife, and to be content with little."[126]

Luther delighted in his children. He believed that "children are a gift of God and come solely through the blessing of God" (Ps. 127:3), a point overlooked by pagans who view children as the result of mere nature and accident.[127] One day, Luther chatted with his seven-year-old son about his doll, and commented on the simplicity and natural playfulness of children, which Luther said makes them "the dearest jesters."[128] The Luther home was full of music, for Luther loved to sing in harmony with his family and guests.[129]

Life was not without sorrow, however. On September 20, 1542, Luther's daughter Magdalene died at age thirteen after a short illness. While the girl was dying, Luther tried to comfort his sobbing wife by saying, "Think where she's going. She'll get along all right."[130]

As Magdalene declined further, he prayed, "I love her very much. But if it is thy will to take her, dear God, I shall be glad to know that she is with thee." He asked the young lady lying in her bed, "Dear Magdalene, my little daughter, you would be glad to stay here with me, your father. Are you also glad to go to your Father in heaven?" She said, "Yes, dear Father, as God wills." Luther exclaimed, "You dear little girl!" and marveled that God had given him such great gifts.[131] He got down on his knees and held his daughter, weeping and still praying for God to spare her, but then said, "Thy will be done."

Magdalene died in his arms. Melanchthon stood by and marveled, "If the love of God for the human race is as great as the love of parents for their children, then it is truly great and ardent." As they laid Magdalene in a coffin, Luther remarked, "It's strange to know that she is surely at peace and that she is well off there, very well off, and yet to grieve so much!" When they buried her, Luther said, "There is a resurrection of the flesh."[132]

---

126 *LW,* 54:218.
127 *LW,* 2:132 (Gen. 9:1).
128 *LW,* 54:334.
129 Scott H. Hendrix, *Martin Luther: A Very Short Introduction* (Oxford, England: Oxford University Press, 2010), 78.
130 *LW,* 54:428.
131 Ibid., 54:430–31.
132 Ibid., 54:431–33.

Luther understood that marriage and child-rearing take place in a world deeply marred by sin and death. He said "bearing one's cross" was one of the primary purposes of marriage.[133] Yet, the believer does not shirk responsibilities such as changing diapers and nursing sick children, and he does not complain at the "bitterness and drudgery." He sees parenting as pleasing to God, a divine service for which sinners are "not worthy." When Christians parent their children by faith in Christ, "God, with all his angels and creatures, is smiling."[134] Thus, Christian family life is part of our "cross-marked vocation," as Gustaf Wingren wrote, where we experience our union with Christ in His crucifixion and resurrection in our ordinary callings.[135] Luther believed that the stresses of family life offer one of the best environments in which to cultivate Christian discipleship.[136]

Conclusion: The Legacy of the Luther Family

Luther died on February 18, 1546. Just a week earlier, he had teased Katie about her anxiety about him, addressing a letter, "Martin Luther to the holy lady, full of worries." He counseled her, "Pray, and let God worry. You have certainly not been commanded to worry about me or yourself. 'Cast your burden on the Lord, and he will sustain you'" (Ps. 55:22).[137]

Katie had many burdens to cast on the Lord after her husband died. She was forced to flee Wittenberg due to the Schmalkaldic War, and she resided elsewhere from November 1546 to January 1547, and again from April to June 1547. During the war, the family's property and possessions were destroyed, leaving Katie impoverished and dependent on the support of others. Next, the plague came to Wittenberg in 1552, forcing the university to retreat to Torgau. In the process of the move, Katie fell in a ditch full of cold water. Seriously weakened, she died on December 20, 1552, not quite fifty-four years old.[138] It is reported that before she died, she declared that she would "cling to Christ like a burr to a dress."[139]

The Luther family lived and died by faith grounded in love. Luther deeply

---

133 *LW*, 4:244 (Gen. 24:1–4).

134 *LW*, 45:39–41, cited in Parsons, *Reformation Marriage*, 150–51.

135 Gustaf Wingren, *Luther on Vocation* (Evansville, Ind.: Ballast, 1994), 57–58.

136 Strohl, "Luther on Marriage, Sexuality, and the Family," in *Oxford Handbook*, 371.

137 *LW*, 50:305–6, cited in Michael A.G. Haykin and Victoria J. Haykin, *The Christian Lover: The Sweetness of Love and Marriage in the Letters of Believers* (Orlando, Fla.: Reformation Trust, 2009), 4.

138 Brecht, *The Preservation of the Church*, 378.

139 Markwald and Markwald, *Katharina von Bora*, 192.

loved his parents, wife, and children. His household became an open book for guests to read of the sanctity of ordinary life shared by a former monk and a former nun. In both his writings and relationships, Martin Luther presented a vision of the family that was full of the angst and ugliness of life in a fallen world and yet was brightened by faith in the Lord.

Luther perpetuated the traditional and biblical understanding of the family as a social state ordered by God in relationships of well-defined authority. At the same time, he gleaned from Holy Scripture a vibrant view of the goodness of women; the honor of sexual intimacy between spouses; the importance of affection, kindness, and trust in the marital relationship; and the sacred calling of raising children in the Lord.

By word and deed, this Reformer helped to restore to European society a model of a truly evangelical domestic life. Just as Luther translated the Bible into the language of the common people, so he translated Christian spirituality into the world of the marriage bed, the cradle, and the dinner table.

Part Two

LUTHER'S THOUGHT

Chapter Five

SCRIPTURE ALONE: LUTHER'S DOCTRINE OF SCRIPTURE

MICHAEL S. HORTON

n 1450, Johannes Guttenberg invented the first printing press known to Europeans. Five years later, he published the first complete book printed with movable type: a Latin Vulgate edition of the Bible. Ironically, though, his first publication was a papal indulgence issued three years earlier. Little could the ingenious inventor have known that his first two printings would collide sixty-two years later, when his presses would be the crucial medium for disseminating a Saxon monk's Ninety-Five Theses against indulgences and a German Bible that corrected serious errors of the Vulgate. After highlighting some key moments in which Luther's view of Scripture was formed, this chapter will summarize that view—mostly in his own words.

Luther laid his eyes on a copy of the Bible for the first time in the university library at Erfurt, when he was twenty years old. His family was reasonably devout, but the Mass was chiefly a theatrical event conducted in Latin, of which the priests themselves typically knew only enough to perform the service. In a lot of towns, Luther said, one would only hear a sermon at Lent.[1] What little one learned directly from church consisted of representations of

---

1 Herman Eikerling, *Luther and His Century: Seven Lectures* (London: Burns and Oates, 1886; repr. Charleston, S.C.: Nabu, 2011), 19–22.

biblical stories and the saints painted on the walls. Luther recalled being fearful as he entered the Gothic doors and was greeted by an ominous relief of Jesus at the last judgment. In contrast to this image, the saints were amiable friends surrounding the most amiable of all: the Virgin Mary, who could be prevailed upon to make her Son more favorably inclined to poor sinners. Holy days involved annual reenactments of the signal events of the gospel, but Jesus' person and work were buried in a heap of saints' days and myriad superstitions, relics, and pilgrimages.

After taking a general master's degree at Erfurt, Luther—against his father's wishes—turned from the study of law to become an Augustinian friar in 1505. In his first year at the monastery, he received, along with the other novitiates, a red leather Bible, but it was taken from him the next year so that he would study physics, the arts, and other subjects. In fact, he recalled that Andreas von Karlstadt, chancellor and chair of the Bible department, did not even own a Bible until many years after he had earned his doctorate. Reflecting on these years in his *Table Talk*, Luther said:

> If I had kept at it, I would have become exceedingly good at locating things in the Bible. At that time no other study pleased me so much as sacred literature. With great loathing I read physics [Aristotle's *Physics*], and my heart was aglow when the time came to return to the Bible . . . I read the Bible diligently. Sometimes one statement occupied all my thoughts for a whole day.[2]

Two years later, Luther was ordained. The abbot of the monastery, Johann von Staupitz, was head of the order in Germany and was a reformer in his own right. He wrote a treatise defending predestination and salvation by grace and encouraging his monks to study the Bible daily.

Luther wore out his psalter. Later, he would call the Psalms "a little Bible," as it testifies to Christ's death and resurrection for sinners.[3] He began to devour the Scriptures. Nevertheless, he reports, "I lost touch with Christ the Savior and Comforter, and made of him the jailer and hangman of my poor soul."[4] Whenever he read of "the righteousness of God," he could only think of

---

2   *LW*, 54:14.
3   "Preface to the Psalms," *LW, Vol. 35: Word and Sacrament I*, ed. E. Theodore Bachman (Philadelphia: Fortress, 1960), 254.
4   Quoted in Kittelson, *Luther the Reformer*, 79.

the righteousness that moves God to condemn the unrighteous. Tormented by fear, Luther spent every hour hoping to become acceptable to God, but despite wearing out his confessor and performing penances, he could not find solace.

Staupitz knew just what to do: send the despairing monk to study the Bible at the University of Wittenberg, founded in 1502 by the abbot and Prince Elector Frederick III. There, he studied Scripture and joined the faculty as professor of Bible in 1512. This was an unusual position in a medieval university, and the fact that it existed before Luther reminds us that he did not rise phoenix-like from the ashes of the medieval church but was indebted to godly believers who knew that the church needed pastors who were steeped in God's Word. In fact, Staupitz was exactly right: the more that Luther wrestled with Scripture, the greater his insight and the satisfaction of his spiritual longing. It did not happen quickly, though. At first, Luther's profound sense of God's righteousness and his own unrighteousness became even more haunting. He lectured on the Psalms (1513–15), then on Romans (1515–16), Hebrews (1517), and Galatians (1519), before returning to the Psalms again (1518–21).

During this period, as he pored over Romans 1–3, the truth hit him like a thunderbolt. True, the righteousness of God condemns all, Jew and Gentile, as Paul argues in Romans 1:16–3:20. But, Paul continues:

> But now the righteousness of God has been manifested apart from the law, although the Law and the Prophets bear witness to it—the righteousness of God through faith in Jesus Christ for all who believe. For there is no distinction: for all have sinned and fall short of the glory of God, and are justified by his grace as a gift . . . to be received through faith. (3:21–25a)

The righteousness *of* God—His attribute—condemns the guilty, but the righteousness *from* God—His gift of righteousness—justifies the ungodly, through faith alone. "Night and day I pondered until . . . I grasped the truth," Luther writes. "Thereupon I felt myself to be reborn and to have gone through open doors into paradise. The whole Scripture took on a new meaning, and whereas before the 'righteousness of God' had filled me with hate, now it became to me inexpressibly sweet in greater love. This passage in Paul became for me a gateway to heaven."[5]

---

5 *Martin Luther's Basic Theological Writings*, 497.

This episode underscores the point that for Luther, *sola Scriptura*—Scripture alone—was inseparable from justification in Christ alone (*solus Christus*), through faith alone (*sola fide*), to the glory of God alone (*soli Deo gloria*). The nature of Scripture depended on its content, and vice versa. The reasoning and experience of the fallen heart yield nothing of this gospel. It is by Scripture alone that the good news is announced to us, and Luther now knew that—experientially—for himself.

After this turning point, Luther says, "The whole Scripture took on a new meaning." Passages that he had pondered over for years suddenly made sense. He came to see that, despite his confusion, and that of the whole church in his day, God addressed him clearly and unmistakably in His Word. No purported Apostle, not even an angel from heaven, could convince him that he had not found Christ in these passages of Scripture. From this rock, Luther could withstand the controversies that were to follow.

It is important to see that Luther was not a dispassionate biblical scholar or theologian. He certainly was not trying to make a name for himself in the academy. For him, Scripture was not simply an authoritative book, but the well to which he returned again and again for life. His experiential wrestling was inseparable from his deep passion for the Bible. Martin Brecht captures well Luther's approach to Scripture: "The monk Luther brought the questions which troubled him to the Scriptures, expecting an answer."[6]

Two years after this discovery, Luther posted his Ninety-Five Theses. The theses questioned the whole practice of indulgences, but there was no mention of justification, the sufficiency of Scripture, or other crucial doctrines. (Luther's 1518 sermon "Two Kinds of Righteousness" reflected a more developed position that reached its most mature expression in his 1535 commentary on Galatians.) As Luther soon learned, though, raising doubts about a lucrative source of revenue was a nasty business; furthermore, it called into question the church's authority over salvation.

At the Leipzig Disputation in 1519, Luther initially sat on the sidelines while Johann Eck debated Andreas von Karlstadt. Rather than hide behind the chancellor, Luther asked permission to join the debate and Eck happily granted his request. Eck pointed out that Pelagians and Arians appealed to Scripture. How then can Scripture alone be our final authority? After all, it is obscure—especially on such weighty and deep matters as salvation. Stepping

---

6 Brecht, *His Road to the Reformation*, 90.

forward, Luther pointed out that both popes and councils had erred and even contradicted each other, while Scripture is clear, consistent, and unerring. Eck's goal was to show that Luther was teaching the same errors as Jan Hus, who had been committed to the flames by the Council of Constance in 1415.

During Luther's time in hiding in Wartburg Castle, he translated the Bible into German, giving birth to the modern German language. Soon, other translations appeared across Europe, fanning a flame that could not be extinguished. Meanwhile, Luther also wrote treatises on papal power, confession, and the church's ministry.

However, during his productive captivity, Wittenberg had become a magnet for extremists like the Zwickau prophets, who proclaimed a kingdom of the Spirit. Even Karlstadt had become radicalized, to the point of rejecting infant baptism and turning the priesthood of all believers into spiritual anarchy. No longer chained to the external ministry of a fallen church, such self-proclaimed prophets announced liberation even from the external Word and, according to some such as Thomas Müntzer, from all human government. Was this making Eck's point that without an infallible interpreter, the infallible Scriptures could not stand? Was Luther in fact opening the door to anarchy in both church and state? In March 1522, Luther had no other choice than to return and to seek to bring evangelical sanity back to a chaotic Wittenberg.

One more debate should be mentioned for understanding how Luther's view of Scripture evolved out of conflict. Desiderius Erasmus was the great Renaissance humanist whose new Greek New Testament "laid the egg that Luther hatched," as some of Luther's contemporaries put it. However, Erasmus eschewed theological controversy. A vocal and even sarcastic critic of external abuses, corruptions, superstitions, and hypocrisy, he nevertheless entered the Reformation debate publicly with *The Freedom of the Will*. The treatise defended what we would today call a semi-Pelagian doctrine of human ability in salvation after the fall. In any event, he argued, the main point is following Jesus, not fighting over doctrine—especially when there are good men on both sides of the debate. Erasmus thought that doctrines such as justification and predestination are unclear from Scripture, so we should simply focus on the simple life of piety that Jesus taught. Luther thundered back in *On the Bondage of the Will*, "The Holy Spirit is not a skeptic, nor are what he has written on our hearts doubts or opinions, but assertions more certain, and more firm, than life itself and all human experience."[7]

---

7 "The Bondage of the Will," in *LW*, 33:24.

Scripture is clear on the most important matters. So if, according to Erasmus, those important matters do not include how God has saved us and how much we should credit and worship Him rather than ourselves, then Luther wondered what Erasmus would put in that category. It was not simply Erasmus' views but his cavalier attitude toward Scripture that most aroused Luther's ire.

Through all of these dramatic episodes—and many others besides, Luther did not waver in his conviction regarding Scripture's truth, authority, clarity, and sufficiency. However, his conviction did mature. He discovered that threats to Scripture came not only from the pope but from radical Protestants who separated the Spirit from His Word. This historical survey provides a context for summarizing Luther's view of Scripture itself.

Sola Scriptura

There was no controversy between Luther and Rome concerning the inspiration of Scripture. In fact, much of today's mainline Protestant and Roman Catholic biblical and theological scholarship would have been regarded by the medieval church as apostate with regard to its view of Scripture. The Scriptures, both sides held, are inerrant. The Council of Trent (condemning the Reformation positions) went so far as to say that the Spirit "dictated" the very words to the Apostles.

The real question had to do with the relation of inspired Scripture to tradition. In other words, is Scripture *alone* God's inspired and inerrant Word, the source and norm for faith and practice? Could the pope say truly that his words are equal to those of Peter and Paul as we find them in Scripture? Are councils infallible in the same way as Scripture? The Council of Trent argued that Scripture and tradition are two streams that form the one river of God's Word. This Word consists not only of "the written books" but also of "the unwritten traditions" that, of course, the Roman pontiff has the privilege of determining. Thus, both Scripture and these traditions the church "receives and venerates with an equal affection of piety and reverence," as both have been "preserved in the Catholic Church by a continuous succession."[8] Therefore, whatever the pope teaches or commands *ex cathedra* (from the chair)—even if it is not based on Scripture—is to be believed by all

---

8   *The Council of Trent, Fourth Session,* trans. J. Waterworth (London: Dolman, 1848), 68–69.

Christians everywhere as necessary for salvation.[9] Ironically, Luther's defense of *sola Scriptura* was condemned as schismatic, but the ancient fathers, both in the East and the West, would have regarded the pretensions of the Roman bishop as an act of separation (schism) from the Apostolic faith.

Long before the Reformation, highly esteemed theologians argued that Scripture alone is normative and that councils simply interpret Scripture, and these interpretations (which may be wrong and amended by further reflection) are to be submitted to by the pope himself. Until the Council of Trent's condemnations of the Reformation teaching, this was an open question. Luther was not the first to argue for Scripture's unique authority even over the pope. After Trent, though, the door was slammed shut on *sola Scriptura* within the Roman Catholic faith.

Luther's problem with the papal church was its corruptions of scriptural faith by addition of myriad doctrines, practices, rituals, sacraments, and ceremonies. Medieval popes increasingly held that they alone were endowed with the Holy Spirit in such a way as to be preserved from error in their judgments. Of course, this idea was not found in Scripture or in the teaching of the ancient fathers. It was an innovation that opened the floodgate to a torrent of novelties, Luther argued:

> When the teaching of the pope is distinguished from that of the Holy Scriptures, or is compared with them, it becomes apparent that, at its best, the teaching of the pope has been taken from the imperial, pagan laws and is a teaching concerning secular transactions and judgments, as the papal decretals show. In keeping with such teaching, instructions are given concerning the ceremonies of the churches, vestments, food, personnel, and countless other puerilities, fantasies, and follies without so much as a mention of Christ, faith, and God's commandments.[10]

How do you adjudicate between truth and error? What if a pope errs, as some medieval councils had in fact declared? Indeed, the fourteenth and early fifteenth centuries saw the schism between two and eventually three rival popes, each claiming St. Peter's throne and excommunicating the others

---

9 Papal infallibility became an official dogma in 1868, at the First Vatican Council. Thus, centuries of debate over the status of pope, councils, and Scripture came.

10 Luther, Smalcald Articles, in *The Book of Concord* (1959), 301.

along with their followers. The Council of Constance ended this tragicomedy by electing a fourth pope to replace the other three. Philip Melanchthon's *Treatise on the Power and Primacy of the Pope* built on Luther's views by drawing together a battery of refutations from Scripture and also from church history to demonstrate the foundation of sand on which the papacy is built.[11]

For Luther, the first plank of *sola Scriptura* is Scripture's nature. As the Holy Spirit's direct revelation through prophets and Apostles, Scripture is in a class by itself. The character of God is at stake in the character of Scripture. Why is Scripture inerrant? "Because we know that God does not lie. My neighbor and I—in short, all men—may err and deceive, but God's Word cannot err."[12] We respect the church fathers and ancient councils as guides, but only God can establish articles of faith: "It will not do to make articles of faith out of the holy Fathers' words or works. Otherwise what they ate, how they dressed, and what kind of houses they lived in would have to become articles of faith—as has happened in the case of relics. This means that the Word of God shall establish articles of faith and no one else, not even an angel."[13]

The second plank is the clarity of Scripture, which was really the heart of the dispute. The Bible is a dark, mysterious, and obscure book, the medieval church taught. No wonder, Luther thought, as he looked back on what he had been taught even as a monk and Bible scholar. But after having studied and translated the Bible for many years, he came to the opposite conclusion. By their own experience, Luther and other Reformers came to see that Scripture is clear on its central teachings. It is the papal church that obscures rather than clarifies. This was what frustrated Luther the most about Erasmus: he seemed to think that Scripture is clear about how we are to live, but obscure about the most central doctrines of the gospel.

In his *Freedom of the Will*, Erasmus alternates between vehement opposition to Luther's teaching and a passive assertion that such doctrines as predestination and free will are obscure in Scripture and unimportant for daily living. Erasmus much preferred Origen (a defender of free will) over Augustine. In fact, he went as far as to conclude concerning Augustine's positions on grace and free will, "What a window to impiety would the public

---

11 Philip Melanchthon, "Treatise on the Power and Primacy of the Pope," in *The Book of Concord* (1959), 320–35.
12 Luther, Large Catechism, in *The Book of Concord* (1959), 444.
13 Luther, Smalcald Articles II, ii, 15, in *The Book of Concord* (1959), 295.

avowal of such an opinion open to countless mortals!"[14] "But if [Scripture] is so crystal clear, why have so many outstanding men in so many centuries been blind, and in a matter of such importance, as those would appear? If there is no obscurity in Scripture, what need of the work of prophecy in the days of the apostles?" But who succeeded the Apostles, he asked, assuming of course that the pope is Peter's successor.

Luther begins his rejoinder, *On the Bondage of the Will*, by tackling Erasmus' denial of Scripture's clarity in its central teachings. Not everything is equally clear in Scripture, but when it comes to election, free will, and justification, its clarity is obscured only by human (and especially papal) ignorance. Don't blame the sun for your lack of sight, he rebuked. "Let wretched men cease to impute, with blasphemous perverseness, the darkness and obscurity of their own heart to the all-clear Scriptures of God."[15] In short, Luther counseled, "If you do not understand this or are not concerned about it, then mind your own affairs and let those understand and be concerned about it on whom God has laid the charge."[16]

This clarity of Scripture is why Luther wrote the Small Catechism to instruct children and new believers in the Bible's basic teachings. In fact, the ecumenical creeds and the new Augsburg Confession, as well as Luther's Small and Large Catechisms, were examples of the fact that the church has been able to arrive at a consensus about the central teachings of Scripture without the pope's intervention.

But the sufficiency of Scripture was also being attacked by the Protestant radicals, whom Luther dubbed "enthusiasts." Meaning "God-within-ism," *enthusiasm* cut the believer loose from any external authority, including Scripture and preaching. Luther was convinced that the enthusiasts, not unlike the pope, imagined that they were God's mouthpiece like the prophets and Apostles of old. We will return to this challenge below.

Interpretation of Scripture

Differences over the nature and sufficiency of Scripture were bound up with different views as to how Scripture should be interpreted. It is hardly surprising that Scripture would be a confusing web of mysteries when its straightforward meaning was buried in layers of mystical and fanciful exegesis.

---

14 *Luther and Erasmus*, 41.
15 Ibid., 44.
16 Ibid., 126.

Sensus Literalis

Every so often, U.S. pollsters ask, "Do you believe that the Bible is to be taken literally?" Luther and other magisterial Reformers would have asked for clarification before answering. They said that Scripture must be interpreted according to its *sensus literalis*, but this means the ordinary sense of the words. In other words, if the passage is an obvious allegory, one interprets it as such; otherwise, one interprets historical narrative, poetry, proverb, parable, apocalyptic, exhortatory, or doctrinal passages according to their genre. Consequently, Christian readers do not interpret John's Apocalypse as if it were a historical narrative or the Hebrew poetry of a psalm as if it were a doctrinal exposition. God works through creaturely means—including the historical, cultural, social, and linguistic background of Scripture's human authors. In terms of basic literary rules at least, the Bible should be read like any other book and Scripture should be interpreted in the light of Scripture.

The medieval church had followed a "fourfold sense" of interpreting Scripture.[17] However, the most important distinction was between literal and allegorical senses. For example, Numbers 27:12 reports, "The LORD said to Moses, 'Go up into this mountain of Abarim and see the land that I have given to the people of Israel.'" The literal sense is straightforward enough: God told Moses to climb the mountain and view the Promised Land. However, "advanced" readers were encouraged to discern the hidden spiritual meaning beneath the ordinary sense. Scores of spiritual manuals appeared that explained how to ascend the spiritual mountain.

This twofold way of interpreting classic texts first appeared when Platonist philosophers were scandalized by portions of Homer's *Iliad* and *The Odyssey*, where the gods were hardly the sort of characters to inculcate virtue in children. The steamy episodes were allegorized so as to teach higher intellectual truths. A similar approach was taken to the Old Testament by the great first-century Jewish Platonist philosopher Philo of Alexandria. In the third century, Origen of Alexandria followed the same approach to both testaments. According to this view, there is a simple meaning of the passage for the simple believer who merely accepts basic Christian doctrine and the deeper spiritual meaning for the advanced. It was usually from the allegorical meaning that one could learn the "moral to the story." Not unlike *Aesop's*

---

17 Besides the literal (i.e., ordinary) sense, there were the typological (promise-fulfillment), tropological (moral), and anagogical (eschatological) meanings.

Fables, the story merely served to make a supposedly higher moral, intellectual, or spiritual point. Just as the body is the "prison-house" of the soul, the literal sense is the outer husk one cuts through in order to discover the seed of truth.

It was therefore not surprising that Scripture should seem dark and obscure, capable of being understood only by the advanced. Luther recalled:

> When I was a monk I was a master in the use of allegories. I allegorized everything. Afterward through the Epistle to the Romans I came to some knowledge of Christ. I recognized then that allegories are nothing, that it's not what Christ signifies but what Christ is that counts. Before, I allegorized everything, even a chamber pot; afterward, I reflected on the histories and thought how difficult it must have been for Gideon to fight with his enemies in the manner reported. If I had been there I would have befouled my breeches for fear. It was not allegory, but it was the Spirit and faith that inflicted such havoc on the enemy with only three hundred men. Jerome and Origen contributed to the practice of searching only for allegories. God forgive them. In all of Origen there is not one word about Christ.[18]

Once again, Luther was not inventing a new idea. Thomas Aquinas, Pierre D'Ailly, and John Duns Scotus had all argued that the ordinary meaning (*sensus literalis*) was to be given at least pride of place, if not the exclusive key to a passage's meaning. Their warnings against the proliferation of fanciful allegorizing went unheeded, but these respected theologians were not judged heretical for issuing them. However, in Luther's case, the papal church was in a reactionary mode.

Ironically, Erasmus and other scholars had recently made the original Greek New Testament accessible, demonstrating the extent to which the Latin Vulgate had mistranslated terms that were crucial to the very doctrines that Luther was defending. This affected terms such as justification (viz., *iustificare*, "to make righteous," when the Greek verb is "to declare righteous") and penance (viz., *poenitentiam agite*, "Do penance!" vs. the Greek word, "Repent!"). As we have seen, Erasmus had no theological reason to provide textual grounds for Luther's arguments; he was simply returning to

---

18 *LW*, 54:46.

the original meaning of the Greek manuscripts. Anyone could understand the issues at stake, but it was crucial to the papal monopoly on scriptural interpretation to encourage more mystical readings so that its straightforward meaning would remain obscure.

Christ at the Center

Christ is the center of the biblical drama, Luther argued, from Genesis to Revelation. Luther repeatedly said that Rome had turned the New Testament into nothing more than a "new law" and Christ into a "new Moses." To preach the Bible without seeing Christ was to not actually preach it at all. And "where Christ is not preached, there is no Holy Spirit to create, call, and gather the Christian church, and outside it no one can come to the Lord Christ."[19]

Jesus and the Apostles spoke of Christ as the center of the Scriptures, and they only had the Old Testament. With Christ as the key, the Old Testament comes alive.[20] "Here you will find the swaddling cloths and the manger in which Christ lies, and to which the angel points the shepherds [Luke 2:12]," Luther said in his preface to the Old Testament. "Simple and lowly are these swaddling cloths, but dear is the treasure, Christ, who lies in them."[21] There is law and gospel in both testaments.[22] Genesis already begins the promise of the Seed who will crush the serpent's head, and this evangelical drama unfolds throughout the history of the patriarchs. The Psalter is "a little Bible," proclaiming "Christ's death and resurrection so clearly."[23] With the New Testament, these promises are announced as fulfilled in Christ. "For it is a testament when a dying man bequeaths his property, after his death, to his legally defined heirs. . . . A poor man, dead in sin and consigned to hell, can hear nothing more comforting than this precious and tender message about Christ; from the bottom of his heart he must laugh and be glad over it, if he believes it is true."[24]

The German Reformer held that Scripture is God's Word because it proclaims Christ. Famously (or infamously), the epistle of James fell short of this test in Luther's evaluation:

---

19 Luther, Large Catechism, in *The Book of Concord* (1959), 416.
20 The gospel is clearly promised throughout the Old Testament, Luther argues. "Prefaces to the Old Testament" (1523), in *LW*, 35:235–333.
21 Ibid., 35:236.
22 Ibid., 35:237.
23 Ibid., 35:254.
24 Ibid., 35:358–59.

Though this epistle of St. James was rejected by the ancients, I praise it and consider it a good book, because it sets up no doctrines of men but vigorously promulgates the law of God. However, to state my own opinion about it, though without prejudice to anyone, I do not regard it as the writing of an apostle; and my reasons follow.

In the first place it is flatly against St. Paul and all the rest of Scripture in ascribing justification to works [2:24]. . . . In the second place its purpose is to teach Christians, but in all this long teaching it does not once mention the Passion, the resurrection, or the Spirit of Christ. He names Christ several times; however he teaches nothing about him, but only speaks of general faith in God. . . . Whatever does not teach Christ is not yet apostolic, even though St. Peter or St. Paul does the teaching. Again, whatever preaches Christ would be apostolic, even if Judas, Annas, Pilate, and Herod were doing it. But this James does nothing more than drive to the law and to its works. Besides, he throws things together so chaotically that it seems to me he must have been some good, pious man, who took a few sayings from the disciples of the apostles and thus tossed them off on paper.[25]

Since James quotes Peter and Paul several times, he must have come after them. The phrase "damning with faint praise" comes to mind when he adds, "for there are otherwise many good sayings in him."[26] As part of the Renaissance "back to the sources" movement, Luther's questioning of the epistle's canonicity was not shocking. Several apocryphal books that Rome had added to the Jewish canon were called into question, and Luther and other Reformers rejected their canonical status. Luther was correct in saying that James was among the disputed texts in the ancient church (recounted in Eusebius' *The Ecclesiastical History*, 2.23.25). However, it was included in the canon for very good reasons, and none of the other Reformers, including Philip Melanchthon, agreed with Luther on this point. In their view, Paul and James were not speaking of "justification" in the same way; for Paul, the question was how we are justified before God, and for James, the question was how our faith is justified (as saving faith) by its fruit. Where the other Reformers came to Scripture expecting to find Christ there, Luther went a step further

---

25 Ibid., 35:395–97.
26 Ibid., 35:397.

by saying that "only that which preaches Christ" is God's Word. He could not have seen then how this implied idea of a canon-within-a-canon would be employed by liberal scholars three centuries later. If he had, I suspect that he would not have introduced such a dangerous approach.

Illumination by the Spirit

John Calvin is famous for his argument in his *Institutes of the Christian Religion* that Scripture remains a closed book apart from the inner testimony of the Spirit, illuminating and convincing us of its inherent truth. However, Luther argued the same point repeatedly.[27] The church is "the mother that begets and bears every Christian," but only "through the Word of God." "The Holy Spirit reveals and preaches that Word, and by it he illumines and kindles hearts so that they grasp and accept it, cling to it, and persevere in it."[28] In fact:

> Where he does not cause the Word to be preached and does not awaken understanding in the heart, all is lost. This was the case under the papacy, where faith was entirely shoved under the bench and no one recognized Christ as the Lord or the Holy Spirit as the Sanctifier. That is, no one believed that Christ is our Lord in the sense that he won for us this treasure without our works and merits and made us acceptable to the Father. What was lacking here? There was no Holy Spirit present to reveal this truth and have it preached.[29]

Where both Rome and the enthusiasts appealed to the Spirit to legitimize their own teachings apart from Scripture, Luther insisted upon the inseparability of the Word and the Spirit. The Spirit does not add new content to revelation, but illumines our hearts to understand and to embrace the Word that He has communicated to us.

The Preached Word

To be sure, the church preceded the written Scriptures—as a complete canon. Luther never questioned that obvious fact. Yet the Word of God created the church, the body of those who call on the name of the Lord (Gen. 4:26). The written Scriptures are the basis, norm, and source for all subsequent preach-

---

27 For example, see *LW*, 23:230; 13:17.
28 Luther, Large Catechism, in *The Book of Concord* (1959), 416.
29 Ibid.

ing, doctrine, and practice. Yet when Luther (as well as Calvin and other Reformers) spoke of the Word of God, the usual reference was to preaching.

Obviously, Luther believed strongly in the power of the written Scriptures; otherwise, he would not have poured so much of his life into translating the Old and New Testaments and seeing to their wide publication. Not just in the monastery, but in the family, regular, daily prayer and Bible reading became part of Reformation piety. "For some years now I have read through the Bible twice every year," he related. "If you picture the Bible to be a mighty tree and every word a little branch, I have shaken every one of these branches because I wanted to know what it was and what it meant."[30]

Nevertheless, Luther said, "The church is a mouth-house, not a pen-house."[31] As Paul said, "Faith comes from hearing, and hearing through the word of Christ" (Rom. 10:17). This emphasis on the *verbum externum* (external Word) is simply a correlate of the idea of salvation by God in Christ *extra nos* (outside of ourselves). We do not descend into our souls or rise up to God, but God comes to us to judge and to save through His speech. Another sinner, in Christ's name and sent by Him through the church's ordination, announces God's Word to us. Luther said, "If you ask a Christian what the work is by which he becomes worthy of the name 'Christian,' he will be able to give absolutely no other answer than that it is the hearing of the Word of God, that is, faith. Therefore, *the ears alone are the organs of a Christian man*, for he is justified and declared to be a Christian, not because of the works of any member but because of faith."[32]

Therefore, preaching is not an indifferent medium but is deemed by God to be suitable for the delivery of a message that is itself saving news. The importance of preaching is highlighted by the fact that justification comes by faith alone, and that faith itself comes through hearing. "There is nothing I want more than to make His gospel known to the world and to convert many people," Luther said.[33] It is only this proclamation of the Word of Christ that keeps the church from perishing at any moment—and, in fact, this proclamation keeps the church advancing in the power of the Spirit.

---

30 *LW,* 54:165.

31 From a church postil in 1522, *WA* 10, I, 48, quoted in Timothy George, *Theology of the Reformers* (Nashville, Tenn.: Broadman, 1988), 91.

32 *LW,* 29:224, emphasis added.

33 *LW, Vol. 26: Lectures on Galatians, 1535, Chapters 1–4,* ed. Walter A. Hansen (St. Louis: Concordia), 379.

Yet again, Luther saw this confidence tested. The year 1541 saw the siege of Buda in Hungary, after the siege of Vienna and the entrance of the Islamic army (the Turks) into Christendom in 1529. The emperor and pope called for sermons in every church and prayers for the defense of the gates. This was ironic, Luther must have thought, since Pope Paul III and Emperor Ferdinand were persecuting the churches of the Reformation, and King Francis I of France, vicious persecutor of the Reformed churches, even allied himself with Sultan Suleiman the Magnificent over Ferdinand. In this context, Luther composed a hymn that was, for understandable reasons, outlawed in Catholic regions. His 1542 hymn "Lord, Keep Us Steadfast in Thy Word" pleads that God's Word would prevail "and curb the Turks' and papists' sword."[34]

As mentioned above, Luther found the opposition forming on two fronts. Besides the pope, there were various self-proclaimed prophets and Apostles who sought to hijack the Reformation for a libertine enthusiasm. His most scathing rebuttal of this movement was his tract *Against the Heavenly Prophets* (1525). [35] It was directed especially at his erstwhile fellow Reformer Karlstadt, who imagined, Luther says, that he "has devoured the Holy Spirit feathers and all."[36] He continues:

> Out of his great mercy, God has again given us the pure gospel, the noble and precious treasure of our salvation. This gift evokes faith and a good conscience in the inner man, as is promised in Isa. 55:1, that his Word will not go forth in vain, and Rom. 10:17, that "faith comes through preaching." The devil hates this gospel and will not tolerate it. Since he has not succeeded hitherto in opposing it with power of sword, he now, as indeed always, seeks victory by deceit and false prophets.[37]

The enthusiasts were fond of contrasting the inner with the outer. Yet, Luther responds, "God has determined to give the inward to no one except through the outward. . . . The oral gospel 'is the power of God for salvation to every one who has faith' (Rom. 1:16)." Of course, the external preaching

---

34 Lutheran Church–Missouri Synod, *Lutheran Service Book* (St. Louis: Concordia, 2006), Hymn 655.

35 "Against the Heavenly Prophets" (1525), in *LW, Vol. 40: Church and Ministry II*, ed. Conrad Bergendoff (Philadelphia: Fortress, 1958), 79–228.

36 Ibid., 40:83.

37 Ibid., 40:146.

and sacraments by themselves will not accomplish anything, but the Spirit accomplishes His work through them.[38] The devil sets about "to reverse this order": a person first has an inward experience and then encounters the outward preaching, baptism, and supper.[39] Fanatics like Karlstadt say that if you follow their path, "you will have the same experience."

> A heavenly voice will come, and God himself will speak to you. . . . With all his mouthing of the words, "Spirit, Spirit, Spirit," he tears down the bridge, the path, the way, the ladder, and all the means by which the Spirit might come to you. Instead of the outward order of God in the material sign of baptism and the oral proclamation of the Word of God he wants to teach you, not how the Spirit comes to you, but how you come to the Spirit. They would have you learn how to journey on the clouds and ride on the wind. They do not tell you how or when, whither or what, but you are to experience what they do.[40]

Another chief culprit was Thomas Müntzer, an ambitious and intelligent neurotic who imagined that he was ordained to lead Germany into the "third age": the era of the Spirit, after the eras of the Father (the law) and the Son (the gospel). According to Müntzer, Paul's counsel to Timothy to "preach the word" (2 Tim. 4:2) referred not to the external Word but to the internal speaking of the Spirit who gives new revelations. Everything external—including Scripture and gospel proclamation, as well as the sacraments and church office—was seen as the grave-clothes of the flesh, part of the false church. Indeed, ordination by the church was unnecessary for those who had apparently become conduits of the Holy Spirit. Fanatics such as Müntzer are as confused about the gospel as the papists, Luther warned, with all of their urgent talk about having an experience that leads finally to a "clean conscience." "How can they know or feel it, when they come and teach of themselves, without a call?"[41]

Müntzer proclaimed himself a prophet and led the Peasants' War that left hundreds dead. For a time, he even took over a German city, resulting in a society that one historian describes as "communist, polygamous, and

---

38 Ibid.
39 Ibid., 40:147.
40 Ibid.
41 Ibid., 40:223.

violent."[42] Müntzer was not alone. Other radical Anabaptist leaders followed similar beliefs, but after Müntzer was toppled, tried, and executed for treason, they decided to take a more pacifist stance.

Of such sects Luther had nothing good to say. When, in his great hymn, he wrote, "That Word above all earthly pow'rs, no thanks to them, abideth; the Spirit and the gifts are ours, through him who with us sideth," he had not only the pope in mind, but these "fanatics." In truth, these radicals were infected with the same love of superstition as the papal clergy. There is always something beyond God's Word that tickles our fancy. But the radical Protestants did not have a corner on "enthusiasm." In fact, in this they were like the pope:

> In these matters, which concern the external, spoken Word, we must hold firmly to the conviction that God gives no one his Spirit or grace except through or with the external Word which comes before. Thus we shall be protected from the enthusiasts—that is, from the spiritualists who boast that they possess the Spirit without and before the Word and therefore judge, interpret, and twist the Scriptures or spoken Word to their pleasure. Müntzer did this and many still do it in our day who wish to distinguish sharply between the letter and the spirit without knowing what they say or teach.
>
> The papacy, too, is nothing but enthusiasm, for the pope boasts that "all laws are in the shrine of his heart," and he claims that whatever he decides and commands in his churches is spirit and law, even when it is above and contrary to the Scriptures or spoken Word.
>
> All this is the old devil and the old serpent who made enthusiasts of Adam and Eve. He led them from the external Word of God to spiritualizing and to their own imaginations, and he did this through other external words. Even so the enthusiasts of our day condemn the external Word, yet they do not remain silent but fill the world with their chattering and scribbling, as if the Spirit could not come through the Scriptures or the spoken words of the apostles but must come through their own writings and words.[43]

---

42 Eugene F. Rice Jr. and Anthony Grafton, *The Foundations of Early Modern Europe, 1460–1559*, 2nd ed. (New York: Norton, 1994), 163–68, 178–83.

43 Luther, Smalcald Articles, in *The Book of Concord* (1959), 312.

"In short," he added, "enthusiasm clings to Adam and his descendants from the beginning to the end of the world." It is "the source, strength, and power of all heresy, including that of the papacy and Mohammedanism. Accordingly, we should and must constantly maintain that God will not deal with us except through his external Word and sacrament. Whatever is attributed to the Spirit apart from such Word and sacrament is of the devil." The prophets always heard God's Word before they exercised their ministry.[44] Even baptism is "nothing else than the Word of God in water."[45]

Because the Word of God—especially the preached Word—is the primary means of grace, it was of utmost concern to Luther to treat the pulpit not as an opportunity for entertainment or pretentious oratory, but for Christ's working by His Spirit to create faith and sustain it to the end. In *Table Talk*, a student reports:

> Rector Bernard von Dölen, minister in Herzberg, complained bitterly about his arrogant auditors who despised the reading of the catechism. Dr. Martin was greatly disturbed and fell silent. Then he said, "Cursed be every preacher who aims at lofty topics in the church, looking for his own glory and selfishly desiring to please one individual or another. What I preach here I adapt to the circumstances of the common people. I don't look at the doctors and masters, of whom scarcely forty are present, but at the hundred or the thousand young people and children."[46]

Once more, this approach assumes that Scripture is clear enough that a sound exposition of it will strike home. With so much at stake, and a Word so powerful for salvation and godliness, ministers dare not get in the way.

Just as the book of Acts relates the growth of the church by the phrase, "And the word of God spread," Luther was convinced that it was God's Word, not his own cleverness, that was reforming the church.

> We should preach the Word, but the results must be left solely to God's good pleasure. . . . I opposed indulgences and all the papists, but never with force. I simply taught, preached, and wrote God's

---

44 Ibid., 313.
45 Ibid., 310.
46 *LW*, 54:235–36.

Word; otherwise I did nothing. And while I slept, or drank Wittenberg beer with my friends Philip and Amsdorf, the Word so greatly weakened the papacy that no prince or emperor ever inflicted such losses upon it. I did nothing; the Word did everything.[47]

Once again, this remark emphasizes that the power of God's Word, read but especially proclaimed, was not simply a theoretical point for Luther, but something that he had experienced himself and witnessed in countless others. Erasmus had hoped for a reform of manners and the outward corruptions of the church, but the radicals ended up being a forest fire that burned itself out. However, Luther knew that the evangelical reform would go forward because its power was God's own speech.

Luther and *Sola Scriptura* Today

As it turns out, Luther's confidence in God's Word was well placed. Five centuries later, translation of the Bible into myriad languages continues unabated. Many Christians, at least in the United States, have several Bibles at home. Missions around the world and at home have spread God's Word with remarkable success. And yet, we still struggle with the same challenges to this Word in our day, even in the church.

First, do we really share Luther's confidence in the power of God's Word—especially proclaimed—to create the world of which it speaks? Or do we think that it needs our help, through the invention of clever techniques and tricks to be more effective in growing churches and reaching the lost?

Second, nearly two centuries after the Reformation, the Enlightenment brought a critical attitude toward all authority external to the individual. Liberal Protestantism created a new papacy of the biblical scholar. How could the average Christian presume to come to the Bible directly, given its purported obvious errors, contradictions, and variant teachings? The scholars alone, it is said, can tell us what the Bible actually says. Increasingly, the average layperson—and many pastors—came to think that the Bible was too complicated and even the actual texts too contested to imagine that one could understand its basic meaning.

Third, there are also the "enthusiasts" who draw thousands, sometimes millions, of followers into their purported revelations and away from the pure

---

47 *LW*, 51:76–77.

milk of God's Word. William McLoughlin reminds us that the effect of pietism in American religious experience (especially culminating in the Second Great Awakening) was to shift the emphasis away from "collective belief, adherence to creedal standards and proper observance of traditional forms, to the emphasis on individual religious experience."[48] If the Enlightenment shifted "the ultimate authority in religion" from the church to "the mind of the individual," pietism and Romanticism located ultimate authority in the experience of the individual.[49] All of this suggests that for some time now, evangelicalism has been as much the facilitator as the victim of modern secularism.

Writing as a self-professed Jewish Gnostic, Harold Bloom has approvingly characterized American religion generally as Gnostic: an *inner* word, spirit, and church set over against an *external* Word, Spirit, and church.[50] Just as the Spirit's inward call is often contrasted with outward means, much of evangelicalism today celebrates the charismatic leader who needs no formal training or external ecclesiastical ordination to confirm a spontaneous, direct, inner call to ministry. Historians may debate whether Protestant enthusiasm is more of a consequence than a cause of the distinctively American confidence in intuitive individualism over against external authorities and communal instruction, but the connection seems obvious. In *Head and Heart*, Catholic historian Garry Wills observes:

> The camp meeting set the pattern for credentialing Evangelical ministers. They were validated by the crowd's response. Organizational credentialing, doctrinal purity, personal education were useless here—in fact, some educated ministers had to make a pretense of ignorance. The minister was ordained from below, by the converts he made. This was an even more democratic procedure than electoral politics, where a candidate stood for office and spent some time campaigning. This was a spontaneous and instant proclamation that the Spirit accomplished. The do-it-yourself religion called for a make-it-yourself ministry.[51]

---

48 William McLoughlin, *Revivals, Awakenings, and Reform* (Chicago: University of Chicago Press, 1980), 25.

49 Ned C. Landsman, *From Colonials to Provincials: American Thought and Culture, 1680–1760* (New York: Twayne, 1997; Ithaca, N.Y.: Cornell University Press, 2000), 66.

50 Harold Bloom, *The American Religion: The Emergence of the Post-Christian Nation* (New York: Simon and Schuster, 1993).

51 Garry Wills, *Head and Heart: American Christianities* (New York: Penguin, 2007), 294.

In the light of this history, Wade Clark Roof's findings are hardly surprising when he reports, "The distinction between 'spirit' and 'institution' is of major importance" to spiritual seekers today.[52] "Spirit is the inner, experiential aspect of religion; institution is the outer, established form of religion."[53] He adds, "Direct experience is always more trustworthy, if for no other reason than because of its 'inwardness' and 'withinness'—two qualities that have come to be much appreciated in a highly expressive, narcissistic culture."[54] In fact, Roof comes close to suggesting that evangelicalism works so well in this kind of culture because it helped to create it.

Stanley Grenz defends this inside-out approach. "Although some evangelicals belong to ecclesiological traditions that understand the church as in some sense a dispenser of grace," he observes, "generally we see our congregations foremost as a fellowship of believers."[55] We share our journeys (our "testimony") of personal transformation.[56] Therefore, Grenz celebrates the "fundamental shift . . . from a creed-based to a spirituality-based identity" that is more like medieval mysticism than Protestant orthodoxy.[57] "Consequently, spirituality is inward and quietistic,"[58] concerned with combating "the lower nature and the world,"[59] in "a personal commitment that becomes the ultimate focus of the believer's affections."[60]

Nowhere in this account does Grenz locate the origin of faith in an external gospel; rather, faith arises from an inner experience. "Because spirituality is *generated from within the individual,* inner motivation is crucial"—more important, in fact, than "grand theological statements."[61]

All of this is at odds with an emphasis on doctrine and especially, Grenz adds, an emphasis on "a material and a formal principle"—referring to the Reformation slogans *sola fide* and *sola Scriptura.*[62] In spite of the fact that the

---

52 Wade Clark Roof, *A Generation of Seekers: The Spiritual Journeys of the Baby Boom Generation* (San Francisco: HarperCollins, 1993), 30.

53 Ibid.

54 Ibid., 67.

55 Stanley J. Grenz, *Revisioning Evangelical Theology: A Fresh Agenda for the 21st Century* (Downers Grove, Ill.: InterVarsity Press, 1993), 32.

56 Ibid., 33.

57 Ibid., 38, 41.

58 Ibid., 41–42.

59 Ibid., 44.

60 Ibid., 45.

61 Ibid., 46. Emphasis added.

62 Ibid., 62.

Scriptures declare that "faith comes by hearing and hearing by the word of Christ," Grenz says, "faith is by nature immediate."[63]

Consistent with his emphasis on the priority of inner experience, Grenz urges "a revisioned understanding of the *nature* of the Bible's authority."[64] Our own religious experience today needs to be included in the process of inspiration.[65] This type of piety offers a surprising and tragic parallel to the enthusiasm that the Reformers faced in the sixteenth century.

Following Luther and Calvin, the Westminster divines confessed that the Spirit blesses "the reading but especially the preaching of the Word" as a "means of grace" precisely because through it the Spirit is "calling us out of ourselves" to cling to Christ.[66] They were asserting that faithful, meditative, and prayerful reading of Scripture in private or family devotions was essential but nevertheless subordinate to the public ministry of the Word in the common life of the church. Just as the Word creates the community, it can only be truly heard, received, and followed in the concrete covenantal exchanges within that community.

Fourth, *sola Scriptura* is often misunderstood in our day in ways that hark back to the sixteenth-century controversy. The slogan does not mean that the Bible is the all-sufficient manual for everything—economics, government, psychological and material well-being, and so forth. The radical Anabaptists scorned all secular learning, but Luther and Calvin sharply rejected the idea that the Bible alone provided everything necessary for our common life in the world. To be sure, what Scripture does reveal changes and informs the way we think about everything, but it does not address every issue or question we have in life. There is an important distinction between God's common grace in general revelation and His saving grace in special revelation. The purpose and scope of Scripture is to announce the good news that we cannot hear from any other source. Scripture delivers heavenly wisdom concerning God's law and the way in which we are to live and relate to others. Yet, above all, it tells us how God has made Christ our "wisdom from God, righteousness, and sanctification and redemption" (1 Cor. 1:30).

Luther never understood *sola Scriptura* to mean that the individual believer can understand the Bible by himself without being part of the wider

---

63 Ibid., 80.
64 Ibid., 88.
65 Ibid., 122.
66 Westminster Shorter Catechism 89.

body of Christ, instructed by faithful ministers. Only the enthusiasts cast off all church authority and read the Bible by themselves without accountability to Christ's body, especially its officers. Luther and the other magisterial Reformers believed that the church is the "mother of the faithful," but that she only conceives her children by means of the Word. Scripture exercises a magisterial authority, but the church is given by Christ a legitimate ministerial authority.

The church nurtures us, corrects us, and instructs us in the faith. It is never safe to leave her care to wander out on our own. This is why the churches of the Reformation accepted the ecumenical creeds as they summarized the Bible's central teachings. The creeds are authoritative because they summarize Scripture, not because of the church's authority.[67] It is why Luther drew up a catechism and Melanchthon penned the Augsburg Confession. We confess God's Word together, holding each other accountable for our interpretations. Scripture's clarity will bring consensus and unity, while our hearts' darkness, obduracy, and love of novelty bring schism.

Fifth, Luther faced opponents like Erasmus who had no trouble submitting to the church's judgments because they did not really take seriously the issues at stake. Why cause division over doctrine? Erasmus said the Bible is chiefly concerned with training in discipleship, not in doctrinal issues. Of course, there is more to Scripture than propositions, but the gospel is at its heart a set of assertions concerning God's saving grace in Jesus Christ—His incarnation, life, death, resurrection, ascension, and return in the flesh. The same challenge of doctrinal indifference is evident on every side. *Doctrine divides, service unites*, we often hear. *Deeds, not creeds.* Luther replies to us as he did to Erasmus, "Abolish the assertions and you abolish Christianity."[68] Christianity is at its best not when it is trying to score points with the academy or win a popularity contest in the culture, but when it is proclaiming the law and the gospel.

Conclusion

Sola Scriptura is not the reason for the divisions in Christendom. Before the rise of the papacy as we know it, Gregory the Great, bishop of Rome, warned that any bishop who claimed the title *universal bishop* was "in his

---

67 Luther, Large Catechism, in *The Book of Concord* (1959), 411.
68 *LW,* 33:21.

swaggering a precursor of the Antichrist."[69] After enduring the schismatic boasts of popes, the Eastern Orthodox churches excommunicated Rome in the eleventh century. Luther never left the Roman Catholic communion; he was excommunicated for preaching what had been promised in the prophets, fulfilled in Christ, and held forth by the Apostles.

Tragically, though, even the churches of the Reformation divided soon after the new light had dawned. One looks upon the divisions of Protestantism today with a broken heart. These divisions began in the opening years of the Reformation itself. And yet, the true test of unity is whether we embrace the gospel that Luther and other Reformers recovered in that remarkable epoch.

It is still the case today that God's Word is obscured and even contradicted by the teachings of the Roman Catholic Church, which continues to teach that Scripture is not sufficient apart from the treasury of popes and councils and—most importantly of all—still rejects as anathema the central affirmation of the gospel, that we are saved by grace alone through faith alone in Christ alone to the glory of God alone. However, only a party spirit could see this corruption of the gospel as a merely Roman Catholic problem. In many Protestant churches, even ones that hail historically from Luther and Calvin, there are distortions as great—sometimes even greater—as those that the Reformers encountered in their day. We need a new Reformation—one that might even sweep through Roman Catholic, Pentecostal, and mainline Protestant churches as well as the smaller confessional churches that seek to uphold "that Word above all earthly pow'rs."

As he grew older, Luther became increasingly aware of his own limitations. Sometimes he wondered, "How can I imagine that I was right and everyone else was wrong?" Yet he kept coming back to the question: Is this what God's Word clearly teaches? He did not decide that alone, but with fellow pastors as well as parishioners—including his wife—who knew God's Word as well.

Luther's view of Scripture was forged on the anvil of life. In a Christmas sermon in 1519, he said that it is not only prayer and meditation, but

---

69 Gregory the Great, *Epistles* 7:33. Gregory adds elsewhere, "If then he shunned the subjecting of the members of Christ partially to certain heads, as if besides Christ, though this were to the apostles themselves, what wilt thou say to Christ, who is the head of the universal Church, in the scrutiny of the last judgment, having attempted to put all his members under thyself by the appellation of universal? Who, I ask, is proposed for imitation in this wrongful title but he who, despising the legions of angels constituted socially with himself, attempted to start up to an eminence of singularity, that he might seem to be under none and to be alone above all?" *Epistles*, 5:18.

also suffering that makes a theologian. Those decades not only of reading, preaching, and translating, but of wrestling and suffering with Scripture only deepened Luther's affection for and dependence on God's Word. The day before he died, he scribbled this note:

> Nobody can understand Vergil in his *Bucolics* and *Georgics* unless he has first been a shepherd or a farmer for five years. Nobody understands Cicero in his letters unless he has been engaged in public affairs of some consequence for twenty years. Let nobody suppose that he has tasted the Holy Scriptures sufficiently unless he has ruled over the churches with the prophets for a hundred years. Therefore there is something wonderful, first, about John the Baptist; second, about Christ; third, about the apostles. "Lay not your hand on this divine Aeneid, but bow before it, adore its every trace." We are beggars. That is true.[70]

---

70 *LW*, 54:476.

Chapter Six

BY FAITH ALONE: LUTHER AND THE DOCTRINE OF JUSTIFICATION

GUY PRENTISS WATERS

There is perhaps no doctrine more closely associated with the teaching and legacy of Martin Luther than justification by faith alone. "The article of justification and of grace is the most delightful, and it alone makes a person a theologian and makes of a theologian a judge of the earth and of all affairs. Few there are, however, who have thought it through well and who teach it aright," he said.[1]

One might think, then, that it would be a fairly simple matter to summarize Luther's views on justification. This task, however, has proven challenging for several reasons. First, Luther's pen produced a prodigious harvest. One scholar has estimated that Luther, between 1516 and 1546, "wrote one or two treatises a month, totaling about four hundred titles in all."[2] Second, as one might expect of an author who published continuously

---

1   *WA*, 25:375, quoted in *What Luther Says*, 704.
2   Lewis W. Spitz, introduction to "Preface to the Wittenberg Edition of Luther's German Writings" in *Selected Writings of Martin Luther, Vol. 1*, ed. Theodore G. Tappert (Minneapolis: Fortress, 2007), 5.

for thirty years, Luther's views on a host of issues developed, matured, and sometimes changed. One may not, then, simply choose at will a statement of Luther's and pronounce it Luther's definitive word on the subject. Third, Luther often wrote in a manner that resists systematization. His hyperbolic style and the occasional nature of many of his writings make it difficult to pinpoint Luther's specific views on subjects even of great importance to him. Fourth, Luther did not think and write in a vacuum. He was a pastor and a churchman. Luther was both shaped by and a shaper of theological and ecclesiastical controversies in his day. The issues and combatants associated with these controversies helped spur Luther to greater theological clarity and depth, not least in the doctrine of justification by faith alone. Fifth, developments after the death of Martin Luther in 1546 pose important questions regarding Luther's views. For instance, did Calvin and the Reformed tradition link arms or part ways with Martin Luther on the doctrine of justification?

Full consideration of these questions is well beyond the scope of this essay.[3] Even so, what can we say about Luther's understanding of justification? By 1519, when he published his first series of lectures on Galatians, the fundamental components of Luther's doctrine of justification by faith alone were in place.[4] Luther had emerged from the controversies launched by the posting of the Ninety-Five Theses with a recognizably Protestant doctrine of justification. In subsequent years, Luther would refine but never reject that doctrine.

And yet, this achievement notwithstanding, it would fall to the younger Genevan Reformer John Calvin to provide a more comprehensive and systematic formulation of the biblical doctrine of justification. Luther and Calvin stood shoulder to shoulder in advancing and defending this doctrine. Calvin, however, articulated—in a manner that Luther did not—the centrality and importance of union with Christ to the New Testament's understanding of justification. It is Calvin's grasp of this point that helps us understand more fully the relationship between one's justification and one's sanctification.

Both Luther and Calvin reflected on the doctrine in the fires of

---

3   See the clear and perceptive treatment of R. Scott Clark, "*Iustitia Imputata Christi*: Alien or Proper to Luther's Doctrine of Justification?" *CTQ* 70 (2006): 269–310, to whose historical analysis I am especially indebted.

4   For these lectures, see *LW, Vol. 27: Lectures on Galatians, 1535, Chapters 5–6; Lectures on Galatians, 1519, Chapters 1–6*, ed. Walter A. Hansen (St. Louis: Concordia, 1963), 151–410. Compare, from the same year, Luther's "Two Kinds of Righteousness," *LW*, 31:297–306, repr. *Martin Luther's Basic Theological Writings*, 119–125.

controversy. Controversy surrounding the doctrine of justification has, sadly, not been confined to the sixteenth century. The evangelical church faces a contemporary challenge to the doctrine of justification by faith alone in the form of what has been called the New Perspective on Paul. A renewed attentiveness to the way in which Luther and Calvin formulated and advocated the biblical doctrine in their day can only help the modern church to do the same in her day.

Luther and Justification

To appreciate Martin Luther's arrival at the biblical doctrine of justification by faith alone, one must first understand the doctrine of salvation that prevailed in the church of Luther's youth. The historian Steven Ozment has well summarized how, for medievals, the way of salvation was fraught with uncertainty.

> For medieval theologians the present life remained an anxious pilgrimage; man lived in unresolved suspense, fearing damnation and hoping for salvation, ever in need of confession and indulgence, discipline and consolation, saintly intercession and the self help of good works. Nothing seemed more impossible than this-worldly certitude of salvation; such was self-deception and presumption at best, seditious rejection of God's church at worst. Saving faith was constantly developing faith, *fides charitate formata*, faith formed by continuous works of love and charity.[5]

The medieval church taught that the believer's justification would not be finally and definitively effected until the day of judgment. On that day, "faith formed by acts of charity (*fides caritate formata*) [would] receive eternal life as full or condign merit (*meritum de condigno*)."[6] While this system of salvation had a place for both faith and grace, it was not a wholly gracious system. One's acceptance before God ultimately rested on one's performance—what one did or did not do with the grace that God supplied. This teaching directly counters the Bible's insistence that we are justified not by any work that we do, but solely on the basis of the imputed righteousness of Jesus Christ (see Rom. 3:21–26, 4:4–5; Eph. 2:8–10; Titus 3:5). As Ozment observes above,

---

5 Steven Ozment, *The Age of Reform, 1250–1550: An Intellectual and Religious History of Late Medieval and Reformation Europe* (New Haven, Conn.: Yale University Press, 1980), 374.

6 Ibid., 233.

medieval theology simply did not permit the ordinary Christian to arrive at an assurance of grace and salvation. People were furthermore dependent on the grace sacramentally dispensed by the church if they were to have any hope of becoming right with God.

Luther's insight into the biblical doctrine of justification by faith alone proved to be the Archimedean point of opposition to this medieval system of salvation and of the recovery of the Bible's teaching on how the sinner is saved. Luther himself recognized the importance and centrality of justification to the Christian life. As he put it in the 1537 Smalcald Articles, "One cannot go soft or give way on this article, for then heaven and earth would fall."[7]

How, then, did Luther himself arrive at the biblical doctrine of justification? Near the end of his life, he relates the moment when justification literally dawned upon him. This so-called Tower Experience—Luther's discovery from Romans 1:17 of the gift of justifying righteousness in the gospel—transported Luther. He said that he "felt" himself "to be reborn and to have gone through open doors into paradise."[8]

Luther himself hints that this insight was the fruit of much studied labor in the Scripture—"night and day I pondered until I saw the connection between the justice of God and the statement that 'the just shall live by faith.'"[9] As Luther elsewhere mused, "I did not learn my theology all at once, but had to search deeper for it, where my temptations took me."[10]

What, then, was the path by which Luther arrived at the biblical doctrine of justification by faith alone? Scholars have vigorously debated this question, but Luther's steps may be traced by considering his lectures on the Psalms (1513–14), his lectures on Romans (1515–16), and his first series of lectures on Galatians (1519).[11] While there is no indication in his lectures on the Psalms that Luther had made his discovery of the gift of righteousness, it is clear that Luther was grappling with the depth and reach of sin in the human

---

7 *Book of Concord* (2000), 301, quoted in Oswald Bayer, *Martin Luther's Theology: A Contemporary Interpretation,* 3rd German ed.; trans. Thomas H. Trapp (Grand Rapids, Mich.: Eerdmans, 2008), 98.

8 Quoted in Bainton, *Here I Stand,* 49. On the scholarly controversies surrounding the date and even the historicity of the event, see Lowell C. Green, "Faith, Righteousness, and Justification: New Light on Their Development Under Luther and Melanchthon" *Sixteenth Century Journal* 4/1 (1972): 65–86.

9 Quoted in Bainton, *Here I Stand,* 49.

10 *WATR,* 1:146, 12–14, as cited at Clark, *"Iustitia Imputata Christi,"* 288.

11 For what follows, see broadly Clark, *"Iustitia Imputata Christi,"* 289–94.

heart.[12] Human beings, Luther concluded, are not good people who do bad things. People are wicked by nature, enemies of God, and incapable of doing anything that could merit God's favor.[13]

Such insights indicated that Luther was deepening himself in "a more thoroughly Augustinian position on original sin and predestination."[14] It would be in his lectures on Romans, however, that Luther would first evidence awareness of the biblical doctrine of justification.[15] Commenting on Romans 3:20, Luther denied that one's deeds could justify him. "The fact is that neither the works which precede nor those which follow justify. How much less the works of the Law! . . . For we are not made righteous by doing righteous works, but rather we do righteous works by being righteous. Therefore grace alone justifies."[16] On the contrary, the righteousness that justifies a person is a righteousness that has come from without, from God. Commenting on Romans 4:7, Luther argued that "we are righteous extrinsically when we are righteous solely by the reckoning of God and not of ourselves or of our own works. For his reckoning is not ours by reason of anything that is in us or in our own power. Therefore our righteousness is neither in us or [sic] in our power."[17]

Even so, there remained points that Luther had yet to clarify and would later clarify. The purely receptive character of faith in justification is absent from his lectures on Romans.[18] The good works that faith produces are not expressly excluded from the basis upon which a person is justified. Neither does Luther distinguish clearly the forensic grace of justification from the transforming grace of inward renewal, prompting at least one scholar to conclude that Luther during this period continued to see a person's justification as at least partially grounded in his sanctification.[19]

By the time that Luther delivered his first series of lectures on Galatians

---

12 Julius Köstlin, *The Theology of Luther in Its Historical Development and Inner Harmony,* 2nd. German ed.; 2 vols.; trans. Charles E. Hay (Philadelphia: Lutheran Publication Society, 1897), 1:92.

13 See the summary at Reinhold Seeberg, *The History of Doctrines* (1895, 1898; repr. Grand Rapids, Mich.: Baker, 1977), 2:229.

14 Clark, "*Iustitia Imputata Christi,*" 289.

15 This is the judgment of Herman Bavinck, *Reformed Dogmatics,* trans. John Vriend (Grand Rapids, Mich.: Eerdmans, 2008), 4:195. For a thorough analysis of these lectures from the vantage point of Luther's understanding of justification, see Bavinck, *Reformed Dogmatics,* 4:189–96.

16 *LW,* 25:242, quoted in Bavinck, *Reformed Dogmatics,* 4:191.

17 Ibid., 25:257, as revised in Clark, "*Iustitia Imputata Christi,*" 290.

18 Green, "Faith, Righteousness, and Justification," 66.

19 Green, following Karl Holl, "Faith, Righteousness, and Justification," 72–73.

in 1519, however, what is widely known as Luther's doctrine of justification was essentially in place. In a brief document written in 1518 (*Acta Augustana*), Luther clarified two matters.[20] First, faith in justification is entirely receptive. Faith does not contribute to the righteousness by which the sinner is justified. It receives the righteousness that God offers in the gospel. Second, justification is not a verdict that lies uncertainly in one's future. It is the believer's present and abiding possession. As Luther would argue in his lectures on Galatians, he who "trust[s] in the name of the Lord," his "sins are forgiven, and righteousness is imputed to" him.[21]

What is the "righteousness" that is imputed to the sinner for justification? In a sermon delivered the same year in which he delivered his first series of lectures on Galatians (1519), Luther argued that this righteousness is "alien righteousness, that is the righteousness of another, instilled from without," the "righteousness of Christ."[22] This righteousness becomes the possession of the sinner "through faith in Christ" and "without our works by grace alone."[23]

In this sermon, it is clear that Luther understands Christ's righteousness chiefly in terms of Jesus' sin-bearing death on the cross, and as "accomplish[ing] the same as that original righteousness [lost in Adam] would have accomplished; rather, it accomplishes more."[24] Luther was careful to distinguish this "alien righteousness" from what he termed "our proper righteousness," that is, the fruit of grace in a justified believer, consisting in three things: "slaying the flesh and crucifying the desires with respect to the self," "love to one's neighbor," and "meekness and fear toward God."[25] These two righteousnesses must be distinguished but never separated, for one's proper righteousness is the "fruit and consequence" of one's alien righteousness.[26]

This transfer of righteousness from Christ to the sinner reflects a larger reality—Christ's possession of the sinner, and the sinner's possession of Christ. "Through faith in Christ, therefore, Christ's righteousness becomes our righteousness and all that he has becomes ours; rather he himself becomes ours. . . . He who trusts in Christ exists in Christ; he is one with Christ, having

---

20 On both which, see Green, "Faith, Righteousness, and Justification," 73–77.
21 *LW*, 27:221 quoted in Clark, "*Iustitia Imputata Christi*," 292.
22 "Two Kinds of Righteousness," in *Martin Luther's Basic Theological Writings,* 119.
23 Ibid., 120.
24 Ibid., 119, 120.
25 Ibid., 120. Luther could also term these two righteousnesses as "passive" and "active," respectively, on which see Köstlin, *The Theology of Luther,* 2:440.
26 "Two Kinds of Righteousness," 121.

the same righteousness as he."[27] Justification, then, takes place in the context of a mutual bond or union between Jesus Christ and the believer. But, for Luther, the sinner is not justified on the basis of this union. As R. Scott Clark notes, "It is clear that Luther did not have the Christian justified on the basis of anything else but Christ's imputed righteousness."[28]

Events subsequent to 1519 saw Luther refining but not modifying this doctrine of justification by faith alone. In the last quarter-century of his life, Luther witnessed challenges to the doctrine from two different theological directions. The first challenge threatened justification as wholly gracious. Luther condemned a "formula of compromise which had been presented at Regensburg in 1541 as a basis of agreement between the Roman Catholics" and Lutherans.[29] Luther categorically rejected any attempt to supplement the imputed righteousness of Christ for justification with the inward, renewing work of the Holy Spirit. Not even one's good works, the necessary fruit of justifying faith, could serve to justify the sinner in any way.

The second challenge understood justification as militating against the law both as "the means to drive sinners to repent" and "as a guide for the ethical life."[30] This challenge emerged from within Lutheranism, attempted to appeal to Luther's own teachings for support, and was spurred by the Lutheran minister Johannes Agricola. For the "Antinomians," as they came to be called, the gospel, not the law, was sufficient to drive men to repent and to direct one in righteous living. In 1539, Luther drafted and circulated a searing letter, *Against the Antinomians*, in which he rejected the Antinomians' positions and upheld the law both as a means to repentance and as a rule of life. In this letter, Luther stressed that he was advancing the position that had always characterized his ministry, namely, that "the law . . . cannot be abolished."[31] In fact, one could not "know what sin is," or "what Christ is [and] what he did for us" apart from the law.[32] Luther was concerned to

---

27 Ibid., 120.

28 Clark, "*Iustitia Imputata Christi*," 292.

29 Köstlin, *The Theology of Luther*, 2:447. For the controversy surrounding Regensburg, see the discussion of Ozment, *The Age of Reform*, 377–78, 405–6. For the way in which Luther, for similar reasons, had earlier and vigorously restated the Protestant doctrine in full fashion at the Disputations of 1536–37, see Clark, "*Iustitia Imputata Christi*," 298–306.

30 Lull and Russell, introduction to "Against the Antinomians" (1539), *Martin Luther's Basic Theological Writings*, 176.

31 "Against the Antinomians," in *Martin Luther's Basic Theological Writings*, 179.

32 Ibid.

uphold justification as a doctrine that did not relax one's obligation to obey the law of God.[33]

How may we summarize Luther's path to the biblical doctrine of justification by faith alone, and his mature understanding of that doctrine? In the years leading up to the posting of the Ninety-Five Theses in 1517, Luther came to embrace two convictions that would underlie his subsequent understanding of the Scripture's teaching on salvation. The first is that human depravity has rendered people incapable of doing anything that could win favor and acceptance from God. The second is that the righteousness by which we are justified is a righteousness that comes from without, as the gracious gift of God.

While these convictions informed Luther's initial protest against indulgences, they did not come to maturation until after the posting of the Ninety-Five Theses. Luther would soon come to realize Scripture's teaching that faith is entirely receptive in justification. Faith does not contribute anything to the imputed righteousness that it appropriates for the sinner's justification. Neither does any part of the Christian's renewal constitute the basis upon which he is justified. Justification is, therefore, not a verdict that lies uncertainly in one's future. It is the believer's present possession that abides into the future, and its sole ground is the imputed merits of Jesus Christ.

Calvin and Justification

Luther's achievement in recovering the biblical doctrine of justification by faith alone is nothing short of monumental. It was an achievement that Luther's younger contemporary, John Calvin, appears to have recognized. In the only extant letter from Calvin to Luther, written in 1545, Calvin could address Luther as a "most distinguished minister of Christ, and my ever-honoured father."[34] Theologians in the Lutheran and Reformed traditions concur that Luther and Calvin were in fundamental agreement concerning the doctrine of justification by faith alone.[35]

---

33 For the way in which Luther understood the Ten Commandments to regulate the believer's life, see his "Treatise on Good Works" (1520), in *Selected Writings of Martin Luther, Vol. 2,* ed. Theodore G. Tappert (Minneapolis, Fortress, 2007), 97–196.

34 *The Selected Works of John Calvin: Tracts and Letters,* vol. 4, eds. Henry Beveridge and Jules Bonnet (repr. Grand Rapids, Mich.: Baker, 1983), 440–42.

35 See, representatively, Bavinck, *Reformed Dogmatics,* 4:200; J.L. Neve, *Churches and Sects of Christendom* (rev. ed.; Blair, Neb.: Lutheran Publishing House, 1944), 286–87.

Without rehearsing the specific details of that agreement, we may pose to Calvin a question that has arisen in our consideration of Luther's doctrine of justification. How did Calvin relate justification and sanctification in such a way as to safeguard the biblical integrity of justification? The specific way in which Calvin addressed this question not only built upon but also advanced Luther's recovery of the biblical doctrine of justification by faith alone.

It is in book 3 of the *Institutes of the Christian Religion* (1559) that we find Calvin's fullest and most mature discussion of justification.[36] We may find answers to the question posed above by attending both to the structure and to the content of book 3. The book opens with an introductory chapter that serves as a seam stitching what Calvin has said in book 2 ("The Knowledge of God the Redeemer in Christ") with what Calvin will say in book 3 ("The Way in Which We Receive the Grace of Christ"). In 3.2, Calvin discusses the grace of faith, and, in 3.3–5, the grace of repentance. After a brief summary of the Christian life in 3.6–10, Calvin undertakes a discussion of justification in 3.11–18.[37]

It is curious that Calvin defers consideration of justification (3.11ff.) until after his discussion of "repentance" or "regeneration" (3.3ff.). Given the importance of justification to the Protestant Reformers, and, as we shall see, its priority, for Calvin, to sanctification, one might have expected Calvin to have placed his discussion of justification nearer the beginning of book 3. Calvin explains his reasoning for this ordering at 3.11.1. He arranged the discussion of book 3 in the way that he did in order to stress "how little devoid of good works is the faith, through which alone we obtain free righteousness by the mercy of God."[38] Calvin, then, had a "polemical" or rhetorical "strategy" in view.[39] He wanted to stress not only the inseparability of justification and

---

36 On the path by which Calvin's published statements on justification in the first edition (1536) of the *Institutes* reached their final form in the last edition (1559), see the brief but illuminating discussion at Richard B. Gaffin Jr., "Justification and Union with Christ: *Institutes 3.11–18*," in ed. David W. Hall and Peter A. Lillback, *A Theological Guide to Calvin's Institutes* (Phillipsburg, N.J.: P&R, 2009), 249–51.

37 I owe the foregoing outline and accompanying headings to Ford Lewis Battles, *Analysis of the Institutes of the Christian Religion of John Calvin* (1980; repr. Phillipsburg, N.J.: P&R, 2001), 20–21.

38 John Calvin, *Institutes of the Christian Religion,* ed. John T. McNeil, trans. Ford Lewis Battles (Louisville, Ky.: Westminster John Knox, 1960), 3.11.1. Compare Calvin's eloquent elaboration of this point at *Institutes* 2.16.19, where he concludes, "since rich store of every kind of good abounds in him, let us drink our fill from this fountain, and from no other."

39 Gaffin, "Justification and Union with Christ," 255.

sanctification, but also the fact that "sanctifying faith, faith functioning for holy living, is the same faith that justifies."[40]

That the faith by which the sinner is justified is a faith that necessarily produces good works is not the only way in which Calvin demonstrates the fundamental inseparability of justification and sanctification. Calvin, at the beginning of book 3, situates the entirety of the application of redemption in the believer's union with Christ.

> How do we receive those benefits which the Father bestowed on his only-begotten Son not for Christ's own private use, but that he might enrich poor and needy men? First, we must understand that as long as Christ remains outside of us, and we are separated from him, all that he has suffered and done for the salvation of the human race remains useless and of no value to us. Therefore, to share with us what he has received from the Father, he had to become ours and to dwell within us. . . . All that he possesses is nothing until we grow into one body with him.[41]

This union with Christ, Calvin continues, is "obtain[ed] . . . by faith," even as "the Holy Spirit is the bond by which Christ effectually unites himself to us."[42] By the Spirit, through the faith that the Spirit gives to the sinner, a person is united with Christ. So united to Christ, he possesses Christ and all the benefits that Christ won for him.

In 3.11.1, Calvin also argues that the particular graces of justification and sanctification are both sourced in Jesus Christ. Through faith, one is united to Christ and, in union with Christ, he receives from Christ both justification and sanctification. Christ was given to us by God's generosity, to be grasped and possessed by us in faith.

> By partaking of him, we principally receive a double grace: namely, that being reconciled to God through Christ's blamelessness, we may have in heaven instead of a Judge a gracious Father; and secondly,

---

40 Ibid. As Gaffin also notes, "this does not mean that faith justifies because it sanctifies or as it functions in sanctification; the role of faith as the sole instrument in receiving justification, [Calvin] makes clear elsewhere, differs from its role in sanctification, ibid," referencing 3.11.7; 3.11.17; 3.14.21; 3.18.8.

41 Calvin, *Institutes*, 3.1.1.

42 Ibid.

MARTIN LUTHER'S 95 THESES

FERDINAND PAUWELS, (1872)

LUTHER BEFORE THE REICHSTAG IN WORMS

ANTON VON WERNER, (1843-1915)

MARTIN LUTHER AS AN AUGUSTINIAN MONK

CRANACH, LUCAS, THE ELDER, (1472-1553)

MARTIN LUTHER IN 1526

CRANACH, LUCAS, THE ELDER, (1472-1553)

MARTIN LUTHER TRANSLATING THE BIBLE

GUSTAV ADOLPH, SPANGENBERG, (1828-1891)

MARTIN LUTHER

CRANACH, LUCAS, THE ELDER, (1472-1553)

that sanctified by Christ's spirit we may cultivate blamelessness and purity of life. Of regeneration, indeed, the second of these gifts, I have said what seemed sufficient.[43]

The believer's union with Christ, then, is the fundamental principle that, for Calvin, demonstrates that justification and sanctification are inseparable but distinguishable.

For Calvin, however, these two benefits are not an undifferentiated and inchoate mass. Nor is Calvin indifferent to their order or relation. In what ways does Calvin distinguish justification and sanctification, and along what lines does he understand them to be distinct graces? In the passage quoted from 3.11.1 above, Calvin mentions "a double grace" (*duplex gratia*) that comes into the possession of an individual when by "faith" he "partak[es] of him (i.e., Christ)." As Muller has noted, Calvin does not expressly enumerate the first grace, but he does mention the "second," namely, "regeneration," of which Calvin has spoken in 3.3–5. Since, for Calvin, "regeneration" and "sanctification" are "virtual synonyms," this "second" grace surely refers to the believer's sanctification.[44] What, then, is the identity of the first grace? It is the theme of Calvin's immediately following sentences in 3.11.1, namely, "justification," which Calvin earlier in 3.11.1 describes in terms of "being reconciled to God through Christ's blamelessness."

Calvin, therefore, expressly distinguishes justification and sanctification. He not only says that these two graces are distinct, but he also explains how they are distinct. Sanctification is an inwardly transformative grace—"sanctified by Christ's spirit," we "cultivate blamelessness and purity of life." Justification, however, is an exclusively forensic grace—by it, we are "reconciled to God" and look upon God not as "a Judge" but as "a gracious Father." Calvin's elaborate definition of justification in 3.11.2–4 serves to confirm and to elaborate his understanding of the exclusively legal and non-renovative character of this benefit.

Calvin, furthermore, argues that the forensic integrity of the grace of justification and a proper understanding of union with Christ go hand in hand.[45] This line of argument surfaces especially in Calvin's polemical interaction

---

43 Calvin, *Institutes,* 3.11.1.

44 So Richard Muller, *Calvin and the Reformed Tradition: On the Work of Christ and the Order of Salvation* (Grand Rapids, Mich.: Baker, 2012), 209.

45 For what follows, I am indebted to the discussion and analysis of Gaffin, "Justification and Union with Christ," 266–69.

with the controversial Lutheran theologian Andreas Osiander at 3.11.5–12. Calvin understood Osiander to teach that "we are substantially righteous in God by the infusion both of his essence and of his quality."[46] In other words, "union with Christ is sharing in Christ's essence, by which his righteousness, specifically the righteousness of his divine nature, is communicated."[47] The believer's righteousness, Osiander argued, is an infused righteousness. This righteousness is the direct result of the believer's participating in the divinity of Jesus Christ with whom he is united. For Calvin, Osiander's doctrine compromised what Scripture teaches concerning both the union between Christ and the believer, and the righteousness that the believer receives from Christ.

> That joining together of head and members, that indwelling of Christ in our hearts—in short, that mystical union—are accorded by us the highest degree of importance, so that Christ, having been made ours, makes us sharers with him in the gifts with which he has been endowed. We do not, therefore, contemplate him outside ourselves from afar in order that his righteousness may be imputed to us but because we put on Christ and are engrafted into his body—in short, because he deigns to make us one with him. Thus is Osiander's slander refuted, that by us faith is reckoned righteousness. As if we were to deprive Christ of his right when we say that by faith we come empty to him to make room for his grace in order that he alone may fill us! But Osiander, by spurning this spiritual bond, forces a gross mingling of Christ with believers.[48]

Calvin resists any understanding of the believer's union with Christ that compromises the personal integrity of either Christ or the believer united with Him. Why is it so important that the personal integrity of Christ and the believer be maintained? It is because it is in the context of such a union that Christ's righteousness is imputed to the sinner. As Richard Gaffin observes, such "a union . . . insures that justifying righteousness is his accomplishment, not theirs, and is theirs solely by being imputed to them."[49] Union with Christ, in other words, helps us understand two realities about our justification.

---

46 Calvin, *Institutes*, 3.11.5, quoted in Gaffin, "Justification and Union with Christ," 266.
47 Gaffin, "Justification and Union with Christ," 266.
48 Calvin, *Institutes*, 3.11.10.
49 Gaffin, "Justification and Union with Christ," 268.

First, the righteousness by which we are justified is solely the accomplishment of Jesus Christ, and in no way that of the sinner. Second, in union with Jesus Christ, all that Christ has accomplished comes into the full and lasting possession of the one united with Him. In the case of justification, Christ's righteousness is imputed to the sinner and received by faith alone. Thus, the sinner, through faith in Christ, stands righteous in the sight of God, and does so entirely by the grace of God. The sinner's works have no justifying efficacy whatsoever. It is Christ's works, made over to the one united with Him, that justify the sinner.

For Calvin, then, union with Christ is the biblical teaching that helps us to understand the proper relation between justification and sanctification. Specifically, union with Christ in Calvin's writings helped to bring clarity to two aspects of justification by faith alone that came under particular scrutiny at the time of the Protestant Reformation. First, union with Christ helps us understand the biblical integrity of the grace of justification. Justification is a benefit that comes into the possession of a person when, in union with Jesus Christ, he receives by faith alone the imputed righteousness of Jesus Christ. Second, union with Christ helps us understand that justification is inseparable from Christ and, therefore, from all the benefits that Christ has won for His people. There is no case of a justified person who is not also being sanctified. The faith by which we receive Christ and His righteousness for justification is no dead faith, but a living faith that works by love. This is not to say that we are in any way justified on the basis of the good works that are the necessary fruit of justifying faith. It is to say that justification and sanctification are both graces sourced in Jesus Christ and, therefore, as inseparable as Christ Himself is inseparable.

It is not that Martin Luther failed to grasp many of these insights. In his 1519 lecture on Galatians 2:21, Luther situates justification by faith alone in the context of a person's union with Christ:

> But he who believes in Christ and by the spirit of faith has become one with Him not only renders satisfaction now to all but also brings it about that they owe everything to him, since he has all things in common with Christ. His sins are no longer his; they are Christ's. . . . Again Christ's righteousness now belongs not only to Christ; it belongs to the Christian.[50]

---

50 *LW,* 27:241, as quoted at Clark, "*Iustitia Imputata Christi*," 292.

In a later lecture (1535) on Galatians 2:20, Luther underscored similar themes:

> But so far as justification is concerned, Christ and I must be so closely attached that He lives in me and I in Him. What a marvelous way of speaking! Because He lives in me, whatever grace, righteousness, life, peace, and salvation there is in me is all Christ's; nevertheless, it is mine as well, by the cementing and attachment that are through faith, by which we become as one body in the Spirit. . . . In this way Paul seeks to withdraw us completely from ourselves, from the Law, and from works, and to transplant us into Christ and faith in Christ, so that in the area of justification we look only at grace, and separate it far from the Law and from works, which belong far away.[51]
>
> By [faith] . . . you are so cemented to Christ that He and you are as one person, which cannot be separated but remains attached to Him forever and declares: "I am as Christ." And Christ, in turn, says: "I am as that sinner who is attached to Me, and I to him. For by faith we are joined together into one flesh and one bone."[52]

The importance of this doctrine, as Luther asserts but does not elaborate, is that it refutes the medieval doctrine of "formed faith" (*fides caritate formata*) as that which justifies.[53] Luther, in other words, understood the Scripture's teaching on union with Christ not only as providing the context in which the Scripture speaks of the sinner's justification, but also as safeguarding the forensic integrity of the grace of justification. Luther also hints here that he understands the grace of sanctification in the same framework of union with Christ: "There is a double life: my own, which is natural or animate; and an alien life, that of Christ in me. . . . Paul, living in himself, is utterly dead through the law but living in Christ, or rather with Christ living in him, he lives an alien life. Christ is speaking, acting, and performing all actions in him."[54] The new life of the Christian, Luther reasons, is a life lived in the Christ who indwells every believer.

---

51 *LW*, 26:167–68.

52 Ibid., 26:168.

53 Ibid., 26:168–69. Luther's closing comment is "I would like to treat this at greater length if I could."

54 Ibid., 26:170.

Calvin's discussion of union with Christ in book 3 of the *Institutes* (1559) does not, therefore, represent a material departure from Luther's understanding of justification. What, then, is Calvin's accomplishment and advance over Luther? It is that Calvin both articulated and demonstrated, with systematic precision and comprehensiveness, union with Christ as the architectonic principle of the Bible's teaching of the application of redemption. In doing so, he both stated and explained how union with Christ ensures the inseparability and the distinct character of the graces of justification and sanctification.

A 'New Perspective' on Justification?

In the last forty years, a substantial challenge to the Reformation's doctrine of justification by faith alone has emerged from academic biblical scholarship.[55] The New Perspective on Paul, as proponents have labeled it, contends that Luther and Calvin profoundly misunderstood Paul's teaching of justification, especially in Galatians and Romans. The New Perspective has not remained confined to the academy but has made its way into the evangelical church. Some claim that the New Perspective offers a more biblically faithful account of justification in Paul than the Reformers had. What, then, do New Perspective proponents claim about justification in Paul? Can the Reformers' doctrine be sustained as true to Paul?

New Perspective proponents argue that Paul has not been properly understood in his first-century Jewish context. When Paul speaks of "the works of the law," they contend, he has in mind particularly those commands of the Jewish law that served to identify and mark out a Jew in distinction from a Gentile. This is the reason why, for instance, circumcision and table fellowship feature so prominently in Paul's discussion of the law in Galatians. In the Christian church, proponents continue, Paul found himself locked in controversy with Judaizing opponents. The nub of the controversy did not concern how the sinner is accepted and accounted righteous. The controversy centered around how the Christian is to be identified before others. Justification in the present, therefore, does not concern how a sinner is forgiven and accounted righteous before God. It is primarily a declaration that

---

55 For a brief introduction to the New Perspective, see my *A Christian's Pocket Guide to Being Made Right with God: Understanding Justification* (Fearn, Ross-shire, Scotland: Christian Focus, 2010). In what follows, I will be primarily interacting with the views of N.T. Wright and, to a lesser extent, James D.G. Dunn, New Perspective proponents who have gained a wide hearing within the evangelical church.

one is a member of the people of God. To be "justified by faith and not by works of the law" does not mean that one is forgiven and accounted righteous before God on the sole basis of the righteousness of Jesus Christ, imputed to the sinner and received through faith alone. Instead, this phrase of Paul's means that one is not declared to be a member of God's people because of such identity markers drawn from the Jewish law as circumcision and the dietary laws. Rather, one is declared to be a member of God's people because of the badge of faith in Christ.

For the New Perspective, justification is not Paul's way of answering the question "What must I do to be saved?" It is the Apostle's way of answering the question, "How may I identify a member of the people of God?" Its primary concern is not salvation but identity.

This is not to say that New Perspective proponents do not believe that Paul provides answers to the question how the sinner may be right with God. Whereas justification in the present primarily concerns how one is identified or marked out as a member of God's people, justification in the future primarily concerns how one is saved. How is one said to be justified on the day of judgment? The verdict of justification, these proponents argue, rests upon two coordinate grounds. The first is the sacrifice of Christ on the cross for sin. The second is the transforming work of the Spirit in a person's life. The work of Christ for us and the work of the Spirit in us combine to justify us on the last day.

The lines between the Reformation and the New Perspective are clear. The Reformation did not deny that justification had implications for the way in which the justified believer is identified and relates to other believers. It nevertheless did not primarily understand justification as referring to inclusion in the people of God. The Reformation did not deny that the justified believer will be "openly acknowledged and acquitted" in the presence of angels and men on the "day of judgment."[56] It did forthrightly deny that a believer's works were, are, or will be even the partial basis of his justification. Because it understood that the sole ground of the sinner's justification is the imputed righteousness of Christ, the Reformation forthrightly affirmed that justification is a present and definitive verdict, and that no justified person can "fall from the state of justification."[57]

One service the New Perspective has provided the church is to stir God's

---

56 Westminster Larger Catechism 90.
57 Westminster Confession of Faith 11.5.

people to reexamine for themselves the biblical foundation of justification by faith alone. Every generation of believers, standing on the shoulders of previous generations of believers, has the responsibility of appropriating and articulating the doctrine for itself. The circulation of error has frequently proven the occasion of that enterprise in the church. The New Perspective challenges the contemporary church to consider afresh the Scripture's teaching about justification.

Luther's and Calvin's doctrines, in fact, are true to the Scripture. What does justification mean for Paul? It is the opposite of condemnation (see Rom. 5:16; 8:33–34). It is, therefore, a verdict that God renders in His courtroom. What, then, does it mean to be declared righteous? On what basis does God make such a declaration? The very heart of our "righteousness," Paul explains in Romans 3:21–26, is the atoning, substitutionary, propitiatory death of Jesus Christ. That death is the crowning act of a lifetime of Jesus' obedience for His people (Phil. 2:8). It is that perfect obedience, along with Jesus' sacrificial death, that constitutes the sole basis upon which a person is justified (Rom. 5:19; 8:3–4).

What are the "works of the law" by which "no one will be justified" (Gal. 2:16)? Those works, Paul explains in Galatians 3:10, are the deeds that the law requires a person to perform. Failure to perform them leaves one under a "curse." The whole range of human activity that Paul catalogs in Romans 3:10–18 shows that "works of the law" (3:20) refers to the law's demands that no sinner is able to meet perfectly (cf. Titus 3:5).

What is the "faith" by which one is justified (Gal. 2:16)? Paul is clear that we are not justified because of faith (much less because of the fruitful activity of faith), but through or by (means of) faith. That is to say, faith is the God-provided instrument by which we receive Christ and His righteousness (Eph. 2:8–10; Phil. 1:29). In the matter of justification, Abraham did not "work" but "believ[ed] in him who justifies the ungodly" (Rom. 4:5). Abraham's character did not factor into God's justifying verdict of Abraham. Abraham, rather, trusted God and His promise of the descendant (Jesus) who would bring blessing to the world (see Gen. 12:1–3; 15:1–6).

For Paul, justification takes place in the context of union with Christ. Paul explicitly teaches this point at 2 Corinthians 5:21: "For our sake he made him to be sin who knew no sin." That is to say, for His people's sake, our sins were laid upon Jesus at the cross. Jesus became the sin-bearer and paid the penalty due to us for sin. What's more, "in him we . . . become the righteousness of God." Paul says two things in that statement. First, we "become the righteousness of God" in just the same way that Jesus became "sin." Jesus' spotless righteousness is imputed to us. Second, this imputation happens in the context of an individual's union with Christ ("in him").

Union with Christ, for Paul, means that we possess Christ, even as He possesses us (see 1 Cor. 6:12–20). In possessing Christ, we share in all the benefits that He won on our behalf. That includes not only justification but also sanctification. We are "in Christ Jesus, whom God made our wisdom and our righteousness and sanctification and redemption" (1 Cor. 1:30). Justification ("righteousness") and sanctification are distinct but inseparable benefits sourced in Jesus Christ, and received when one is united to Him by faith.

Conclusion

Martin Luther's rediscovery of the doctrines of grace five hundred years ago was a remarkable achievement and an incalculable service to the church. Luther emerged from a concerted study of the Scripture with the dual conviction that the sinner is saved by grace alone and that this central truth had been profoundly obscured in the church of his day. As we have seen, Luther came to a more precise understanding and articulation of the doctrine of justification over a period of several years. It would fall to Calvin to articulate systematically and comprehensively the doctrine in its biblical fullness.

The doctrine of justification at the time of the Reformation was recovered and advanced in the flames of controversy—the medieval way of salvation that characterized church teaching throughout Luther's and Calvin's lives; the teaching of Agricola and the Roman Catholic–Lutheran dialogue at Regensburg in Luther's later years; and the teaching of Osiander in Calvin's later years. Challenges to the doctrine are nothing new. In our generation, the New Perspective on Paul challenges the evangelical church to articulate afresh the unchanging, biblical doctrine of justification. Luther and Calvin serve us well today in the twenty-first century. They do so, of course, in their bequeathal to us of the fruits of their study of the Scripture. But they also serve us in the example that they have left us.

The doctrine of justification by faith alone is a prized treasure in the church's possession. That treasure may never be taken for granted. It is retained only through hard, patient, and persistent toil in the Word of God. But, they would surely insist, how could we possibly give anything less to the Savior who has given us nothing less than Himself?

Chapter Seven

GRACE ALONE: LUTHER AND THE CHRISTIAN LIFE

SINCLAIR B. FERGUSON

The muscles on the preacher's face tightened as his gaze turned directly toward me. He carefully enunciated some such words as these: "Without this, thousands will perish in hell. It is imperative that you make your donation."

I was watching television, steeling myself mentally against the intimidating, spiritually blackmailing logic of a contemporary televangelist as he urged me to donate to his ministry lest the lost be damned—and part of the guilt rest on my conscience. I suspected there might be not a few lonely listeners who were taking note of the toll-free number to call with their pledge, many of them donating from their meager incomes. Words attributed to a sixteenth-century Dominican friar echoed down the corridors of the intervening five hundred years:

Wenn die Münze im Kästlein klingt,
die Seele in den Himmel springt

As soon as the coin in the coffers rings
The soul from purgatory springs

A little knowledge of Scripture and of the history of the church protects us from such gospel-offending tactics. But in the early sixteenth century, few people had much knowledge of either. And so, when the skilled preacher and sometime inquisitor Johann Tetzel (1464–1519) came to town offering indulgences, many found his preaching as irresistible as that of his modern counterparts. He seemed to know his Bible. And the weight on one's conscience of failing to relieve loved ones of the pangs of purgatory was an overwhelming motivation for obtaining an indulgence, whatever the financial cost. Thus, Tetzel urged his hearers:

> "Seek ye the Lord while he may be found ... while he is near" (Isa. 55.6); work, as John says, "while it is day," for "the night cometh when no man can work (John 9:4).—Do you not hear the voices of your dead parents and other people, screaming and saying: "'Have pity on me, have pity on me ... for the hand of God hath touched me' (Job 19.21)? We are suffering severe punishments and pain, from which you could rescue us with a few alms, if only you would." Open your ears, because the father is calling to the son and the mother to the daughter.[1]

Indulgence?

The Roman Catholic Church has always, officially, carefully guarded the theology and wording surrounding the granting of an indulgence. It is "a remission before God of the temporal punishment due to sins whose guilt has already been forgiven."[2] In effect, an indulgence reduces, or even eliminates, the time a soul spends in purgatory. Unsurprisingly, the only scriptural reference in the two-plus-page exposition of indulgences in *The Catechism of the Catholic Church* is a general encouragement to put off the old man and put on the new.[3] Even given their unscriptural nature or substantiation, Johann Tetzel was certainly pushing the envelope.

But indulgences were simply the tip of the iceberg of late-medieval Roman Catholic theology and practice. They were, however, the straw that

---

1   Quoted in Oberman, *Luther: Man between God and the Devil*, 188.
2   *The Catechism of the Catholic Church* (San Francisco: Ignatius, 1994), 370.
3   Eph. 4:22, 24.

broke the camel's back where Luther was concerned (although he must have been surprised by the eventual consequences of his reaction). The financial fleecing of his flock, not to mention the spiritual danger indulgences posed, stimulated the thirty-three-year-old monk/scholar/pastor to nail his Ninety-Five Theses to the door of the Castle Church in Wittenberg.

Originally, of course, the theses were intended for academic debate. They were, after all, written in Latin. One thing that is immediately striking about them, however, is that to a degree beyond his Reformation forerunners, Luther saw that the root problem with the church was not merely life but doctrine. Doctrine, he understood, shapes life and practice. He commented in later life (if with a little Luther-like exaggeration):

> Doctrine and life must be distinguished. Life is bad among us, as it is among the papists, but we don't fight about life and condemn the papists on that account. Wycliffe and Huss didn't know this and attacked [the papacy] for its life. I don't scold myself into becoming good, but I fight over the Word and whether our adversaries teach it in its purity. That doctrine should be attacked—this has never before happened. This is my calling. Others have censured only life, but to treat doctrine is to strike at the most sensitive point.[4]

For this reason, the theses were the beginning of his progressive public dismantling of the entire late-medieval sacramental system of salvation.

For almost a decade, Luther was a work in progress. October 31, 1517, was roughly the halfway point in his pilgrimage from seeking a gospel that would assure him of salvation, to the full-grown attack on the church's theology expressed in 1520 in his *On the Babylonian Captivity of the Church* and *On the Freedom of a Christian*. By January 1523, he was openly saying (as he noted in a sermon on Luke 2:41–52), that if Mary, the mother of our Lord, could be mistaken about Jesus, then the church could be too.[5]

This dismantling was already hinted at in the opening statement of the Ninety-Five Theses:

---

4 *LW*, 54:110.

5 *The Complete Sermons of Martin Luther*, ed. John N. Lenker, trans. S.E. Ochsenford (Grand Rapids, Mich.: Baker, 2000), 2:25.

When our Lord and Master Jesus Christ said "Repent," he intended that the entire life of believers should be repentance.[6]

Here Luther, set free from the Vulgate's mistranslation of the Greek verb *metanoeō* (repent) by the Latin *poenitentiam agite* (do penance) was, in effect undermining the whole late-medieval *ordo salutis* (way of salvation).[7] It is only within this context that we can fully appreciate how Luther viewed the biblical teaching on becoming and living as a Christian by grace alone, through faith alone, in Christ alone.

A Medieval Order

The "way of salvation" with which Luther and his contemporaries were familiar had the following taxonomy:

The power of baptism lay in the way in which initial grace was infused into the recipient.

The rest of life, governed by the sacraments of the church, essentially involved a progress in this grace or a return to it. Penance was the way in which the backslidden individual was restored, providing the so-called second plank—an opportunity to begin again to cooperate with God's grace in developing a personal righteousness consummated if and when faith was fully formed by perfect love for God. It was widely held that it was almost always *if* and not *when*.

Two features marked this progress. One was that the individual was responsible *facere quod in se est*,[8] that is, to do what lay within his powers to cooperate with sacramentally given grace in progressing toward actual righteousness.[9] The problem was, of course, as Luther was acutely aware, that man is by nature hopelessly *incurvatus in se* (turned in on himself).[10] This pattern simply turned him in even further to find the grounds for justification. The real need was to be turned out of oneself to discover salvation in Jesus Christ.

---

6 *Martin Luther's Ninety-Five Theses*, 47.

7 Paradoxically, given his later conflict with Erasmus (1469–1536), this was possible only because of the latter's publication of his edition of the Greek New Testament in 1516.

8 The phrase is especially associated with Gabriel Biel (1420–95).

9 Luther has a "purple passage" on this phrase in his discussion of Galatians 2:20. See Martin Luther, *Commentary on St Paul's Epistle to the Galatians*, trans. Philip S. Watson, (London: James Clark, 1953), 174. The phrase is probably the forerunner of the still-used "Heaven helps those who help themselves."

10 See Luther's comments in *Luther: Lectures on Romans*, ed. and trans. Wilhelm Pauck, Library of Christian Classics (London: S.C.M., 1961), XV:159, 225.

Two, the goal in view in the individual's progress through this *ordo salutis* was for unformed faith (*fides informis*) to develop progressively toward a more perfect righteousness manifested in a faith fully formed by love (*fides caritate formata*). When faith was thus suffused with perfect love for God, the individual was in fact righteous (*iustus*). Therefore, God could righteously justify him since he was in fact justifiable and had become so by grace. Against this background, the Reformation doctrine of the justification of the ungodly was, it was claimed, a legal fiction and not a reality.[11]

Justification by Faith—but Not Alone?

The problem here was subtle: the church taught justification by grace. Medieval theology was replete with discussions of grace and how one receives it.

The Reformers, however, detected more than one fatal misstep. For one thing, grace was regarded as more or less a substance infused into the individual, not the disposition of God toward the individual. For another, when Luther in essence asked, "Spell out what you mean by 'grace,'" he realized that (to use Paul's language) "grace is no more grace."[12] For, in the biblical usage, there is no room for contribution or cooperation in God's justifying grace. It is free and unconditional, not in any sense earned or congruent with anything in us. It is precisely the justification of the ungodly, and it is not based on anything God's grace has accomplished in us. Rather, justification is grounded in what God has done in Christ outside of us.

Luther's Discovery

Luther had himself embodied as well as observed the implications of the medieval view. When it came to *facere quod in se est*, few had done more than the young Augustinian monk to progress toward righteousness:

> I almost fasted myself to death, for again and again I went for three
> days without taking a drop of water or a morsel of food. I was very
> serious about it. . . . I chose twenty-one saints and prayed to three
> every day when I celebrated mass; thus I completed the number

---

11 It is probably in view of this criticism that in his mature *Institutes*, Calvin expounds sanctification and the Christian life *before* treating justification. Both are united in Christ and are therefore inextricably linked with and inseparable from one another. Thus justification by grace *through faith alone* could not be accused of antinomianism. See Calvin, *Institutes*, book 3.

12 Rom. 11:6.

every week. I prayed especially to the Blessed Virgin, who with her womanly heart would compassionately appease her Son.

Luther provides his own commentary on this:

"The most pious monk is the worst scoundrel" because "he denies that Christ is the mediator and high priest and turns him into a judge."[13]

Inevitably, Luther found himself confronted with the question: "How can I be sure that I have done enough? How can I know that the love I feel for God has so suffused my being that he is able to say '*Justus es*—you are justified'?" The truth was, as he later wrote, addressing Erasmus:

If I lived and worked to all eternity, my conscience would never reach comfortable certainty as to how much it must do to satisfy God. Whatever work I had done, there would still be a nagging doubt [*scrupulus*] as to whether it pleased God, or whether He required something more.[14]

For this reason, he hated the expression "the righteousness of God."

That expression "righteousness of God" was like a thunderbolt in my heart. When under the papacy I read, "In thy righteousness deliver me" (Ps. 31:1) and "in thy truth," I thought at once that this righteousness was an avenging anger, namely the wrath of God. I hated Paul with all my heart when I read that the righteousness of God is revealed in the gospel (Rom. 1:16, 17). Only afterward, when I saw the words that follow—namely that it's written that the righteous shall live through faith (Rom. 1:17)—and in addition consulted Augustine, was I cheered. When I learned that the righteousness of God is his mercy, and that he makes us righteous through it, a remedy was offered to me in my affliction.[15]

---

13 *LW*, 54:339–40.
14 Martin Luther, *The Bondage of the Will*, trans. J.I. Packer and O.R. Johnston, (London: James Clarke, 1957), 313–14.
15 *LW*, 54:308–9.

In fact, within the church's articulation of the *ordo salutis*, it was beyond the realm of the possible for an ordinary individual to enjoy the assurance of faith. And this, in turn, meant that it was impossible to "enjoy" God Himself.[16]

Luther owed a great deal to the vicar general of his order in Germany (the Observant Augustinians), who—although he did not follow Luther in his breach with Rome—pointed him to the heart of the gospel:

> My good Staupitz said, "One must keep one's eyes fixed on that man who is called Christ." Staupitz is the one who started the teaching [of the gospel in our time].[17]

Luther's eventual breakthrough led to a fresh understanding of what it meant to be a Christian, sovereignly and graciously justified, counted righteous through faith alone, brought into union with Christ.

A Sovereign God

Salvation is therefore, for Luther, first and foremost the work of a sovereign God. Divine sovereignty is more frequently associated with Calvin than with Luther. But this is partly due to the systematic character of Calvin's writing[18] and to the fact that later Lutheranism tended to play down this aspect of its founder's teaching. But in some places, the German Reformer's writing tempts one to ask, "Is Luther also among the Calvinists?" For, contrary to the *facere quod in se est* of medievalism, Luther was profoundly conscious that by nature we are totally depraved and therefore totally disabled spiritually. Neither biblical commands nor our moral obligations to live for God's glory should be misread as assuming or implying our ability to fulfill them. *Homo incurvatus in se* is incapable of converting himself to God.[19]

This is, in effect, one of the main themes of what is often regarded as Luther's finest and most careful piece of theological writing, *On the Bondage*

---

16 Contrast Paul's teaching on the inner logic of the gospel in relationship to the assurance it provides, Rom. 5:1–11.

17 *LW*, 54:97.

18 Doubtless also his treatise *On the Eternal Predestination of God*.

19 This helps to explain why Luther tended to categorize the law, alongside sin, Satan, and death, as our enemy. He saw that it cannot effect what it commands and therefore only condemns us. In this sense, when he used the law in responding to the question of the lawyer (Luke 10:27–37), Jesus Himself becomes an "unfriendly, ungracious man." This is counterbalanced for Luther by the fact that "the Samaritan of course is our Lord Jesus Christ himself." *Complete Sermons of Martin Luther*, 3.1, 3, 27.

of the Will, an eloquent response to and polemic against Erasmus' *The Free-dom of the Will*. Here, Luther argues that since even the best of men who fulfill all the rites and requirements of their church—specifically, men like the Pharisee Nicodemus—are blind to and incapable of entering the kingdom of God, our only hope is for God Himself to move toward us in electing grace:

> What in the way of effort and endeavour does he [Nicodemus] leave undone? He confesses Christ to be true, and to have come from God, he refers to his signs, he comes by night to hear and discuss further. Does he not seem to have sought by the power of "free-will" all that pertains to godliness and salvation? But see what shipwreck he makes.[20]

Over against Erasmus, therefore, Luther vigorously contends that such passages as Romans 9:15ff. refer to the absolute sovereignty of God in distinguishing election and salvation. He will not allow Paul's use of Malachi 1:2–3 ("I have loved Jacob but Esau I have hated") to be reduced merely to different roles in the service of God: "It is not only an external lordship and servitude that is there being treated of, but everything that belongs to the people of God—that is, the blessing, word, Spirit and promise of Christ and the eternal kingdom."[21]

At every exegetical crux in Romans 9—including the hardening of the heart of Pharaoh and the imagery of the potter and the clay—Luther and Calvin occupy a similar perspective. Indeed, Luther's language outdoes that of his younger contemporary in vigor and the manner in which he excoriates his opponents. Why such vigor? Because for Luther, the only hope for human depravity and inability lies in a radical divine sovereignty.

Grace Alone Availeth

Salvation is therefore by grace and not by merit. In one sense, this second point simply amplifies the first. But for Luther, it has a special significance.

When Luther introduced his lectures on Romans (given in 1515–16, but remarkably never published until the twentieth century), he saw the function of the letter through the lenses of God's call to Jeremiah:

---

20 Luther, *Bondage of the Will*, 305–6.
21 Ibid., 225.

The sum and substance of this letter is to pull down, to pluck up, and to destroy all wisdom and righteousness of the flesh (i.e., of whatever importance they may be in the sight of men and even in our own eyes), no matter how heartily and sincerely they may be practised, and to implant, establish, and make large the reality of sin (however unconscious we may be of its existence).[22]

This included destroying the subtle theological distinction between congruent merit (*meritum de congruo*) and condign merit (*meritum de condigno*). In the first, as we cooperate with God, we are fitted for God's further gift of grace. Strictly speaking, God is not obliged to give us this, but since, as the popular saying goes, "heaven helps those who help themselves," such grace could be anticipated. This grace further enables the individual to do such works that God in justice would reward with eternal life (i.e., condign merit).

This theology, which escapes the crassest forms of Pelagianism, nevertheless devolves into a more subtle form of semi-Pelagianism. But the more subtle the theology, the greater the danger. The insistence that the individual acts to cooperate with grace—with the implication that he becomes a person to whom it is appropriate to show grace—in effect destroys all that grace really means.

What Luther clearly grasped was a vital biblical principle: The moment I ground grace in anything in myself, present in any measure through myself, no matter by what means produced, grace has forfeited the right to be called grace. Luther grasped the Pauline principle that it is not because of anything in an individual that he becomes the object of God's saving grace or is distinguished from another.[23] Rather, as Luther would write tersely on his deathbed, "We are beggars," or more fully in his great paraphrase of Psalm 130:

Thy love and grace alone avail
To blot out my transgression;
The best and holiest deeds must fail
To break sin's dread oppression.
Before thee none can boasting stand,
But all must fear thy strict demand

---

22 *Luther: Lectures on Romans*, XV:3.

23 Luther's comments on the extent of the atonement are in keeping with this ("Christ did not die absolutely for all." See *Luther: Lectures on Romans*, XV:252.

And live alone by mercy.
Therefore my hope is in the Lord
And not in mine own merit;
It rests upon His faithful Word
To them of contrite spirit
That he is merciful and just;
This is my comfort and my trust.
His help I wait with patience.[24]

Luther was, after all, an *Augustinian* monk.

Faith Alone

Salvation, which is of God alone, by grace alone, is also ours through faith alone. Herein lay the heart of the matter for Luther. Salvation in the fullest sense is ours finally in the resurrection. But our present justification guarantees this final consummation. Justification itself is not ours as the hoped-for goal of the elongated experience of a sacramental *ordo salutis* producing in us an imperfect righteousness that leaves us still in need of the fires of purgatory to complete the work. Rather, amazingly, wonderfully, graciously, we are justified in Christ the moment we come to Him. The judgment of the last day has been brought forward in Christ to the present day. At the cross, Christ took our place as condemned; in the tomb, Christ rose again, free from the judgment and condemnation He bore in our place. He thus became the guarantee both of our justification in the present day and our resurrection in the last day.[25] Christ—with all the blessings of justification—is the believer's "the hour I first believed."[26]

Intriguingly, in the modern theological context, over against both Erasmus and Jerome long before him, Luther simply will not allow that the *works*—without which we are justified—are merely the ceremonial works of the law.[27]

---

24 "From Depths of Woe I Raise to Thee," trans. Catherine Winkworth, 1863.
25 Rom. 4:24–25.
26 The words are from John Newton's hymn "Amazing Grace," verse 2.
27 It may be worth noting here that the view often associated with the New Perspective on Paul, that "the works of the law" in Paul refer to the Jewish "boundary markers" of the ceremonial law, is by no means a novel perspective. Luther was conscious of its pedigree in his day stretching back beyond his immediate protagonist Erasmus to Jerome. This is a sure indication to us that in adopting the view that Paul refers to "the works of the law" in their totality (i.e. inclusive of, not exclusive of, the "moral" law of the Ten Commandments) Luther was not doing so as a poorly

That we are justified apart from works does not mean that works have no place in the Christian life. The very reverse is the case. The Ninety-Five Theses had already stressed that loving actions toward neighbors are far more important than purchasing indulgences.[28] Indeed, on one occasion, Luther uttered the *bon mot* "I should be called *Doctor Bonorum Operum*—Doctor of Good Works."[29] For rather than denying their importance, the way of faith guarantees them. The tree that has now become good will bear good fruit. As Paul notes in Galatians 5:6, love is the fruit of faith, for "faith work[s] by love."

Luther writes pointedly in this connection:

> They [the scholastic theologians] read this place of Paul through coloured glass (as the saying is), and pervert the text after their own dreams. For Paul saith not: Faith which *justifieth* by love, or: Faith which maketh acceptable by love.[30] Such a text they do invent and forcibly thrust it into this place.... Paul... saith that works are done by faith through love, and not that a man is justified by love.... He saith not: Charity is efficacious, but: Faith is efficacious, and not: Charity worketh, but: Faith worketh.[31]

In Christ Alone

Salvation that is of God alone, by grace alone, through faith alone, is ours only in Christ alone. In *On the Freedom of a Christian*, Luther underscored the "incomparable benefit" of faith in Christ, namely, union with Him:

> Faith unites the soul with Christ as a bride is united with her bridegroom... it follows that everything they have they hold in common, the good as well as the evil. Accordingly the believing soul can boast

---

equipped sixteenth-century exegete unfamiliar with alternatives. Rather, he specifically rejects the view that has gained considerable currency in some contemporary scholarship. See, e.g. *The Bondage of the Will*, 284: "It is not true that Paul is speaking here only of ceremonial works."

28 See especially theses 43–46.

29 See Oberman, *Luther: Man between God and the Devil*, 77. Luther is probably referring here to the fact that those who had been named as "Doctors of the Church" all acquired what amounted to Latin nicknames, thus Aquinas was known as *Doctor Angelicus* (the angelic doctor), Alexander of Hales as *Doctor Irrefragibilis* (the irrefutable doctor), etc.

30 The allusion being clearly to the idea of *fides caritate formata*, so that the person is essentially justified on the basis of the perfect love for God (= righteousness) which has been wrought in them.

31 Luther, *Commentary on St Paul's Epistle to the Galatians,*, 465.

and glory in whatever Christ has as though it were its own, and whatever the soul has Christ claims as his own. Let us compare these and
we shall see inestimable benefits. Christ is full of grace, life, and salvation. The soul is full of sins, death, and damnation. Now let faith
come between them and sins, death, and damnation will be Christ's,
while grace, life, and salvation will be the soul's; for if Christ is a
bridegroom, he must take upon himself the things that are his bride's
and bestow upon her the things that are his. If he gives her his body
and very self, how shall he not give her all that is his? And if he takes
the body of the bride, how shall he not take all that is hers? . . . Who
can understand the riches of the glory of this grace?[32]

At last, in Christ, there is freedom from the guilt and power of sin. But, as
Luther famously notes on the opening page of *On the Freedom of a Christian*,
this is double-sided:

A Christian is a perfectly free Lord of all, subject to none.
A Christian is a perfectly dutiful servant of all, subject to all.[33]

These paradoxical statements find their proper harmonization in Christ.
The Master of all became the servant of all. And we are united to Him. Now
we share in His conquest of all the powers that have ensnared us and held us
in bondage.

As baptized Christians, we are delivered from the dominion of sin. We
have been baptized into union with Christ, in whose death sin's reign was
broken and its dominion ended. It is true, we are not yet delivered from its
presence, and therefore the Christian is engaged in a daily and lifelong battle
against it. But we battle in the resources of our union with Christ.

Commenting on Galatians 2:20—"I am crucified with Christ"—Luther
draws out the implications:

Even as Christ himself was crucified to the law, sin, death and the
devil, so that they have no further power over him; even so, I through
faith being now crucified with Christ in spirit, am crucified and dead

---

32 "The Freedom of a Christian," in *Three Treatises,* trans. W.A. Lambert, rev. J.J. Grimm (Philadelphia: Fortress, 1970), 286–87.
33 Ibid., 277.

to the law, sin, death and the devil, so that they have no further power over me, but are now crucified and dead unto me. Paul speaketh not here of crucifying by imitation or example. . . . But he speaketh here of that high crucifying, whereby sin, the devil and death are crucified in Christ, and not in me. Here Christ doth all himself alone. But I believing in Christ, am by faith crucified also with Christ, so that all these things are crucified and dead also unto me.[34]

If by "all these things" Luther includes "are crucified and dead also unto me," as certainly some of his followers did, then he is less careful with his language here than Paul's words require. It is perhaps understandable that conclusions he himself repudiated were drawn from his words, as for example in his pupil and friend Johannes Agricola's conclusion that believers are not only dead to the law, but the law is dead to them.[35]

But Luther's main point here is biblical. Union with Christ sets the believer free from the dominion of powers that enslaved him before he came to Christ. Now he is empowered to live as Christ's free man—in obedience to His Word as His servant, no longer under the reign of sin but under the reign of Christ, no longer condemned by the law but finding increasingly that through the Spirit the law's directives are fulfilled in our lives.[36] Yes, the believer dies, but the sting of death has been drawn, and the believer through it enters into eternal life.

Satan Defeated

The Christian has also been set free from bondage to Satan. Attention has sometimes been given to Christ's victory over Satan as a central aspect in Luther's understanding of the atonement,[37] but his emphasis on the Christian's freedom from Satan's power has been largely ignored.[38] But for Luther

---

34 Luther, *Commentary on St Paul's Epistle to the Galatians*, 166–67.

35 In Rom. 7:1–4, Paul uses the analogy of a husband's dying with the consequence that his wife is "released from the law" (v. 3) and is thus free to marry another and is not condemned by the law as an adulteress. In his application of the analogy to the believer, however, Luther underlines that it is the believer, not the law, who has died.

36 For Luther, the law always had love in view: "When we examine the laws of Moses, we find they all treat of love." *Complete Sermons of Martin Luther*, 3.1, 21.

37 Most notably in Gustav Aulen's *Christus Victor* (London: S.P.C.K., 1931).

38 A point well made in Oberman, *Luther: Man between God and the Devil*, 104: "Luther's world of thought it wholly distorted and apologetically misconstrued if his conception of the Devil is dismissed as a medieval phenomenon and only his faith in Christ retained as relevant or as the

himself, this was vital. The disregard of this emphasis is all the more striking because in Luther, it is unavoidable. It is no accident that Christ's conquest of the evil one, and ours through Christ, is the central motif of his "*Ein' feste Burg ist unser Gott*":

A mighty fortress is our God, a bulwark never failing . . .

For still our ancient foe doth seek to work us woe;
His craft and power are great, and, armed with cruel hate,
On earth is not his equal.

Did we in our own strength confide, our striving would be losing;
Were not the right Man on our side, the Man of God's own choosing:
Dost ask who that may be? Christ Jesus, it is He;
Lord Sabaoth, His Name, from age to age the same,
And He must win the battle.

And though this world, with devils filled, should threaten to undo us,
We will not fear, for God hath willed His truth to triumph through us:
The Prince of Darkness grim, we tremble not for him;
His rage we can endure, for lo, his doom is sure,
One little word shall fell him.[39]

We should heed Luther's word about Satan's "craft." Luther's life story conveys a profound awareness of this as a reality in the Christian life, and his writings display a keen sense of Satan's subtlety and deceptiveness. Thus, in his exposition of Genesis 3, he notes:

But if, as is proper, we consider these matters a little more carefully, we shall find that this was the greatest and severest of all temptations; *for the serpent directs its attack at God's good will and makes it his business to prove from the prohibition that God's will towards man is not good.*

---

only decisive factor. Christ and the Devil were equally real to him. . . . There is no way to grasp Luther's milieu of experience and faith unless one has an acute sense of his view of Christian existence between God and the Devil: without a recognition of Satan's power, belief in Christ is reduced to an idea about Christ—and Luther's faith becomes a confused delusion in keeping with the tenor of his time."

39 J.A. Alexander's translation.

Therefore Satan here attacks Adam and Eve in this way to deprive them of the Word and to make them believe his lie after they have lost the Word and their trust in God.[40]

This distortion of the character of God (the attack on His good will) and deprivation of the truth about God (exchanging the truth for a lie[41]) were for Luther a central insight into the controversies of his own time. It was not because he was medieval that he pictured a "world all devils o'er" but because he believed that the whole world lies in the power of the evil one.[42] He thus detected Satan's malignant influence in distorting the Word of God and depriving the church of the gospel, not only in Eden but in sixteenth-century Europe.

While it is true that "this slyness and villainy of Satan is imitated by all the heretics,"[43] Luther saw that he had a yet more subtle work among God's people: turning the gospel into another law. Here is one fascinating comment:

> In a conflict with the devil it isn't enough to say, "This is the Word of God," for it is the devil's greatest [trick] to take away one's weapon when fear suddenly strikes. . . . He is hostile to us. We don't know a hundredth part of what he knows. . . . It is the supreme art of the devil that he can make the law out of the gospel. . . . The devil turns the Word upside down.[44]

People hear the good news of forgiveness in the gospel. Forgiveness is not based on any prequalification. But Satan is a "sour soul." The result? People respond by saying they will live better lives, try harder, and endeavor to be better. The Word has indeed been turned upside down. To overcome the devil, therefore, the believer must rest in all the blessings that are freely given to him in Christ and rejoice in them. Thus, at the end of the day, the gospel turns the devil upside down.

---

40 *LW*, 1:148, emphasis mine.
41 Rom. 1:25.
42 1 John 5:19.
43 *LW*, 1:148.
44 *LW*, 54:105. Recorded by Viet Dietrich, who as a student had boarded with Luther, acted as his amanuensis, and also accompanied him to both the Marburg Colloquy in 1529 and to the Diet of Augsburg the following year.

Implications

What, then, do the sovereignty of God, salvation by grace, justification by faith, and new life in union with Christ mean for the living of the Christian life? For Luther, they carry four implications:

The first implication is the knowledge that the Christian believer is *simul iustus et peccator*,[45] at one and the same time justified and yet a sinner. This principle, to which Luther may have been stimulated by John Tauler's *Theologia Germanica*, was a hugely stabilizing principle: in and of myself, all I see is a sinner; but when I see myself in Christ, I see a man counted righteous with His perfect righteousness. Such a man is therefore able to stand before God as righteous as Jesus Christ—because he is righteous only in the righteousness that is Christ's. Here we stand secure.

The second implication is the discovery that God has become our Father in Christ. We are accepted. One of the most beautiful accounts found in Luther's *Table Talk* was, perhaps significantly, recorded by the somewhat melancholic, yet much loved, John Schlaginhaufen:

> God must be much friendlier to me and speak to me in friendlier fashion than my Katy to little Martin. Neither Katy nor I could intentionally gouge out the eye or tear off the head of our child. Nor could God. God must have patience with us. He has given evidence of it, and therefore he sent his Son into our flesh in order that we may look to him for the best.[46]

Third, Luther emphasizes that life in Christ is necessarily life under the cross.[47] If we are united to Christ, our lives will be patterned after His. The way for both the true church and the true Christian is not via the theology of glory (*theologia gloriae*) but via the theology of the cross (*theologia crucis*). This impacts us inwardly as we die to self and outwardly as we share in the sufferings of the church. The medieval theology of glory must be overcome by the theology of the cross. For all their differences in understanding the precise nature of the sacraments, Luther and Calvin are at one here. If we are united with Christ in His death and resurrection, and marked out thus by our

---

45 A recurring note in Luther, e.g., *Luther: Lectures on Romans*, 127, 208, 322.

46 *LW,* 54:127.

47 For copious references to this principle in Luther, see Walther von Loewenich, *Luther's Theology of the Cross*, trans. Herbert J.A. Bouman (Minneapolis: Augsburg, 1976), 112–43.

baptism (as Paul teaches in Rom. 6:1–14), then the whole of the Christian life will be a cross-bearing:

> The Cross of Christ doth not signify that piece of wood which Christ did bear upon his shoulders, and to the which he was afterwards nailed, but generally it signifieth all the afflictions of the faithful, whose sufferings are Christ's sufferings, 2 Cor. i.5: "The sufferings of Christ abound in us"; again: "Now rejoice I in my sufferings for you, and fulfil the rest of the afflictions of Christ in my flesh, for his body's sake, which is the Church" &c. (Col. i.24). The Cross of Christ therefore generally signifieth all the afflictions of the Church which it suffereth for Christ.[48]

The believer's union with Christ in His death and resurrection and its outworking in daily experience thus became, for Luther, the spectacle lenses through which the Christian learns to view every experience in life. This—the *theologia crucis*—is what brings everything into sharper focus and enables us to make sense of the ups and downs of the Christian life:

> It is profitable for us to know these things, lest we should be swallowed up with sorrow or fall to despair when we see that our adversaries do cruelly persecute, excommunicate and kill us. But let us think with ourselves, after the example of Paul that we must glory in the cross which we bear, not for our sins, but for Christ's sake. If we consider only in ourselves the sufferings which we endure, they are not only grievous but intolerable; but when we may say: "Thy sufferings (O Christ) abound in us"; or, as it is said in Psalm xliv: "For thy sake we are killed all the day," then these sufferings are not only easy, but also sweet, according to this saying: "My burden is easy, and my yoke is sweet" (Matt. xi.30).[49]

Fourth, the Christian life is marked by assurance and joy. This was one of the hallmarks of the Reformation, and understandably so. The Reformation's rediscovery regarding justification—that, instead of working toward a hoped-for arrival at it, the Christian life actually begins with it—brought

---

48 Luther, *Commentary on St Paul's Epistle to the Galatians*, 558.
49 Ibid., 559.

stunning deliverance, filling mind, will, and affections with joy. It meant that one could now begin to live in the light of a settled future in glory. Inevitably, that light reflected back into the present life, bringing intense relief and release.

Standing on Your Head

For Luther, the Christian life is a gospel-grounded, gospel-built, gospel-magnifying life that exhibits the free and sovereign grace of God and is lived out in gratitude to the Savior who died for us, yoked to Him in cross-bearing until death is swallowed up in victory and faith becomes sight.

Perhaps, in 1522, as they sat listening to Luther preaching one Sunday in the church at Borna, some of his congregation wondered what lay at the heart of this gospel that had so excited, not to say transformed, Brother Martin. Could it possibly be for them too? Luther had read their minds. He had come into the pulpit well prepared to answer their question:

> But what is the Gospel? It is this, that God has sent his Son into the world to save sinners, Jn. 3, 16, and to crush hell, overcome death, take away sin and satisfy the law. But what must you do? Nothing but accept this and look up to your Redeemer and firmly believe that he has done all this for your good and freely gives you all as your own, so that in the terrors of death, sin and hell, you can confidently say and boldly depend upon it, and say: Although I do not fulfil the law, although sin is still present and I fear death and hell, nevertheless from the Gospel I know that Christ has bestowed on me all his works. I am sure he will not lie, his promise he will surely fulfil. And as a sign of this I have received baptism. . . .
>
> Upon this I anchor my confidence. For I know that my Lord Christ has overcome death, sin, hell and the devil for my good. For he was innocent, as Peter says: "Who did no sin, neither was guile found in his mouth." 1 Pet. 2, 22. Therefore sin and death were not able to slay him, hell could not hold him, and he has become their Lord, and has granted this to all who accept and believe it. All this is effected not by my works or merits; but by pure grace, goodness and mercy.[50]

---

50 *Complete Sermons of Martin Luther*, 1.2, 373.

Luther once said, "If I could believe that God was not angry at me, I would stand on my head for joy."[51] Perhaps that very day some of those who heard him preach responded and experienced the "confidence" of which he spoke. Who knows but some of the younger hearers later wrote to their friends in turn and told them that they had gone home and stood on their heads for joy?

---

51 *WA*, 176.6f, cited by Oberman, *Luther: Man between God and the Devil*, 315.

Chapter Eight

CHRIST ALONE: LUTHER ON CHRIST, THE SACRAMENTS, AND THE CHURCH

W. ROBERT GODFREY

When Martin Luther posted his Ninety-Five Theses for public debate among scholars at the University of Wittenberg on October 31, 1517, he was still an unknown Augustinian monk who had not yet recovered the gospel from the Scriptures. But already, in various theses he anticipated interests that would grow and clarify for him over time. For instance, thesis 32: "They will be condemned eternally, together with their teachers, who believe themselves sure of their salvation because they have letters of pardon."[1] In this thesis, he writes of the salvation that he would later understand clearly in terms of the work of Christ, of the indulgences that were a corrupt outgrowth of medieval abuses of the sacraments, and of the teachers who as leaders in the church were leading Christians seriously astray. In this chapter, we will look at the mature thought of Luther on Christ, the sacraments, and the church.

---

1   *Martin Luther's Ninety-Five Theses*, 31.

Christ

Luther recovered for the church from the Bible the centrality of the person and work of Christ in redemption. He stripped away various medieval errors and accretions so that Christ shone clearly as the light of the world. His writing on the work of Christ was often remarkably simple and brief. He especially highlighted that Christ had accomplished all that was needed for the salvation of His people in His life, death, and resurrection. For example, Luther wrote in 1522: "Therefore one must teach as follows: 'Behold, Christ died for you! He took sin, death, and hell upon Himself and submitted Himself. But nothing could subdue Him, for He was too strong; He rose from the dead, was completely victorious, and subjected everything to Himself. And He did all this in order that you might be free from it and lord over it. If you believe this, you have it.'"[2]

Similarly, he taught in his Large Catechism (1529):

> There was no counsel, no help, no comfort for us until this only and eternal Son of God, in his unfathomable goodness, had mercy on our misery and wretchedness and came from heaven to help us . . . Jesus Christ, the Lord of life and righteousness and every good and blessing. He has snatched us, poor lost creatures, from the jaws of hell, won us, made us free, and restored us to the Father's favor and grace . . . he who has brought us back from the devil to God, from death to life, from sin to righteousness, and now keeps us safe there.[3]

In very consistent terms, Luther wrote later in *On the Councils and the Church* (1539): "Christ, who is a king of righteousness in us through his precious blood, death, and resurrection, with which he blotted out our sin for us, made satisfaction, reconciled God, and redeemed us from death, wrath, and hell."[4] Jesus is truly the complete redeemer, saving His own from death, the devil, and the Father's wrath, and bringing to them life, forgiveness, and righteousness.

Luther stressed that the work of Christ was the foundation of the certainty and dependability of the promises of Jesus. As he had struggled with

---

2 "Sermons on the First Epistle of St. Peter," *LW*, 30:13.
3 Large Catechism, in *The Book of Concord* (1959), 414.
4 "On the Councils and the Church," *LW*, 41:140.

terrible temptations as a monk and found peace with God in the promises of the Word, so he wanted everyone to experience that peace. He taught that salvation came to everyone who trusted the promises of Jesus. He wanted to make clear that the promise and the presence of Jesus are objectively true and available even where there is no faith. Faith does not create the promise or make Jesus the Savior; rather, faith simply rests on the saving Jesus.

The Work of Christ and the Will of the Father

Luther often made his thought on the work of Christ clearer as he related it to the will of the Father and to the preaching of the law and the gospel.[5] He insisted that the love and saving purpose that we see in the work of Jesus reveals and expresses precisely the love and purpose of the Father:

> The first thing you see in this Person of Christ is that He does not look at anyone with a sour face, treat anyone in an unfriendly manner, or frighten and drive anyone away from Him; He invites and draws all men to Him in the kindliest manner, both with His words and with His bearing. He shows Himself as a servant who wants to help everybody. Furthermore, He lets Himself be crucified for you and freely sheds His blood. All this you see with your eyes; and with your ears you hear nothing but friendly, sweet, and comforting words, such as: "Let not your hearts be troubled" (John 14:1); "Come to Me, all who labor and are heavy-laden" (Matt. 11:28); "Whoever believes in Me shall not be lost, but have eternal life" (John 3:16), etc., etc. The Gospel of St. John is full of such verses. From this you can infer with certainty that He is not hostile to you but wants to show you all grace and goodness. Cling to this; hold firmly to it; do not permit your eyes and your thoughts to stray beyond this; and let nothing else that occurs to you lead you off the right path.
>
> And as you now hear and see Christ revealing Himself to you, you can rest assured that the Father is disposed toward you in like manner. . . . Christ states: "The words that I say to you I do not speak on My own authority," but they are the Father's words. And at another place we read (John 6:40): "This is the will of My Father, that everyone who sees the Son and believes in Him should have eternal life."

---

5   For a fuller discussion of some of these themes, see W. Robert Godfrey, "The Spiritual Vitality of Martin Luther," in *The Divine Fire* (London: The Westminster Conference, 1996), 7–26.

He who grasps this in faith cannot think that God is angry with him or will reject and condemn him. For here there is neither a word nor a sign of disfavor, but only friendly, gracious words, a loving and kind look, in short, sheer fervor and ardor of ineffable, fatherly, and sincere love.[6]

Luther fervently called everyone to look to Jesus and to find the mercy of the Father rich and abundant in Him. He did not want anyone to doubt the willingness of God to save all who come to Jesus. The Father and the Son are so united in purpose that the Christian need never worry that the will of the Father is any different from the words and promises of the Son.

The Work of Christ in the Preaching of the Law and the Gospel

For Luther, the work of Christ came to sinners outwardly in God's institutions and inwardly by the Holy Spirit and faith. Both the outward and the inward were necessary. He wrote:

Now when God sends forth his holy gospel he deals with us in a two-fold manner, first outwardly, then inwardly. Outwardly he deals with us through the oral word of the gospel and through material signs, that is, baptism and the sacrament of the altar. Inwardly he deals with us through the Holy Spirit, faith, and other gifts. But whatever their measure or order the outward factors should and must precede. The inward experience follows and is effected by the outward. For he wants to give no one the Spirit or faith outside of the outward Word and sign instituted by him, as he says in Luke 16[:29], "Let them hear Moses and the prophets." Accordingly Paul can call baptism a "washing of regeneration" wherein God "richly pours out the Holy Spirit" [Titus 3:5]. And the oral gospel "is the power of God for salvation to every one who has faith" (Rom. 1[:16]).[7]

The Christian must give priority to the outward institutions of the Word, both in preaching and in the sacraments. As God came to us in the incarnation, so He continues to come through outward means to accomplish His

---

6 LW, Vol. 24: Sermons on the Gospel of St. John, Chapters 14–16, ed. Jaroslav Pelikan (St. Louis: Concordia, 1961), 60.

7 "Against the Heavenly Prophets in the Matter of Images and Sacraments," in LW, 40:146.

purpose. They are the means that God has appointed and through which He works by His Spirit.

Luther always stressed that we find God in His institutions, His appointed means, not in our creations or our experiences. We must use God's ways to come to Him. Luther rejected the inventions of Rome and the claims of the Spirit's revelations among the Anabaptists. Only the institutions established in the Bible connect us to Jesus. Luther boldly declared that he would rather have Jesus present in the preaching of the Word than in person: "Thus He comes to us through the gospel. Yes, it is far better that he comes through the gospel than that he would now enter in through the door; for you would not even know him even though he came in. If you believe then you have; if you do not believe then you do not have."[8]

For Luther, true preaching must always have two elements: the law and the gospel. We cannot know God or ourselves without these two truths. Of the law in preaching, he wrote: "The Law only shows sin, terrifies, and humbles; thus it prepares us for justification and drives us to Christ."[9] The law must be preached regularly to God's people who never outgrow their need of its humbling work. Luther insisted:

> To those who are smug and have altogether discarded the fear of God, God's blows and wrath must be presented in order that they may be warned by the example of others and cease to sin. . . . Therefore those who, influenced by I know not what reasons, maintain that the Law should not be preached in the church are pernicious teachers. Would you actually not teach the Law where there is a real people of the Law, namely, the greedy, the proud, adulterers, usurers, idolaters, etc.? Would you use the promises of the New Testament to increase the smugness of those who were smug before? Indeed, God wants the destruction of Sodom by fire and that lake of asphalt to be conspicuous to this day and to be spoken of in sermons and made known among all posterity, in order that at least some may be reformed and may learn to fear God. . . . Today you may encounter many who are offended by the necessary preaching of the Law and shun it, for they maintain that their consciences are burdened when

---

8 *WA,* 10 III:349, *LW,* 51:114 quoted in Paul Althaus, *The Theology of Martin Luther,* trans. Robert C. Schultz (Philadelphia: Fortress, 1975), 193n30.

9 *LW,* 26:126.

they hear that sort of thing. But are they not fine Christians? They do not give up sinning; they are addicted to greed, to wrath, to lust, to reveling, etc. When they hear these sins censured, they are offended and do not want their consciences burdened. Shall we for this reason let everyone do what he pleases and declare him blessed? Not at all; for you hear that the destruction of Sodom by fire is to be set before all succeeding generations and indeed before the very church of God, in order that men may learn to fear God.[10]

Luther called the law a "hammer"[11] that must be used to smash smugness and indifference.

While Luther stressed the condemning function of the law as primary, he was no antinomian. Rather, he expected that those who were carefully instructed in the law and who fled for refuge to Christ would live lives of love and real good works, not works invented to please human notions of ascetic holiness:

Paul is an outstanding interpreter of the commandments of God. For he compresses all of Moses into a very brief summary and shows that in all his laws, which are almost endless, nothing is contained except this very brief word: "You shall love your neighbor as yourself." Reason, of course, is offended at this stinginess and paucity of words, when it is stated so briefly "Believe in Christ" and "You shall love your neighbor as yourself." Therefore it despises both the doctrine of faith and the doctrine of truly good works. To those who have faith, however, this stingy and paltry phrase "Believe in Christ" is the power of God (Rom. 1:16), by which they overcome sin, death, and the devil, and obtain salvation. So also serving another person through love seems to reason to mean performing unimportant works such as the following: teaching the erring; comforting the afflicted; encouraging the weak; helping the neighbor in whatever way one can; bearing with his rude manners and impoliteness; putting up with annoyances, labors, and the ingratitude and contempt of men in both church and state; obeying the magistrates; treating one's parents with respect; being patient in the home with a cranky

---

10 *LW*, 3:222–23.
11 *LW*, 26:316.

wife and an unmanageable family, and the like. But believe me, these works are so outstanding and brilliant that the whole world cannot comprehend their usefulness and worth; indeed, it cannot estimate the value of even one tiny truly good work, because it does not measure works or anything else on the basis of the Word of God but on the basis of a reason that is wicked, blind, and foolish.[12]

Luther was strong and clear that the law teaches us that Christians must love their neighbor. He certainly taught a third use of the law. We will return to Luther's third use of the law in more detail later in considering his doctrine of the church.

When the law has been preached to crush all self-righteousness in sinners, then the gospel must be presented. The two are necessary, but must be sharply distinguished. The true preachers and the true Christians are the ones who know the law and the gospel and know when and how to apply each to the Christian's conscience. He wrote:

Both the Law and the Gospel must be taught and considered. It is a mistake to confine yourself to one of the two. The Law serves no other purpose than to create a thirst and to frighten the heart. The Gospel alone satisfies the thirst, makes us cheerful, and revives and consoles the conscience. Lest the teaching of the Gospel create lazy, gluttonous Christians who think they need not perform good works, the Law tells the old Adam: "Refrain from sin! Be pious! Desist from this, and do that!" Then, when the conscience becomes depressed and realizes that the Law is not a mere cipher, man becomes frightened. And then he must give ear to the voice of the Gospel. When you have sinned hearken to the Teacher, Christ who says: "Come to Me! I will not let you die of thirst but will give you drink."[13]

For Luther, the gospel is purely and simply the promise of forgiveness through the work of Jesus: "Thus when I hear that Jesus Christ died, took away my sin, gained heaven for me, and gave me all that He has, I am hearing the Gospel."[14] To hear the gospel is to hear Jesus, who in the gospel is present to save.

---

12 *LW*, 27:56.
13 *LW, Vol. 23: Sermons on the Gospel of St. John Chapters 6–8*, ed. Jaroslav Pelikan (St. Louis: Concordia, 1959), 272.
14 *LW*, 30:45.

Christians always need to hear the gospel because they are always in need of forgiveness:

> Further we believe that in this Christian church we have the forgiveness of sins, which is granted through the holy sacraments and absolution as well as through all the comforting words of the entire Gospel. Toward forgiveness is directed everything that is to be preached concerning the sacraments and, in short, the entire Gospel and all the duties of Christianity. Forgiveness is needed constantly.[15]

The forgiveness that we constantly need was for Luther the great message and gift of the preaching of the gospel and of the gospel sacraments.

Sacraments

For Luther, as Christ is present to save in the preaching of the gospel, so Jesus is present in the same way in the sacraments. Much of Luther's energy went to defining and defending the sacraments as real means by which Jesus is present for and a blessing to His people. Luther was often misunderstood by other Protestants on this point, as if his view of the sacraments were magical, superstitious, or divorced from faith. He insisted that God always uses material things to administer His blessings and that the sacraments are a certain, reliable statement of the gospel as a visible Word. He wrote: "Because it is one thing if God is present, and another if He is present for you. He is there for you when He adds His Word and binds Himself, saying, 'Here you are to find me.'"[16] For Luther, Jesus had bound Himself to be found in the sacraments. Those who mocked or minimized the sacraments mocked God and did not understand His ways. He insisted: "Our fanatics, however, are full of fraud and humbug. They think nothing spiritual can be present where there is anything material and physical, and assert that flesh is of no avail. Actually the opposite is true. The Spirit cannot be with us except in material and physical things such as the Word, water, and Christ's body and in his saints on earth."[17]

Luther rejected all mechanical or magical ideas of the sacraments, but he

---

15 Luther, Large Catechism, in *The Book of Concord* (1959), 417.

16 *WABr*, 3:379, quoted in Mark U. Edwards Jr., *Luther and the False Brethren* (Stanford, Calif.: Stanford University Press, 1975), 96.

17 *WABr*, 3:404–5, quoted in Edwards, *Luther and the False Brethren*, 97.

was adamant that they be understood as real ways in which Christ is present. The sacraments are Christ's institutions, and He is present in them regardless of whether anyone receives them in faith. Faith does not make a sacrament; God does. It is for that reason that Luther spoke so strongly about the power of the sacraments.

Baptism

Luther stressed the objective promise of Christ contained in baptism: "To be baptized in God's name is to be baptized not by men but by God himself."[18] Further, "In Baptism, therefore, every Christian has enough to study and to practice all his life. He always has enough to do to believe firmly what Baptism promises and brings—victory over death and the devil, forgiveness of sin, God's grace, the entire Christ, and the Holy Spirit with his gifts. In short, the blessings of Baptism are so boundless that if timid nature considers them, it may well doubt whether they could all be true."[19] Specifically, he wrote of the blessing of baptism: "To appreciate and use Baptism aright, we must draw strength and comfort from it when our sins or conscience oppress us, and we must retort, 'But I am baptized! And if I am baptized, I have the promise that I shall be saved and have eternal life, both in soul and body.'"[20]

At the same time, Luther insisted that faith must receive the sacrament for it to be saving. He wrote:

True, one should add faith to baptism. But we are not to base baptism on faith. . . . Whoever allows himself to be baptized on the strength of his faith, is not only uncertain, but also an idolater who denies Christ. . . . But a baptism on the Word and command of God even when faith is not present is still a correct and certain baptism if it takes place as God commanded. Granted, it is not of benefit to the baptized one who is without faith, because of his lack of faith, but the baptism is not thereby incorrect, uncertain, or of no meaning.[21]

Baptism actually has no saving benefit to the individual unless it is received in faith.

---

18 Luther, Large Catechism, in *The Book of Concord* (1959), 437.
19 Ibid., 441f.
20 Ibid., 442–43.
21 "Concerning Rebaptism," in *LW*, 40:252.

The Lord's Supper

In his own day, Luther found himself attacked by Roman Catholics, by Anabaptists, and by some Protestants for his teaching on the Lord's Supper. Luther insisted that he simply taught and believed what he found in the Bible. He summarized his teaching in this way:

> Now, what is the Sacrament of the Altar? Answer: It is the true body and blood of the Lord Christ in and under the bread and wine which we Christians are commanded by Christ's word to eat and drink. . . . It is true, indeed, that if you take the Word away from the elements or view them apart from the Word, you have nothing but ordinary bread and wine. But if the words remain, as is right and necessary, then in virtue of them they are truly the body and blood of Christ. . . . No matter whether you are unworthy or worthy, you here have Christ's body and blood by virtue of these words which are coupled with the bread and wine.[22]

The fruit of the presence and promise of Christ in the supper was clear for Luther: "In other words, we go to the sacrament because we receive there a great treasure, through and in which we obtain the forgiveness of sins. . . . Therefore, it is appropriately called the food of the soul since it nourishes and strengthens the new man."[23]

Luther fervently maintained the presence of Christ in the Lord's Supper against all opposition:

> Here again our clever spirits contort themselves with their great learning and wisdom, bellowing and blustering, "How can bread and wine forgive sins or strengthen faith?" Yet they know that we do not claim this of bread and wine—since in itself bread is bread—but of that bread and wine which are Christ's body and blood and with which the words are coupled. These and no other, we say, are the treasure through which forgiveness is obtained. This treasure is conveyed and communicated to us in no other way than through the words, "given and poured out for you." Here you have both truths,

---

22 Luther, Large Catechism, in *The Book of Concord* (1959), 447f.
23 Ibid., 449.

that it is Christ's body and blood and that these are yours as your treasure and gift. Christ's body can never be an unfruitful, vain thing, impotent and useless. Yet, however great the treasure may be in itself, it must be comprehended in the Word and offered to us through the Word, otherwise we could never know of it or seek it.[24]

Luther always insisted that the Word and the sacraments must be kept together as to their realities and their effects because they were both the saving institutions of God.

Yet again, Luther was clear that only the believer receives the blessing of Christ promised in the supper: "It is he who believes what the words say and what they give, for they are not spoken or preached to stone and wood but to those who hear them, those to whom Christ says, 'Take and eat,' etc. And because he offers and promises forgiveness of sins, it cannot be received except by faith. . . . But he who does believe has nothing, for he lets this gracious blessing be offered to him in vain and refuses to enjoy it."[25]

As Luther insisted on the outward means of grace, so he also insisted on the inward ways of God, particularly the Holy Spirit and faith. The Holy Spirit graciously works faith in the heart of God's elect through the Word. The inward work of the Spirit to give the gift of faith was central to Luther. He wrote, "In the Word comes the Spirit, and gives faith where and to whom He will," and again, "God gives the Holy Spirit, who works faith where and when He will in those who hear the Gospel."[26]

The Church

As a priest, monk, and professor in 1517, Luther faced a church that was amazingly complex. The varieties of its institutions, offices, and activities seemed almost endless. To oversimplify, parishes, cathedrals, shrines, chapels, monastic establishments, schools, and charities were served and supervised

---

24 Ibid.

25 Luther, Large Catechism, in *The Book of Concord* (1959), 450. The language of Luther here is remarkably similar to that of Calvin in his *Institutes*, 4.17, 32, and 33: "In his Sacred Supper he bids me take, eat, and drink his body and blood under the symbols of bread and wine. I do not doubt that he himself truly presents them, and that I receive them." And "this is the wholeness of the Sacrament, which the whole world cannot violate: that the flesh and blood of Christ are no less truly given to the unworthy than to God's elect believers. At the same time, it is true, however, that, just as rain falling upon a hard rock flows off because no entrance opens into the stone, the wicked by their hardness so repel God's grace, that it does not reach them."

26 Quoted in Köstlin, *The Theology of Luther*, 2:300.

by deacons, priests, ordained and lay monks, bishops, cardinals, and the pope. As Luther's knowledge of the Bible and his reforming vision grew, he became convinced that the church Christ had established was, in contrast, a simple reality. As early as 1522, he wrote:

> The belly-preachers have also perverted the precious words "holy" and "spiritual" for us; they have called their priestly and monastic estate holy and spiritual. . . . They have done the same thing with the name "church" by asserting that the pope and the bishops are the church. When they wilfully do what they please, they say that the church has commanded it. Holiness does not consist in being a monk, priest, or nun, in wearing tonsures and cowls. It is a spiritual word which states that inwardly we are sincerely holy in the spirit before God. And his [Peter's] real reason for making this statement was to point out that nothing is holy but the holiness that God works in us.[27]

He gave a full statement of his doctrine of the church in his 1539 treatise *On the Councils and the Church,* his response to the pope's summons of an ecumenical council to consider proposals for reform in the church.

In this treatise, Luther first discusses the history of ecumenical councils and their proper work. He concludes that however valuable ancient councils were, they could not rival the Scriptures for the clarity or completeness of their teaching of Christian truth: "In summary, put them all together, both fathers and councils, and you still will not be able to cull from them all the teachings of the Christian faith, even if you culled forever. If it had not been for Holy Scripture, the church, had it depended on the councils and fathers, would not have lasted long."[28]

Next, Luther turns to the real character of the church. For him, the church is essentially the life and ministry of the local congregation: "Now, wherever you hear or see this word preached, believed, professed, and lived, do not doubt that the true *ecclesia sancta catholica,* 'a Christian holy people' must be there, even though their number is very small."[29] Luther expands on this basic understanding of the church in answering a most basic question for Christians: "But how will or how can a poor confused person tell where such

---

27 *LW,* 30:6.
28 *LW,* 41:52.
29 Ibid., 41:150.

Christian holy people are to be found in this world?"[30] As Christians found themselves living in a world with two competing claimants to the title of the true church, they faced the question as to how they could tell which was the real church of Christ. Luther presented several characteristics that Christians should look for in order to recognize the church. His discussion, interestingly, paralleled Reformed considerations of the marks of the church. But Luther was presenting more than marks. His full discussion really explicated his doctrine of the church, particularly through seven elements of its visible life.

The Word

"First, the holy Christian people are recognized by their possession of the holy word of God."[31] Luther always returned to the foundational importance of the Scriptures and the gospel in his approach to any doctrinal question. The church must have and cherish the revelation of God. "And even if there were no other sign than this alone, it would still suffice to prove that a Christian, holy people must exist there, for God's word cannot be without God's people, and conversely, God's people cannot be without God's word."[32]

Baptism

"Second, God's people or the Christian holy people are recognized by the holy sacrament of baptism, wherever it is taught, believed, and administered correctly according to Christ's ordinance."[33] The church possessed and administered the sacrament of baptism as taught in the Bible, a visible expression of the gospel.

The Lord's Supper

"Third, God's people, or Christian holy people, are recognized by the holy sacrament of the altar, wherever it is rightly administered, believed, and received, according to Christ's institution. This too is a public sign and a precious, holy possession left behind by Christ by which his people are sanctified so that they also exercise themselves in faith and openly confess that they are Christian, just as they do with the word and baptism."[34] Again, the sacrament

---

30 Ibid., 41:148.
31 Ibid.
32 Ibid., 41:150.
33 Ibid., 41:151.
34 Ibid., 41:152.

of the Lord's Supper must be treasured by the church as Christ has taught it in the Bible.

Discipline

"Fourth, God's people or holy Christians are recognized by the office of the keys exercised publicly. That is, as Christ decrees in Matthew 18[:15–20], if a Christians sins, he should be reproved; and if he does not mend his ways, he should be bound in his sin and cast out. If he does mend his ways, he should be absolved. That is the office of the keys."[35] For Luther, the real church exercised discipline over its members. This element of Luther's understanding has often been missed, but he was crystal clear about it.

Biblical Offices

"Fifth, the church is recognized externally by the fact that it consecrates or calls ministers, or has offices that it is to administer."[36] Luther recognized that the Bible established office in the church—not the sacral caste of priests—but the minister who faithfully preached the Word and administered the sacraments.

Luther's focus on the simplicity and importance of the congregation came to quite radical expression, for his day, in his belief that in principle the congregation has the right to call its own minister. As early as 1523, he had written a treatise titled *That a Christian Assembly or Congregation Has the Right and Power to Judge All Teaching and to Call, Appoint, and Dismiss Teachers, Established and Proven by Scripture.*[37] Ministers were not a mysterious order created and imposed by a hierarchy, but were to emerge from the congregation.

Worship

"Sixth, the holy Christian people are externally recognized by prayer, public praise, and thanksgiving to God. Where you see and hear the Lord's Prayer prayed and taught; or psalms or other spiritual songs sung, in accordance with the word of God and the true faith; also the creed, the Ten Commandments, and the catechism used in public, you may rest assured that a

---

35 Ibid., 41:153.
36 Ibid., 41:154.
37 *LW,* 39:305–14.

holy Christian people of God are present."[38] The church was visible in its simple, Word-centered worship.

Suffering

"Seventh, the holy Christian people are externally recognized by the possession of the sacred cross. They must endure every misfortune and persecution, all kinds of trials and evil from the devil, the world, and the flesh."[39] Since the servant was not greater than the master, as Jesus had taught, the church would suffer in this world as it served Christ faithfully.

Luther derived these seven points from the first table of the Ten Commandments and recognized that, though these elements were never perfect in the church, they were truly present: "These are the true seven principal parts of the great holy possession whereby the Holy Spirit effects in us a daily sanctification and vivification in Christ, according to the first table of Moses. By this we obey it, albeit never as perfectly as Christ. But we constantly strive to attain the goal, under his redemption or remission of sin, until we too shall one day become perfectly holy and no longer stand in need of forgiveness."[40]

These seven characteristics were only the beginning of what could be said about the church. He said:

> In addition to these seven principal parts there are other outward signs that identify the Christian church, namely, those signs whereby the Holy Spirit sanctifies us according to the second table of Moses. . . . We need the Decalogue not only to apprise us of our lawful obligations, but we also need it to discern how far the Holy Spirit has advanced us in his work of sanctification and by how much we still fall short of the goal, lest we become secure and imagine that we have now done all that is required. Thus we must constantly grow in sanctification and always become new creatures in Christ![41]

Luther taught the positive value of the law in a clear and remarkable way in this treatise. As Luther wrote in 1539, he was not only concerned to refute the Roman understanding of the church, but also to respond to the false teaching of antinomianism in his own ranks. He was as strong in rejecting

---

38 *LW,* 41:164.
39 Ibid.
40 Ibid., 41:165–66.
41 Ibid., 41:166.

the antinomians as in rejecting the pope. He stated powerfully that the Holy Spirit truly sanctified Christ's people:

> The Christians, however, are a people with a special call and are therefore called not just *ecclesia*, "church," or "people," but *sancta catholica Christiana*, that is, "a holy Christian people" who believe in Christ. That is why they are called a Christian people and have the Holy Spirit, who sanctifies them daily, not only through the forgiveness of sin acquired for them through Christ (as the Antinomians foolishly believe), but also through the abolition, the purging, and the mortification of sins, on the basis of which they are called a holy people . . . there is always a holy Christian people on earth, in whom Christ lives, works, and rules, *per redemptionem*, "through grace and the remission of sin," and the Holy Spirit, *vivificationem et sanctificationem*, "through daily purging of sin and renewal of life," so that we do not remain in sin but are enabled and obliged to lead a new life, abounding in all kinds of good works, as the Ten Commandments or the two tables of Moses' law command, and not in old, evil works.[42]

He made particularly clear the importance of the Ten Commandments for the Christian life:

> For they [the Antinomians], having rejected and being unable to understand the Ten Commandments, preach much about the grace of Christ, yet they strengthen and comfort only those who remain in their sins, telling them not to fear and be terrified by sins, since they are all removed by Christ. They see and yet they let the people go on in their public sins, without any renewal or reformation of their lives. Thus it becomes quite evident that they truly fail to understand the faith and Christ, and thereby abrogate both when they preach about it. How can he speak lightly about the works of the Holy Spirit in the first table—about comfort, grace, forgiveness of sins—who does not heed or practice the works of the Holy Spirit in the second table, which he can understand and experience, while he has never attempted or experienced those of the first table?[43]

---

42 Ibid., 41:143f.
43 Ibid., 41:147.

Luther's commitment to the necessity of holiness in the life of the Christian was not something new in the face of the antinomian controversy. In 1522, for example, he had clearly taught about "genuine and true faith": "It must not be an indolent and sleepy faith and only a dream. No, it must be a living and active thing, so that one devotes oneself to it with all confidence and clings to the Word, no matter what happens, in order that we may press forward through fortune and misfortune."[44] He also wrote then, "Therefore since the Lord Christ is now completely yours through faith, and you have received salvation and all His blessings, you must henceforth let it be your concern to cast off all wickedness, or all that is evil, and all guile."[45]

Conclusion

Throughout his life as preacher and Reformer, Luther recognized how tempting it was for Christians to tire of Christ, the sacraments, and the church and to look for something new:

> For we always must have something new, Christ's death and resurrection, faith and love, are old and just ordinary things; that is why they must count for nothing, and so we must have new wheedlers (as St. Paul says). And this serves us right since our ears itch so much for something new that we can no longer endure the old and genuine truth, "that we accumulate," that we weigh ourselves down with big piles of new teachings. This is just what has happened and will continue to happen.[46]

Luther believed that the devil used this desire for the new and unbiblical to advance his evil kingdom. Luther expressed that powerfully in these terms: "Now when the devil saw that God built such a holy church, he was not idle, and erected his chapel beside it, larger than God's temple . . . the devil is always God's ape, trying to imitate all God's things and to improve on them."[47] In Luther's day, as in ours, the church was always overshadowed by the devil's chapel, but it never was destroyed.

---

44 *LW*, 30:28.
45 Ibid., 30:47.
46 *LW*, 41:127f.
47 Ibid., 41:167f.

In the last sermon that he preached, three days before his death, Luther lamented again that people so despised the gracious institutions of God. They still wanted something special and exciting like a pilgrimage or a holy relic. But he called on them to rest in the simplicity and abundance of God's provision in Christ, His sacraments, and His church:

Oh, people say, what is that [preaching]? After all, there is preaching every day, often many times every day, so that we soon grow weary of it. What do we get out of it? All right, go ahead, dear brother, if you don't want God to speak to you every day at home, in your house and in your parish church, then be wise and look for something else: in Trier is our Lord God's coat, in Aachen are Joseph's pants and our blessed Lady's chemise; go there and squander your money, buy indulgence and the pope's secondhand junk; these are valuable things! You have to go far for these things and spend a lot of money; leave house and home standing idle!

But aren't we stupid and crazy, yes, blinded and possessed by the devil? There sits the decoy duck in Rome with his bag of tricks, luring to himself the whole world with its money and goods, and all the while anybody can go to baptism, the sacrament, and the pulpit! How highly honored and richly blessed we are to know that God speaks with us and feeds us with his Word, gives us his baptism, the keys [absolution], etc.! But these barbarous, godless people say: What, baptism, sacrament, God's Word?—Joseph's pants, that's what does it! It is the devil in the world who makes the high personages, the emperor and the kings, oblivious to such things and causes them to allow themselves to be so grossly duped and fooled and bespattered with filth by these first-class rascals and liars, the pope and his tonsured shavelings. But we should listen to God's Word, which tells us that he is our schoolmaster, and have nothing to do with Joseph's pants or the pope's juggling tricks.[48]

---

48 *LW,* 51:390f.

Chapter Nine

THE GLORY OF GOD ALONE: LUTHER ON VOCATION

GENE EDWARD VEITH

hristians today often struggle over how they can have a strong marriage and how they can be good parents. They worry about the extent to which they should get involved in politics. They wonder how Christians can exercise some kind of influence on the culture as their forebears did. On another level, many Christians just feel beaten down by the world. They feel their spiritual lives getting pushed to the margins by the pressures of having to make a living, the endless family obligations, and the mundane demands of everyday life. Some Christians compartmentalize their lives, cultivating a Sunday-morning piety that has little to do with the other six days of the week. Others attempt valiantly to live out their faith in every dimension of their lives, but they are not sure how to do that. Is it by witnessing all the time, to customers, colleagues, employees, and passersby? Is there a certain way of being a Christian office worker, factory hand, or service provider? Don't we have to do pretty much the same thing as the non-Christians in all of these fields?

Christians resolve these conflicts in different ways. Some embrace the world, becoming worldly. Others escape the world, becoming otherworldly. The biblical principle of being "in the world" without being "of the world" (John 17:13–18) is confusing and seems impossible to realize.

How to live faithfully in the world is, of course, a perennial challenge in the Christian life. But few Christians today realize that these puzzles were largely resolved, both biblically and practically, by Reformation theology. All of these modern difficulties—in families, the workplace, the culture—are definitively addressed and in many cases solved by the doctrine of vocation.

Luther's doctrine of vocation is one of his most important contributions to the Christian church, next only to his reemphasis on the gospel and on the Word of God. John Calvin and the other Reformers embraced what Luther taught about vocation, with Calvin, as we shall see, applying it in some innovative ways. But strangely, over the last few centuries, vocation has largely faded from memory, even for Reformation Christians. Where it has been remembered, the doctrine of vocation has often been shrunk into a narrow little category—having to do with how you perform your job—as opposed to what it was for Luther and Calvin—namely, the theology of the Christian life.

For Luther, the doctrine of vocation has to do with God's providence, how He governs and cares for His creation. Vocation is at the heart of Luther's ethics and is the locus for the good works that are the fruits of faith. Vocation for Luther is where we grow in sanctification, where we bear the crosses that drive us to prayer and build our faith, where we love and serve our neighbors, and where we live out the implications of the gospel.[1] Far from being an abstract explanation or some theoretical point of dogma, vocation is eminently practical, giving specific guidance for everyday life and the problems that arise.

The doctrine of vocation was the impetus and inspiration for the enormous social and cultural changes brought on by the Reformation—in the new spiritual value placed upon the family, the goal of universal education, the unparalleled social mobility, new ventures in economics and government—and it has the potential to spark a similar social reformation today. But its spiritual implications are of greater importance. *Vocation*, after all, is simply the Latinate word for "calling," and learning again how to respond to God's call in every dimension of our lives—including what seems most ordinary—will spark a reformation of Christian spirituality.

---

1 The definitive treatment of Luther's theology of vocation is Wingren, *Luther on Vocation*. For contemporary applications, see my book *God at Work: Your Christian Vocation in All of Life* (Wheaton, Ill.: Crossway, 2002). Also my book written with my daughter Mary Moerbe, *Family Vocation: God's Calling in Marriage, Parenting, and Childhood* (Wheaton, Ill.: Crossway, 2012).

Vocation and God's Providence

Vocation is not just about what we are to do, though it includes that. For Luther, vocation is first of all about what God does. We often talk about what God is doing in our lives; vocation is about what God is doing *through* our lives. God bestows His gifts—such as physical life, daily bread, earthly protection, the teaching of His Word—primarily by means of human beings' carrying out their vocations (such as, for these examples, parents, farmers, magistrates, and pastors).

Vocations, according to Luther, are "masks of God." We see our parents who gave us life, the farmer who grew the grain that went into the bread we ate for breakfast, the police officers who protect us from crime, and the pastor who preached the gospel that we received in faith. But looming behind them is God Himself, who works through them. God hides Himself—that is, He is present but not visible—in the ordinary human beings who bless us by their actions day by day. And He hides Himself in us to bless others through our actions. As Luther says in his commentary on Psalm 147:

> What else is all our work to God—whether in the fields, in the garden, in the city, in the house, in war, or in government—but just such a child's performance, by which He wants to give His gifts in the fields, at home, and everywhere else? These are the masks of God, behind which He wants to remain concealed and do all things. Had Gideon done nothing but take the field against Midian, the Midianites would not have been beaten; and God could certainly have beaten them without Gideon. He could give children without using men and women. But He does not want to do this. Instead, He joins man and woman so that it appears to be the work of man and woman, and yet He does it under the cover of such masks.[2]

Luther emphasized that God works through means—the Word and sacraments in His spiritual kingdom, and vocation and His created order in His earthly kingdom. God does not have to work through means. He created Adam from the dust and Eve from Adam's body, rather than from a father and a mother. When the Israelites were in the wilderness, He gave them manna

---

2 "Commentary on Psalm 147," in *LW, Vol. 14: Selected Psalms III*, ed. Jaroslav Pelikan (St. Louis: Concordia, 1958), 114.

as their daily bread, rather than having it come from farmers, millers, and bakers. But God has chosen to give His gifts primarily and usually through other people. Today, though He might perform a miraculous healing, more normally He heals by means of doctors, nurses, pharmacists, and other medical professionals. But a person who is healed by physicians should still thank God for the healing, just as we should thank God at every meal for the food He provides by means of those who prepared it.

Our vocations are multiple, according to Luther, and God calls us to service in the four "estates" that He has built into creation as institutions that make human life possible: the church, the household, the state, and the "common order of Christian love." These—and not the man-made orders of monasticism—are "the holy orders and true religious institutions established by God."[3] In the estate of the church,

> All who are engaged in the clerical office or ministry of the Word are in a holy, proper, good, and God-pleasing order and estate, such as those who preach, administer sacraments, supervise the common chest, sextons and messengers or servants who serve such persons. These are engaged in works which are altogether holy in God's sight.[4]

Thus, Luther, while critiquing monasticism, affirmed the local congregation, with its parish pastor and other church workers who serve God's people, as opposed to the monks who withdraw from them in pursuit of their own private holiness.

But whereas the church had been considered as the only arena for a life of perfect holiness—reserved for those who "had a vocation," a special calling to be a priest, a monk, or a nun—Luther insisted that the other estates are likewise realms of vocation and holiness:

> All fathers and mothers who regulate their household wisely and bring up their children to the service of God are engaged in pure holiness, in a holy work and a holy order. Similarly, when children and servants show obedience to their elders and masters, here too is pure holiness, and whoever is thus engaged is a living saint on earth.[5]

---

3 "Confession Concerning Christ's Supper" (1528) in *LW, Vol. 37: Word and Sacrament III*, ed. Robert H. Fischer (Philadelphia: Fortress, 1961), 364.
4 Ibid.
5 Ibid.

The estate of the household includes above all the family, which itself contains multiple callings: husbands and wives in marriage; fathers and mothers in fatherhood and motherhood; sons and daughters in childhood. Luther included in this estate the labor by which households make their livings. In the sixteenth century, long before the Industrial Revolution, work was largely centered in the home. Peasant farmers, shopkeepers, and craftsmen such shoemakers and blacksmiths all plied their trades in their homes, with the entire family pitching in. Luther's understanding of the interconnectedness of the family and the work it pursues is reflected in the Greek word *oikonomia*, meaning "the management and the regulation of the resources of the household,"[6] the term from which we derive our word *economy*. Thus, the estate of the household includes both the family vocations and the vocations of the workplace.

The third estate is that of the civil government, the state, which includes, more generally, the society and the culture: "Moreover, princes and lords, judges, civil officials, notaries, male and female servants and all who serve such persons, and further, all their obedient subjects—all are engaged in pure holiness and leading a holy life before God."[7] Not just government officials but "all their obedient subjects"—that is, all members of a particular society—have a calling as citizens, which is a vocation of "pure holiness."

And then Luther goes beyond the specific roles God has given us to play in this world to an overarching estate: "Above these three institutions and orders is the common order of Christian love, in which one serves not only the three orders, but also serves every needy person in general with all kinds of benevolent deeds, such as feeding the hungry, giving drink to the thirsty, forgiving enemies, praying for all men on earth, suffering all kinds of evil on earth, etc."[8] Here is another of Luther's great phrases: "the common order of Christian love." This is the realm of informal human interactions—friendships, conflicts, occasions for compassion—in which God also calls us to serve others.

Vocation and Good Works

Under medieval Catholicism, someone who wanted to live a pure and holy life would seek a "vocation" in a religious order. But that required (and still requires) a vow of celibacy, thus repudiating the vocations of marriage, par-

---

6 The Catholic Encyclopedia Online, "Political Economy," by F. O'Hara, accessed May 20, 2015, http://www.newadvent.org/cathen/12213b.html.
7 "Confession Concerning Christ's Supper," in *LW*, 37:365.
8 Ibid.

enthood, and the family. It also required a vow of poverty, thus repudiating the economic vocations. It also required a vow of obedience, which involved at that time coming under the authority of the church hierarchy instead of the civil authorities. In rejecting the clerical vows of celibacy, poverty, and obedience, Luther insisted that the seemingly secular estates that God had ordained for human life are precisely the places where Christians are to live out their faith.

Luther taught this on the basis of Scripture. "Only let each person lead the life that the Lord has assigned to him, and to which God has called him" (1 Cor. 7:17). According to this verse, God assigns us to a certain "life" and calls us to that life. The Apostle Paul teaches that Christ is hidden in marriage, gives instructions to parents and their children, and says that servants should work as if they were serving God instead of their masters, who are reminded that they too are servants of God (Eph. 5:22–6:9). The Apostle also teaches that God works through earthly rulers to punish wrongdoers and to bless those who do good by making a peaceful society possible (Rom. 13:1–7; cf. 1 Peter 2:13–14). The Ten Commandments themselves are vocational, as Luther emphasizes in the Small Catechism, teaching our duties to God, but also to our parents, to our spouse, to our fellow members of society (by not killing them), to the economic order (by not stealing or coveting other's possessions), and to the law courts (by not bearing false witness).

The commandments of Scripture, as Jesus tells us, can be summarized by the injunction to love God "with all your heart and with all your soul and with all your mind" and to "love your neighbor as yourself" (Matt. 22:34–40). Loving God is not something we can do in our sinful natures; rather, it is a function of God's love for us and His gift of Jesus Christ for our salvation. The Apostle John makes this explicit: "In this is love, *not that we have loved God* but that *he loved us* and *sent his Son to be the propitiation for our sins*" (John 4:10, emphasis added). Thus, our relationship with God and our love for Him do not depend in any way upon our own initiatives or good works, but only on Christ, to whom we are united by faith. "We love because he first loved us" (John 4:19). And this love for God, which is our response to the gospel of our salvation, carries over into love for our neighbors. "Beloved, if God so loved us, we also ought to love one another" (John 4:11).

"God does not need our good works," Gustaf Wingren observes in summarizing Luther in his Advent sermon, "but our neighbor does."[9] Our good

---

9 Wingren, *Luther on Vocation*, 10. See "Gospel for the First Sunday in Advent," *LW*, *Vol. 75: Church Postils I*, eds. Benjamin T.G. Mayes and James T. Langebartels (St. Louis: Concordia,

works are not to be spiritual exercises that we are supposedly doing for God to acquire merit before Him. Rather, what God, having reconciled us to Himself, requires is for us to love and serve our neighbors. And this is done precisely in vocation.

The problem of monasticism, according to Luther, is that while it emphasizes the saving power of good works, the works it requires—mortifications, rituals, devotional exercises—are not really "good" at all. "For whom is it helpful?"[10] he asks. The good works that God requires are to be acts of love and service to our neighbors. "If you find you have a work that you do for the benefit of God or of His saints or of yourself and not only for your neighbor," Luther says, "know that such a work is not good."[11]

The monastery and the cloister, with their vows against the estates that God has established for human relationships, purposefully shut out the neighbor. Indeed, the monks and nuns who were considered the holiest were the hermits and anchoresses, those who lived absolutely alone, devoting themselves to God, but having no contact whatsoever with a neighbor. In contrast, God calls those who want to serve Him to do so by serving their neighbors. Thus, a Christian who is acting in vocation—a mother who is changing her baby's diapers, a little boy who is doing his chores—is doing a holier work than that of all the man-made asceticisms of the monasteries. In Luther's colorful and comical language, "A miller's maid, if she believes, does more good, accomplishes more, and I would trust her more if she only takes the sack from the donkey than all the priests and monks [do] if they sang themselves to death day and night and tormented themselves until they bleed."[12] In turn, each vocation has its particular neighbors to love and serve:

A man is to live, speak, act, hear, suffer, and die for the love and service of his wife and child, the wife for the husband, the children for the parents, the servants for their masters, the masters for their servants, the government for its subjects, the subjects for their government,

---

2013), 41–44. A postil is a sermon written to be read in all of the churches in a jurisdiction. Luther's postils were a means of teaching the evangelical congregations as a whole and so had a broad influence.

10 Ibid., 75:43.

11 Ibid., 75:44.

12 Ibid., 75:44. See also "The Estate of Marriage," in *LW, Vol. 45: Christian in Society II*, ed. Walther I. Brandt (Philadelphia: Fortress, 1962), and the explanation of the fourth commandment in Luther's Large Catechism.

each one for his fellow man, even for his enemies, so that always one is the other's hand, mouth, eye, foot, even heart and mind.[13]

In marriage, the husband's neighbor is his wife, and he is called to love and serve her. The wife's neighbor is her husband, and she is called to love and serve him. Likewise with parents and children, rulers and citizens, pastors and the members of their congregation—they are all called to love and serve each other. In the workplace, employers ("masters") and employees ("servants") do good to each other, and together they love and serve their customers with the fruits of their labor.

Vocation and the Christian Life

Here is how Luther defines "a true and complete Christian life": "Faith brings and gives Christ to you as your own with all His possessions. Love gives you to your neighbor with all your possessions."[14] Faith comes first, through the gospel, whereupon faith bears fruit in works of love for the neighbor. This is "faith working through love" (Gal. 5:6). This sense of the Christian life as the interplay between faith and love is the theme of one of Luther's greatest works, *On the Freedom of the Christian*. "A Christian lives not in himself, but in Christ and in his neighbor," Luther writes. "He lives in Christ through faith, in his neighbor through love. By faith he is caught up beyond himself into God. By love he descends beneath himself into his neighbor."[15]

> Just as our neighbor is in need and lacks that in which we abound, so we were in need before God and lacked his mercy. Hence, as our heavenly Father has in Christ freely come to our aid, we also ought freely to help our neighbor through our body and its works, and each one should become as it were a Christ to the other that we may be Christs to one another and Christ may be the same in all, that is, that we may be truly Christians.[16]

Christ is in vocation, and when we love and serve our neighbor, He Himself is working through us to bless the person in need. Likewise, Christ is

---

13 Ibid.
14 Ibid., 75:42.
15 "The Freedom of the Christian," in *LW*, 31:371.
16 Ibid., 31:367–68.

hidden in our neighbor (Matt. 25:31–46), so that when we love and serve "the least of these," we are loving and serving Him. Being "Christs to one another" means more than simply being benevolent. Christ sacrificed Himself for us. And so we must sacrifice ourselves for others.

Jesus said, "If anyone would come after me, let him deny himself and take up his cross daily and follow me" (Luke 9:23). Bearing the cross means more than suffering; it means suffering for someone. The cross is the instrument of sacrifice. Taking up our cross does not here refer to martyrdom; rather, we are to take up our cross "daily," in the course of our everyday vocations. The sacrifice called for here is of the self. When we love and serve our neighbor, at some level, we deny ourselves—what we want, what we would rather do—for the sake of the neighbor. The father who works at his job until he is physically exhausted to make ends meet for his family, or who drives his children to soccer practice when he would much rather be doing something else, is presenting his body as a "living sacrifice" for his family (Rom. 12:1). These sacrifices are often very small and are often a joy to offer. But whereas the world today sees marriage, parenthood, and work in terms of self-fulfillment, the Bible describes them all in terms of self-denial.

When the Apostle Paul talks about marriage as having to do with Christ and the church, he is not just talking about patterns of authority but also patterns of sacrifice. Wives are to submit to their husbands, a sacrifice of herself for him; husbands are to "love [their] wives, as Christ loved the church and gave himself up for her" (Eph. 5:25). The husband is in the role of Christ, not to lord it over his wife but to emulate His sacrifice for the church by giving Himself up for His bride. In fact, the Bible describes all authority that vocation may bring in terms of service and sacrifice:

And Jesus called them to him and said to them, "You know that those who are considered rulers of the Gentiles lord it over them, and their great ones exercise authority over them. But it shall not be so among you. But whoever would be great among you must be your servant, and whoever would be first among you must be slave of all. For even the Son of Man came not to be served but to serve, and to give his life as a ransom for many." (Mark 10:42–45)

Many Christian books on marriage focus on the question, "Who has to obey whom?" even as they try to solve marital problems in terms of the world's ideal of self-fulfillment. But a biblical and vocational approach to marriage offers a completely different paradigm, bringing the gospel into the relationship and showing quarreling couples how to live out their faith in love for each other.

Luther writes extensively about bearing the cross in vocation.[17] Though people today evaluate their marriages, jobs, and other vocations according to how "successful" they are—to the point of abandoning those vocations when they bring pain instead of pleasure—Luther acknowledges the trials and sufferings that these vocations can bring. These drive us to prayer and to greater dependence on Christ, who takes our cross into His cross, which causes us to grow in our faith.[18] Christ also turns our crosses into acts of sacrifice for the neighbor.

For Luther, the doctrine of vocation has to do with the priesthood of all believers. That does not mean that all believers get to be pastors. A priest is someone who offers a sacrifice. In our relationship to God, Christ is our only priest, and His sacrifice for our sins was once and for all (Heb. 7). Roman Catholicism taught that Christ's sacrifice is reenacted in the Mass. This is why ministers in the Roman Catholic Church are called "priests," a term Protestants avoid for their ministers. And yet, all Christians are called to take up their crosses and to present their "bodies as a living sacrifice" (Rom. 12:1). The Apostle Peter begins his own discussion of vocation by teaching that we are to be "a holy priesthood, to offer spiritual sacrifices acceptable to God through Jesus Christ" (1 Peter 2:5), going on in that chapter and the next to talk about submission to authority, masters and servants, husbands and wives. Thus, Luther connected the priesthood of all believers to the sacrifices of vocation. "The Christian brings his sacrifice as he renders the obedience, offers the service, and proves the love which his work and calling require of him," Vilmos Vatja writes, summarizing Luther. "The work of the Christian in his calling becomes a function of his priesthood, his bodily sacrifice. His work in the calling is a work of faith, the worship of the kingdom of the world."[19]

To be sure, we often sin in our vocations. We want to be served rather than to serve, using our callings for our own self-aggrandizement instead of for the good of our neighbor.[20] We sometimes sin against our vocations.

---

17 Wingren, *Luther on Vocation*, 50–63.
18 Ibid., 184–99.
19 Vilmos Vatja, *Luther on Worship* (Philadelphia: Muhlenberg, 1958), 169.
20 Wingren, *Luther on Vocation*, 6.

Some doctors use their God-given medical skills to abort or euthanize their patients rather than caring for them. Some husbands are cruel to their wives instead of loving and serving them. Some pastors teach their flock falsehoods rather than the Word of God.

Luther wrote his Small Catechism so that it would help Christians scrutinize their vocations. It includes a "Table of Duties," which consists of "certain passages of Scripture for various holy orders and estates whereby these are severally to be admonished as to their office and duty.[21] These "holy orders" are not those of monasticism but of pastors and their hearers, rulers and subjects, husbands and wives, employers and workers, all arranged in dyads of neighbors, giving the Bible passages that pertain to their offices. In the section of the catechism on "Confession," the question asks, "What sins should we confess?"

> Here consider your station according to the Ten Commandments, whether you are a father, mother, son, daughter, master, mistress, servant; whether you have been disobedient, unfaithful, slothful; whether you have grieved any person by word or deed; whether you have stolen, neglected, or wasted aught, or done other injury.[22]

With this self-examination, applying the Ten Commandments to one's vocation, the Christian is then enjoined to repent and to confess those sins before God and also the pastor—whether individually or in corporate worship—and then to receive Christ's forgiveness, which He conveys by means of the pastor as he proclaims the gospel.

Thus, for Luther, the spiritual life is not to be carried out alone in a hermitage, nor in constant "church work" seven days a week. The spiritual life of faith working in love is played out in our marriages, in what we do with our children, in the workplace, in the culture, and in the communities where God has placed us. To be sure, vocation is where evangelism happens naturally, as parents raise their children in the Lord and workers share their faith with their colleagues. But it is not necessary to always spiritualize what we do by using it as a pretext for churchly activities. The vocation itself—on the factory floor or the office cubicle, in the home, or the community—has value in God's sight. It is the place of love and service, sin and forgiveness, faith and sanctification.

---

21 *Luther's Small Catechism* (St. Louis: Concordia, 1943), 25.
22 Ibid., 19.

"In all our religious and ethical life," the Swedish theologian Einar Billing said, "we are given to an incredible overestimation of the extraordinary at the expense of the ordinary."[23] Vocation brings the Christian life into the ordinary, real world of our everyday lives. Luther wrote:

> If you are a manual laborer, you find that the Bible has been put into your workshop, into your hand, into your heart. It teaches and preaches how you should treat your neighbor. Just look at your tools—at your needle or thimble, your beer barrel, your goods, your scales or yardstick or measure—and you will read this statement inscribed on them. Everywhere you look, it stares at you. Nothing that you handle every day is so tiny that it does not continually tell you this, if you will only listen.[24]

Conclusion

What happened to the doctrine of vocation? "Calvin's view of vocation largely stands in continuity with Luther's view," Brandon Jones says, though the later Reformer made some new applications.[25] When vocation is addressed in the *Institutes*, Calvin sounds very much like Luther:

> Therefore each individual has his own kind of living assigned to him by the Lord as a sort of sentry post. . . . The Lord's calling is in everything the beginning and foundation of well-doing. . . . No task will be so sordid and base, provided you obey your calling in it, that it will not shine and be reckoned very precious in God's sight.[26]

Luther discouraged people from leaving their callings, whereas Calvin encouraged them to be open to new callings from God. But when Luther

---

23 Einar Billing, *Our Calling* (Philadelphia: Fortress, 1964), 29.

24 *LW, Vol. 21: The Sermon on the Mount and the Magnificat*, ed. Jaroslav Pelikan (St. Louis: Concordia, 2007), 237.

25 Brandon C. Jones, "Reforming Luther on Vocation: A reassessment of Martin Luther's theology of vocation in light of Gilbert Meilaender's works" (lecture, ETS Annual Meeting, 2009), 7, http://www.academia.edu/205930/Reforming_Luther_on_Vocation.

26 Calvin, *Institutes*, 3.10.6. The early editions ended with a section "On the Christian Life," culminating in this passage (at 2.7.24–25). Thus, vocation was, in effect, the last word in the *Institutes*. In the fifth and sixth editions, the work was reorganized, so that this material appears in book 3. But it was also published separately in an extremely popular handbook titled *Golden Booklet of the True Christian Life*.

exhorts Christians to remain where they are, it is nearly always in the context of assuring them that they do not have to enter a monastery to live the highest Christian life.[27] Luther was writing in the context of the late-medieval social order and its feudal economy, in which peasants remained peasants and sons followed the trade of their fathers. But very soon, thanks in part to the doctrine of vocation as well as the Reformation schools, social mobility exploded. Luther stressed the offices of the vocations rather than the individuals who held them. Calvin encouraged Christians to consider their personal gifts, talents, and inclinations in finding a calling. Calvin applied vocation to the burgeoning middle class and to the tradesmen, merchants, and manufacturers of the emerging modern economy.[28] This was fully realized in the writings and actions of the Puritans and their heirs.

But eventually, in all of this, *vocation* became narrowed in its meaning. The word that once referred to all of God's estates and to His calling Christians to service in all of the dimensions of their lives became just another synonym for *job*. Luther probably used the term in reference to the family callings (marriage, parenthood, childhood) more than he did to the workplace. So does Scripture, with the key text 1 Corinthians 7:17—"Let each person lead the life that the Lord has assigned to him, and to which God has called him"—referring specifically to marriage.

But today, not only the workplace but the family and the culture have been drained of their spiritual significance. Medieval attitudes about what constitutes good works, the compartmentalization of life, and church work as more spiritually significant than "secular" concerns have reasserted themselves even among evangelical Christians. Meanwhile, today's secularists are finding that family, work, and the society have been drained of meaning. The consequences are a shallow worldliness, futile attempts to remake God-ordained institutions on human terms, and temporary exhilaration crashing down into despair. The doctrine of vocation has never been more relevant or more urgent.

---

27 See, for example, *LW,* 3:62. Brandon Jones makes this same point.

28 For these differences between Luther and Calvin on vocation, see Max Stackhouse, "Vocation," in *The Oxford Handbook of Theological Ethics,* eds. Gilbert Meilaender and William Werpehowski (Oxford, England: Oxford University Press, 2005), 198–99.

Part Three

LUTHER'S LEGACY

Chapter Ten

CORRECTLY AND PROFITABLY READ SCRIPTURE: LUTHER THE BIBLICAL SCHOLAR

AARON CLAY DENLINGER

Martin Luther's credentials as a Reformer would hardly seem to require verification. He is, indeed, likely to be seen by many as *the* Reformer of his day—the man who triggered the Reformation as such with his protest against the sale of indulgences; the man who put his finger on fundamental flaws in the medieval church's views on authority and salvation; and the man who subsequently articulated the principles of *sola Scriptura*, *sola gratia*, *sola fide*, *solus Christus*, and *soli Deo gloria* that came to define Protestantism.

Yet *Reformer* is not a label Luther would have readily applied to himself. He simply did not view himself as the proper agent of the changes that were taking place around—and ultimately through—him. In his estimation, the Word of God was the proper agent of those changes. God accomplishes His purposes, Luther understood, by means of His Word (cf. Isa. 55:11), and God's purpose in Luther's day, it seemed obvious, was to rouse the church from its theological and moral stupor. Luther's own part in that process, to his thinking, was merely to facilitate the reach of God's Word.

Luther expressed this conviction rather colorfully in a sermon preached in Wittenberg on March 10, 1522. Reflecting on the relative roles that he and God's Word had played in the surprising events of recent years, he observed: "I simply taught, preached, and wrote God's Word; otherwise I did nothing. And while I slept, or drank Wittenberg beer with my friends Philip and Amsdorf, the Word so greatly weakened the papacy that no prince or emperor ever inflicted such losses upon it." Lest his listeners miss the point, Luther repeated: "I did nothing; the Word did everything."[1]

Luther's convictions regarding Scripture's authority and his role as a preacher of God's Word are considered elsewhere in this book. It is the particular task of this chapter to examine Luther's identity as a biblical scholar, especially as that identity found expression in his efforts to translate and interpret Scripture. Translating and interpreting the Bible were, after all, two important aspects—even more so than sleeping and drinking Wittenberg beer—of the "nothing" Luther did behind the scenes of the "everything" ultimately accomplished by God's Word in his day.

Luther as Translator of the Bible

When Luther preached that sermon in Wittenberg on March 10, 1522, he had, in fact, very recently completed his translation of the New Testament into German.[2] In one of the more famous episodes of his life, Luther had been "kidnapped" en route from Worms to Wittenberg in May 1521 by order of his prince, Elector Frederick the Wise, and tucked away—for his own protection—in Wartburg Castle in Eisenach. During the early months of his time there, he took advantage of the forced break from his normal duties to advance the Reformation with his pen, writing works that criticized monasticism and the Roman Catholic Mass. He also began to think seriously about translating portions, at least, of the New Testament into German. In early December, he paid a short, secret visit to Wittenberg, where Philip Melanchthon—his close friend and disciple, and professor of Greek at the University of Wittenberg— encouraged him to tackle translation of the New Testament in its entirety, thus honoring the essential unity of that testament. Luther heeded Melanchthon's advice and, upon returning to Eisenach, threw himself wholly into the task, completing the project in the remarkably short span of eleven weeks,

---

1 *LW*, 51:77. Editorial comments from original text omitted.
2 For a fuller treatment of Luther's efforts at Bible translation, see especially Eric W. Gritsch, "Luther as Bible Translator," in Donald K. McKim, ed., *The Cambridge Companion to Martin Luther* (Cambridge, England: Cambridge University Press, 2003), 62–72.

just before leaving the Wartburg for good. Published the following September (and so dubbed the September Testament), Luther's German New Testament was an immediate best seller.

Back in Wittenberg, Luther lost no time in launching efforts to translate the Old Testament into German. This task ended up taking considerably longer than had his translation of the New Testament. Though Luther now enjoyed direct assistance from both Melanchthon and Matthew Aurogallus, professor of Hebrew at the University of Wittenberg, he and his colleagues were hindered in their efforts by their busy schedules (including, as of 1525, the demands of married life for Luther), bouts of illness for Luther (kidney stones and gallstones), and political events in Germany that required one or more of them to spend time away from Wittenberg. There was also, of course, the inherent difficulty of the task. Luther had translated, on average, eleven pages per day of the New Testament into German while in the Wartburg. By way of comparison, he and his colleagues took four days to translate three particularly difficult lines from the book of Job in 1524.

Their work progressed in stages. By 1523, they had completed the Pentateuch. The next year saw the finished translation of the historical books (Joshua to Esther) and poetical books (Job to Song of Solomon), leaving only the prophetic books—which proved particularly reluctant to "speak German," as Luther put it—to be completed. No matter their resistance, Luther had completed translation of the Minor Prophets by 1526 in conjunction with his university lectures on those books. Translation of Isaiah, a labor Luther compared to that of childbirth, was completed by 1528. The Reformer knew something about childbirth by then—his son Hans and daughter Elizabeth were born in 1526 and 1527, respectively. Whether Katie, his wife, would have conceded that her husband's efforts to render biblical Hebrew into German were comparable to hers in childbearing remains uncertain. By 1530, translation of the book of Daniel was complete. Though the end of their project was clearly in view, Luther guessed that the events prophesied in Daniel that culminated in the end of the world would probably beat them to the finish line. As it happened, the world continued, and the Prophets in their entirety were completed by 1532.

The first entire Luther Bible, comprising both Old and New Testaments, proceeded from the press of the Wittenberg printer Hans Lufft in September 1534. When Luther died twelve years later, half a million copies of this and subsequent editions of his German Bible were in circulation. While German printers profited greatly from producing these editions, Luther, interestingly, never earned a dime—or rather, a guilder—from the Bibles sold. He never requested royalties. His aim, of course, was not to turn a profit, but to put God's Word into the hands of the people in language they could understand, to have them hear it read and preached, and so ultimately to see sinners reconciled to God through faith in the person and work of the One whom it proclaims. Luther's success in this regard defies statistical analysis.

Before considering Luther's translation of the Bible in more detail, it is important to acknowledge—as has not always been done—that Luther was not the first person to translate the Bible into German. Portions of Scripture—namely, certain psalms and extracts from the gospels—existed in German translation as early as the ninth century, having been commissioned by the Emperor Charlemagne to assist in the conversion of Germanic peoples to Christianity within his realm. By the fourteenth century, a complete German Bible was in circulation in the Holy Roman Empire. This late-medieval translation was revised and reproduced, following the introduction of the printing press to Europe in the mid-fifteenth century, more than a dozen times before Luther ever began his own translation work. The Roman Catholic Church held no official position on the legitimacy of these German vernacular Bibles, but one can discern a certain discomfort on her part with such works and the access they granted the laity to the sacred text. In 1486, the archbishop of Mainz issued a provincial prohibition of unauthorized printings of German Bibles, arguing that the German language was inherently ill-suited to communicate the sacred matter of Scripture, and that, regardless, the German people weren't capable of grasping that matter, whatever language they encountered it in.[3]

What, then, set Luther's translation of the Bible apart from these previous efforts? The first thing that made Luther's work unique was the sources he used for translation. Much like the fourteenth-century English version of Scripture produced by John Wycliffe and his followers, the German translations of Scripture produced before Luther were based upon the Latin Vulgate, which had served as the medieval church's standard version of the Bible. Although Luther consulted the Vulgate—as well as existing German versions of the Bible—his translation was ultimately based on the best available Greek and Hebrew texts of Scripture. Luther, in other words, translated from the languages in which Scripture was originally penned.

---

3   Schaff, *History of the Christian Church*, 7:344.

The failure of previous translators to consult the original Greek and Hebrew texts of Scripture was no real fault of their own. Knowledge of Greek and Hebrew had all but vanished in Western Europe in the centuries after the collapse of the Western Roman Empire and the influx of Germanic tribes into European lands. The Vulgate had become the church's de facto official version of Scripture partially, to be sure, because of its merits as a translation, but even more so because of the inability of anyone to read Scripture in its original languages. In the years immediately preceding the Reformation, however, a circle of scholars known as humanists had labored to revive interest in the languages of antiquity and to recover classical texts—Scripture included—in their original languages. Toward those ends, the prince of humanist scholars, Desiderius Erasmus, had produced in 1516 a critical edition of the Greek New Testament, having compared all the Greek manuscripts available to him in order to arbitrate textual variants and capture, as much as possible, the exact, original words of the various writings contained in the New Testament.

Luther worked from the second, revised edition of Erasmus' Greek New Testament, published in Basel in 1519, when he translated the New Testament into German. For translation of the Old Testament, he and his colleagues relied on a copy of the Masoretic text of the Hebrew Scriptures produced in 1494 by the Italian Jewish printer Gerson ben Moses Soncino.

Of course, translation of the Bible into German from Greek and Hebrew required a significant degree of aptitude in those languages. Luther had begun studying the biblical languages while still a monk in Erfurt. He had utilized the Hebrew Scriptures in his university lectures on the Psalms in 1513–15 and the Greek New Testament in his lectures on Romans, Galatians, and Hebrews in 1515–19. As of 1518, he had availed himself of Melanchthon's presence at Wittenberg to improve his knowledge of biblical Greek. Even so, Luther's abilities in the biblical languages remained modest. Fortunately, his translation team included experts in Greek and Hebrew like Melanchthon and Aurogallus. Melanchthon's linguistic abilities can be measured by the fact that he had published commentaries on classical authors, had translated Greek poets into Latin, and had written a Greek grammar before graduating from his teens.

A further distinguishing feature of Luther's Bible was its accuracy, readability, and—indeed—beauty in the German language. Luther shed some light upon his own philosophy of translation into German in a 1530 open letter on the subject.[4] In that letter, he observed that he and his colleagues had sought to translate Scripture into the kind of German that was spoken by "the mother in the home, the children on the street, [and] the common man in the marketplace." "We must," he noted, "be guided by their language, the way they speak, and do our translating accordingly. That way they will understand it."[5]

By Luther's own admission, producing a German text that was faithful to the original sources but nevertheless readable—and so, ultimately, understandable—was no easy task. He reckoned that few folk would realize, upon reading the finished product, how much he and his colleagues had struggled over certain biblical passages. "One now runs his eyes over three or four pages and does not stumble once—without realizing what boulders and clods had once lain there where he now goes along as over a smooth-planed board. We had to sweat and toil there before we got those boulders and clods out of the way, so that one could go along so nicely."[6]

Nevertheless, Luther felt some frustration as of 1530 with the success of his German Bible as it then stood. He commented that he and his colleagues had aimed for "good German" in their work, but "unfortunately" had "not always reached or hit upon" the same.[7] A desire to improve the existing translation of the New Testament and, by 1530, most of the Old Testament resulted in the establishment in 1531 of the *Collegium Biblicum* (Bible guild), a circle of six or so Wittenberg scholars who met weekly in Luther's home to revisit and revise the standing German translation of Scripture. The men who made up this group were selected not just because they were knowledgeable in one or more of the ancient languages—Latin, Greek, Hebrew, and Aramaic—but also because they represented discrete regions of Germany, and so could collectively ensure that the translation of a given passage decided upon would be understood by as broad a range of German speakers as possible.

Luther's Bible guild outlived the initial publication of the entire German Bible in 1534. Once the whole of Scripture had been translated, Luther and his colleagues began revising the entire text. In fact, Luther spent the rest of his life improving his translation of both testaments, thus justifying the opinion of one scholar that he was "obsessed with the right way to translate

---

4   *LW*, 35:175–202.
5   Ibid., 35:189.
6   Ibid., 35:188.
7   Ibid., 35:190–91.

the Bible."[8] With the help of his colleagues, he ultimately produced no less than five unique editions of the entire German Bible, the last completed in 1545, one year before his death.[9] His goal with every change made to the text was greater faithfulness to the meaning of the biblical Author/authors and better German—that is, German that would be more easily comprehended by the people.

Unsurprisingly, Roman Catholic polemicists raised questions early on about the accuracy of Luther's German Bible. They specifically accused him of importing his own "heretical" ideas about salvation into Paul's discussion of justification in the book of Romans. Luther's translation of Roman 3:28 had Paul stating that "man is justified by faith *alone* [German *allein*] apart from works of the law," while the Greek text merely stated that "man is justified by faith apart from works of the law." Luther freely admitted that the word "alone" was absent from the Greek original, but argued that good German required the word "alone" to capture the "sense" of Paul in translating this passage. He explained that Germans—when affirming one thing and denying another—regularly modify the thing affirmed with the word "alone." So, for example, a German speaker would say, "I have *allein* eaten and *nicht* [not] yet drunk," even if the essentially equivalent phrase "I have eaten and *nicht* yet drunk" would suffice.[10]

Luther provided further examples of this grammatical phenomenon in German, all toward the vindication of his translation of Paul. In sum, he displayed complete confidence that his translation of Romans 3:28 had captured "the sense of the text" and had communicated the same in words that were "clear and vigorous" and, ultimately, true to "the way [Germans] speak." His Roman detractors, needless to say, were no more impressed by his apology for his rendering of Romans 3:28 than they were by his description of them as "blockheads" who sat staring at the word *allein* in his translation "like cows at a new gate," uncertain what to make of it because, in the end, they understood neither the science of translation nor the German language as it was spoken by the people.[11]

---

8   Orrin Robinson, "Luther's Bible and the Emergence of Standard German," in David E. Wellbery et al., eds., *A New History of German Literature* (Cambridge, Mass.: Harvard University Press, 2004), 233.

9   Schaff, *History of the Christian Church*, 7:348.

10   *LW*, 35:188–89.

11   Ibid.

Ironically, the very same Roman Catholic figures who criticized the accuracy of Luther's translation of the Bible into German ultimately provided testimony to the merits of Luther's work. Shortly after the release of Luther's German New Testament in 1522, Duke George of Saxony, a strong opponent of Luther's reform, banned Luther's translation from his territories and ordered the confiscation of existing copies—measures that only increased sales of the work. George subsequently commissioned the Roman Catholic scholar Jerome Emser, a man who claimed to have discovered no fewer than 1,400 errors in Luther's translation, to produce an alternative, orthodox German translation of the New Testament to counter the spread and influence of Luther's work. Emser's translation appeared in 1527 and subsequently saw numerous editions under the guidance of Johann Eck between 1534 and 1558. But a comparison of Emser's translation to Luther's reveals that Emser largely copied Luther's work, editing the text when appropriate to make certain passages sound less supportive of Luther's reforming ideas. "The Papists steal my German," Luther complained, "and they do not thank me for it, but rather use it against me."[12] Of course, such plagiarism of Luther's translation served as a kind of backhanded compliment to the quality of the Reformer's work.

Whatever judgments have been made over the centuries regarding the accuracy of Luther's Bible translation, nearly all have conceded the literary and aesthetic merits of the German text he produced. His translation made significant use of techniques such as rhyme and alliteration, devices that were principally intended to make Scripture as memorable as possible to those reading or hearing it—perhaps for the very first time—in their native tongue. An example of rhyme can be found in Luther's translation of Proverbs 8:14. Where our English versions read "I have counsel and sound wisdom" (ESV), Luther's German reads "*Mein ist beides, Rat und Tat*" (literally, "mine is both advice and help"). An example of alliteration can be found in Luther's rendering of Mark 14:33. Where our English versions describe the Savior in Gethsemane as "greatly distressed and troubled" (ESV), Luther's German describes Christ as "*zittern und zagen*" (literally, "trembling and wavering").[13]

Scholars agree that Luther produced a work of remarkable literary quality, even if this was not his foremost goal. Luther possessed "an extraordinary

---

12 Quoted in Schaff, *History of the Christian Church*, 7:351.
13 Ruth H. Sanders, *German: Biography of a Language* (Oxford, England: Oxford University Press, 2010), 147.

ear for language and a literary talent unparalleled in his place and time."[14] Needless to say, nonnative German speakers will find it difficult to fully appreciate the literary merits and aesthetic appeal of Luther's translation. Perhaps the best witness to Luther's accomplishment for those who do not speak German is the eighteenth-century composer Johann Sebastian Bach, who set Luther's German translation of Scripture to music in numerous pieces. So, for instance, Bach's *St Matthew Passion* comprises the exact text of Luther's translation of chapters 26 and 27 of Matthew's gospel. It is no accident that Luther's words sit so comfortably against the backdrop of Bach's music. The congruity between Luther's text and Bach's music stems from the inherent beauty of each.

One could gauge the ultimate success of Luther's translation of the German Bible—beyond questions of accuracy, readability, and aesthetic appeal—by its sheer staying power. Luther's Bible remains the most widely read and preached translation of Scripture among German speakers today. More telling testimony to the success of Luther's translation of the German Bible—at least by the standards of Luther's ultimate goal as noted above— came from another of Luther's Roman antagonists, Johann Cochlaeus. Three years after Luther's death, Cochlaeus was still complaining, in his biography of the Reformer, about the impact that Luther's translation of Scripture had made in Germany: "Even shoemakers and women and every kind of unlearned person, whoever of them . . . had somehow learned German letters, read it most eagerly as the font of all truth. And by reading and rereading it they committed it to memory and so carried the book around with them in their bosoms. Because of this, in a few months they . . . did not blush to dispute about the faith and the Gospel, not only with laypeople of the Catholic party, but also with priests and monks."[15] Had Luther been alive to read this, he would, one suspects, have discovered in it the greatest endorsement that his efforts at translation could have received.

Luther as Interpreter of the Bible

The first printing of Luther's German New Testament in 1522 came to be known as the September Testament not simply, or even primarily, because it was published in September, but because it was succeeded by a revised

---

14 Robinson, "Luther's Bible," 233.
15 Elizabeth Vandiver et al., eds., *Luther's Lives: Two Contemporary Accounts of Martin Luther* (Manchester, England: Manchester University Press, 2002), 106.

edition—the December Testament—within only three months' time. Luther made no significant changes to the biblical translation itself in the December Testament. He merely added marginal notes and prefaces to each book of the New Testament, thereby producing something akin to what today might be called a study Bible. In this, we see Luther's concern, from the very first, not just to grant the people access to Scripture in language they could understand, but also to guide them in their reading and understanding of Scripture.

Indeed, guiding others in their reading and understanding of Scripture was Luther's principal vocation, at least to his thinking. From 1512, when Luther was appointed chair of biblical studies at Wittenberg, until his death in 1546, Luther lectured two to three times per week during term time, always expositing discrete books of the Bible. His exegetical and interpretive efforts reached an audience beyond Wittenberg's student population in the form of biblical commentaries based upon his lectures. Luther ultimately produced commentaries on the Old Testament books of Genesis, Deuteronomy, the Psalms, Ecclesiastes, Song of Solomon, Isaiah, and all the Minor Prophets, as well as the New Testament books of Romans, Galatians, 1 Timothy, Titus, Philemon, Hebrews, 1 and 2 Peter, Jude, and 1 John. His level of engagement with the biblical text seems to have deepened as he aged—his exegetical labors in the book of Genesis occupied him from 1535 to 1545 and ultimately filled eight volumes of the English edition of his works. Of course, Luther's biblical interpretation also found expression in his many sermons and—for that matter—in his polemical and theological treatises. Indeed, exegesis and interpretation of the Bible lay at the root of everything Luther ever wrote or said in service to the church. A proper appreciation for Luther, then, requires paying some attention not just to what he believed, but also—and, in some sense, more fundamentally—to how he read the Bible and thus arrived at what he believed.[16]

Luther's starting point in biblical interpretation was his conviction that "the Holy Scriptures did not grow on earth," but are "the Word of God," having been "spoken by the Holy Ghost."[17] Given its identity as "the Word of God," Scripture ultimately validates and interprets itself. To seek confidence that Scripture is God's Word, or to seek Scripture's meaning from some other source than Scripture itself, would be to acknowledge some word above

---

16 For a fuller treatment of Luther's approach to biblical interpretation, see especially Arthur Skevington Wood, *Luther's Principles of Biblical Interpretation* (London: Tyndale, 1960).

17 Quoted in Wood, *Luther's Principles*, 12.

God's Word. But Scripture knows no "masters, judges, or arbiters" in Luther's view. It knows "only witnesses, disciples, and confessors."[18] Thus, he rejected Rome's claim that Scripture requires validation from the institutional church to be recognized as the Word of God.[19] He likewise rejected Rome's claim to possess—whether in church councils or in the person of the pope—the exclusive right and requisite spiritual gift to interpret Scripture. In claiming some unique prerogative and ability to interpret Scripture, "the Pope," Luther quipped, "pretends to drink malmsey out of the same cask from which others . . . get water."[20]

Against such Roman presumption, Luther insisted that Scripture "belongs equally to everybody."[21] His conviction that "everybody" could, at least in theory, read and understand Scripture's message was rooted in his assumption that Scripture is fundamentally clear in its teaching (and so ultimately accessible to every Christian). "There is not on earth," he wrote, "a book more lucidly written than the Holy Scripture."[22] Luther's insistence on Scripture's clarity found expression, among other places, in his mid-1520s conflict with Erasmus—the very man whose Greek New Testament served Luther's translation needs—concerning the effects of sin upon human choices. Erasmus prefaced his defense of "free will" with the claim that scriptural teaching on many matters is rather *un*clear, including—somewhat ironically—that matter regarding which he intended to expound Scripture's meaning. "The deeper we go" into "some secret places of Scripture," Erasmus wrote, "the darker and darker it becomes."[23] Luther replied by acknowledging that God keeps some (indeed most) things to Himself (see Deut. 29:29), but he insisted that when God speaks—as He has done in every word of Scripture—He intends to be understood.

Of course, Luther, like every student of Scripture, knew the experience of reading the Bible and struggling at times to make sense of it. His defense of Scripture's clarity, then, requires some nuancing. He drew an important distinction between the "subject matter" of Scripture and the various

---

18 *LW*, 26:58.

19 On Luther's notion of Scripture's self-authentication, see Althaus, *Theology of Martin Luther*, 75–76.

20 Quoted in Wood, *Luther's Principles*, 6.

21 Ibid. Luther did, however, privilege a corporate, churchly interpretation of Scripture over any private individual's judgment of Scripture's meaning. This is evidenced in his ongoing call for a "truly free council" to meet and adjudicate the theological controversies of his day on the basis of Scripture's teaching.

22 Ibid., 17.

23 *Luther and Erasmus*, 38.

"texts"—some more grammatically challenging than others—that constitute Scripture and so advance the "matter" in question. It is, he insisted, the "subject matter" that is always clear—"the subject matter of the Scriptures . . . is all quite accessible"—even though specific "texts" might prove "obscure and abstruse . . . because of our ignorance of their vocabulary and grammar."[24] A further obstacle to our understanding of Scripture, no matter the clarity of Scripture's "matter," is discovered in our sinful resistance to Scripture's teaching and/or insistence that Scripture conform to our demands for what God ought to reveal to us. "Scripture simply confesses the trinity of God and the humanity of Christ," Luther observed in illustration of his point. "There is nothing here of obscurity or ambiguity. But how these things can be, Scripture does not say . . . , nor is it necessary to know."[25]

An important principle for reading and understanding the Bible is implied by Luther's nuanced understanding of Scripture's clarity. That principle, alluded to previously, is that Scripture itself must interpret Scripture. When confronted with a puzzling passage, the Bible reader should let clearer biblical texts shed light upon more difficult texts. "If the words are obscure in one place, yet they are plain in another."[26] One should also be careful to interpret individual texts of Scripture in a way that conforms to the overall teaching of the Bible. Luther criticized contemporaries who, in defense of one error or another, failed to "quote Scripture in its entirety." To properly interpret discrete passages in Scripture, one must "have regard to the whole of Scripture."[27]

But what does "the whole of Scripture" teach? What, ultimately, is the "subject matter" of Scripture, which Luther deemed perfectly clear? "Take Christ out of the Scriptures," Luther wrote to Erasmus, "and what will you find remaining in them?"[28] Or, to put the matter positively: "All of Scripture everywhere deals only with Christ."[29] Luther made this assertion with regard to both testaments of Scripture. The New Testament reveals Christ in a rather straightforward way, while the Old Testament constitutes "the swaddling clothes and the manger in which Christ lies."[30] Luther took his cue in

24 Ibid., 110.
25 Ibid., 112.
26 Ibid., 111.
27 Quoted in Wood, *Luther's Principles*, 22.
28 *Luther and Erasmus*, 110.
29 Quoted in Althaus, *Theology of Martin Luther*, 74.
30 Quoted in Wood, *Luther's Principles*, 33.

this regard from Christ's own testimony concerning the Old Testament Scriptures: "It is they that bear witness about me" (John 5:39). The surest method, then, of interpreting any given passage of the Bible is to look for the One whom Scripture in its entirety reveals. "If . . . you would interpret well and truly, set Christ before you, for He is the man to Whom it all applies."[31]

Luther's assertion that "Scripture everywhere deals only with Christ" requires several qualifications. First, it should be noted that while Luther commonly identified Christ as the single subject of Scripture (as in the quotes above), he regularly observed elsewhere that Scripture comprises two distinct "words" of God: law and gospel. So, for instance, he wrote in his *On the Freedom of a Christian* that "the entire Scripture of God is divided into two parts: commandments and promises."[32] God's commandments (law) "show us what we ought to do but do not give us the power to do it." God's promises (gospel), on the other hand, reveal Jesus Christ to us—the One who has fulfilled God's law on our behalf and suffered the penalty for our sins, thereby securing for us forgiveness of sins and eternal fellowship with God. Luther's distinction between "commandments and promises" is not a distinction between Old and New Testaments: law and gospel are interwoven throughout Scripture from beginning to end.

Luther's acknowledgment of "two parts" to Scripture could, upon the surface, seem to contradict his assertion that Christ—who is uniquely revealed in the gospel "part" of Scripture—constitutes the whole of Scripture's subject matter. But closer attention to Luther's teaching on law and gospel resolves any apparent contradiction in his doctrine. God's commandments are, Luther explained, ultimately "intended to teach man to know himself, that through them he may recognize his inability to do good and may despair."[33] Human despair, however, is never God's final goal. God leads sinners "to despair" so that they might "seek . . . help . . . from someone else"—namely, Jesus Christ, who has lived and died in the stead of sinners. God's commandments, in other words, ultimately serve the interest of God's promises. Luther's recognition of commandments and promises in Scripture—"words" of God that must not be confused—does not, then, ultimately oppose his assertion that "Scripture everywhere deals only with Christ." It reminds us, rather, that the identification of Christ as the exclusive content of Scripture was not intended

---

31 Ibid., 34.
32 *LW,* 31:348.
33 Ibid.

to provide license to discover Christ in passages in forced or awkward ways—some passages, the Reformer realized, lead to Christ by another route than direct proclamation of Him.

Second, it should be noted that "Christ" entailed, for Luther, both the person and the work of the Savior. In other words, the content of Scripture was ultimately, in Luther's perspective, "Christ and him crucified" (1 Cor. 2:2). Luther's medieval predecessors had developed their own method for discovering Christ in places of Scripture that did not obviously speak of Him. They had insisted that Scripture has both a literal and one or more nonliteral meanings: an *allegorical* meaning that might reveal Christ or some aspect of Christian doctrine; a *tropological* meaning that served to reinforce Christian morals; and/or an *anagogical* meaning that pointed to future (eschatological) events in the life of the church and the world. Medieval interpreters, then, had not been entirely remiss in finding Christ in the whole of the Bible. They had, in fact, discovered Him in some of the most unlikely places. But the "Christ" yielded by their allegorical readings of Scripture was typically one who merely intended—perhaps in explicit correspondence to the tropological meaning of a text—to reinforce God's law, either by promulgating or modeling the same.

Luther had little patience for those who buried, with their allegorical "monkey-tricks," the plain meaning of Scripture.[34] "When I was a monk," he admitted, "I allegorized everything. But after lecturing on the Epistle to the Romans, I came to have some knowledge of Christ. For therein I saw that Christ is no allegory."[35] He had even less patience for those who, by virtue perhaps of their allegorical exegesis, turned Christ into a mere expounder of divine law, whether by His teachings or His perfect example. He denounced those who preached the "works, life, and words" of Christ with no greater goal than improving their listeners' "conduct of life."[36] In Luther's view, the "Christ" whom "Scripture everywhere" reveals is a "Christ" disclosed in plain words and, even more significantly, a "Christ *for* you and me"—a "Christ," in other words, who is God's gift to us.[37]

---

34 Quoted in Wood, *Luther's Principles*, 24.

35 Ibid., 25. Luther's instructions to look for Scripture's "literal" meaning should not be confused with advice to read Scripture in a literalistic fashion. So, for instance, Luther's interpretive approach left ample room for discerning Christ in OT types. Scholars agree that many of the "spiritual" meanings that OT interpreters discovered in the biblical text were simply rechristened the "literal" or "plain" meaning by Luther.

36 *LW*, 31:357.

37 Ibid. Emphasis mine.

Luther made this point most clearly in his 1521 work *A Brief Instruction on What to Look for and Expect in the Gospels.* "Be sure," he lectured his readers, "that you do not make Christ into a Moses, as if Christ did nothing more than teach and provide examples as the other saints do, as if the gospel were simply a textbook of teachings or laws." A "Christ" who is only a positive role model "is no more help to you than some other saint"; the "gospel" of "Christ" our perfect example "cannot . . . be called gospel" at all.

Proper reading and understanding of Scripture, then, entails discovering and accepting Christ "as a gift, as a present that God has given you and that is your own." Luther explained: "This means that when you see or hear of Christ doing or suffering something, you do not doubt that Christ himself, with his deeds and suffering, belongs to you. On this you may depend as surely as if you had done it yourself; indeed as if you were Christ himself." Only when Christ has been thoroughly digested as gift can "you take him as your example, giving yourself in service to your neighbor just as you see that Christ has given himself for you."[38]

The "Christ" whom "Scripture everywhere" reveals, then, is a Christ, finally, who demands the human response of faith. One must believe that God offers him this extraordinary gift and accept it for what it truly is, a priceless treasure freely given. "When you lay hold of Christ as a gift which is given you for your very own and have no doubt about it, you are a Christian. [Your] faith redeems you from sin, death, and hell."[39] With a view toward faith as the proper response to Christ as properly revealed—i.e., Christ as God's gift to sinners—in Scripture, Luther could ultimately claim that Scripture contains "nothing but Christ *and* the Christian faith."[40]

In bringing this brief consideration of Luther's approach to biblical interpretation to a close, it may perhaps be useful to observe Luther in the act of interpreting Scripture—that is, to see how Luther applied these principles to a specific text. While any number of passages might serve our purpose in this regard, I have chosen to review Luther's treatment of Genesis 3:14–15: "The Lord God said to the serpent, 'Because you have done this, cursed are you above all livestock and above all beasts of the field; on your belly you shall go, and dust you shall eat all the days of your life. I will put enmity between you and the woman, and between your offspring and her offspring;

---

38 *LW*, 35:120.
39 Ibid.
40 Quoted in Wood, *Luther's Principles*, 33. Emphasis mine.

he shall bruise your head, and you shall bruise his heel'" (ESV). Luther's comments on these words well illustrate a number of his basic principles of biblical interpretation as outlined above, and illumine, moreover, critical differences between his approach to Scripture and that of his medieval predecessors.[41]

Genesis 3:14–15 records God's words of judgment upon the serpent that persuaded Adam and Eve to break God's law by eating the forbidden fruit (Gen. 2:16–17; 3:1–7). Numerous biblical exegetes in pre-Reformation times had deemed the biblical account of Adam and Eve's fall—especially with regard to the role played therein by the talking serpent—unfruitful for doctrinal or practical purposes if received purely as a historical episode. Thus, they had resorted to allegorical interpretation of the text, making the serpent and his offspring (or "seed")—and, for that matter, Adam, Eve, and every other entity referenced in the passage—symbols of realities encountered in the everyday experience of average Christians.[42] In Luther's comments on this text, he intentionally distanced himself from such "allegorists" and promised a "historical and literal" analysis of the passage in which "Adam remains Adam," "the woman remains a woman," and "the serpent remains a serpent," albeit "one dominated by Satan."

God's words of judgment, directed in the first instance to "a real serpent," must, therefore, be accepted at face value. "Before sin," Luther judged, the serpent "walked upright" and was "most pleasing to man, as . . . puppies are today." By virtue of God's judgment, the serpent now "creeps on the ground" and has become "more frightful and more hated than all the other animals." Moreover, the serpent has been banished from the "dinner party" that other beasts perpetually attend and consigned to a permanent diet of "raw earth."

Luther acknowledged, however, that God's words were equally—indeed, ultimately—directed at Satan, who was "hidden within the serpent." Indeed, the serpent, "being an irrational animal, did not understand" God's words of judgment, "but Satan did, and he was the one whom God had especially in mind." Luther's assumption that Satan lay "hidden within the serpent" was informed by biblical texts that identify Satan as "the father of lies" who

---

41 Luther's commentary on Gen. 3:14–15 is found in *LW,* 1:182–98. All following quotes are taken from these pages unless otherwise referenced.

42 For a brief but informative discussion of literal and allegorical exegesis in the patristic and medieval periods, see Heiko A. Oberman, *Forerunners of the Reformation: The Shape of Late Medieval Thought* (repr., Cambridge, England: James Clarke, 2002), 281–94.

"prowls around like a roaring lion, seeking someone to devour" (John 8:44; 1 Peter 5:8).[43] His reasoning on this point well illustrates his principle of letting clear biblical texts interpret less clear biblical texts. Who but the "father of lies," after all, could tell that very first lie, "You shall not surely die" (Gen. 3:4)? "When we must make statements about Satan," Luther advised his readers, "let us fall back on other Scripture proofs that are pertinent, sure, and strong."

Luther resisted the temptation—freely indulged by his allegorizing predecessors—to discover some aspect of Satan's condemnation in *every* word of judgment addressed to the serpent. One need not, for example, discover a reference to Satan's loss of his angelic "form and stature" in the words "on your belly you shall go," even if we can be sure that Satan's fall did result in his deformity. In any case, Satan's share in the judgment pronounced by God finds expression primarily in the subsequent words of Genesis 3:15: "I will put enmity between you and the woman, and between your offspring and her offspring; he shall bruise your head, and you shall bruise his heel." Luther discovered in these words prophetic testimony to "the ultimate destruction of Satan's tyranny": "it is not the tail and not the belly of the serpent but the head itself, that is to be crushed and trodden underfoot by the Seed of the woman."

"Satan," Luther judged, "understood this threat well." Thus "he has continued to rage against human nature with such great hatred." But while God's words of judgment in this text are directed at Satan, they are not, in the final analysis, "spoken by God for the devil's sake." Indeed, "God does not regard [Satan] worthy of His condemnation." God speaks these words of judgment, rather, "for the sake of Adam and Eve"—that is, so "they may hear this judgment and be comforted by the realization that God is the enemy of that being which inflicted so severe a wound on man." While "the allegorists" had seen Adam and Eve as literary symbols of faculties that exist in every human being (reason, the affections, etc.), Luther viewed Adam and Eve as historical individuals who had sinned and stood in need of pardon (which, remarkably, God was willing to extend).

God's words of judgment to Satan, then, are words of promise—that is, gospel—to Adam and Eve. "Here grace and mercy begin to shine forth from the midst of the wrath which sin and disobedience aroused. Here in the midst of most serious threats the Father reveals His heart; this is not a father who

---

43 See also Rom. 16:20.

is so angry that he would turn out his son because of his sin, but one who points to a deliverance, indeed one who promises victory against the enemy that deceived and conquered human nature."

The divine mercy extended to Adam and Eve finds its basis, according to Luther, in the promised triumph over Satan by "the Seed of the woman," who is none other than "the Son of God." It is here, in discerning the identity of that "Seed" that will crush the serpent's head, that Luther's Christ-centered reading of Scripture shines and the contrast between Luther's interpretative approach to Scripture and that of his medieval predecessors is most pronounced. Pre-Reformation interpreters of Scripture had identified the "Seed of the woman" not as Jesus Christ, but as Mary, the mother of Christ, largely because medieval versions of the Latin Vulgate had rendered the pronoun in the biblical phrase "he will crush your head" as feminine. In other words, Genesis 3:15 in the Vulgate read "*she* will crush your head" (*ipsa conteret caput tuum*), despite the lack of any basis for such a reading in the Hebrew text.

Luther was appalled by this medieval mistake and the honor it ultimately stole from Christ. "How damnable," he wrote, "that through the agency of foolish exegetes Satan has managed to apply this passage, which in fullest measure abounds in the comfort of the Son of God, to the Virgin Mary!" He rejoiced that, with access to Scripture in its original languages, the proper reference and meaning of Genesis 3:15 could now be "restored." It should be noted that the specific crime committed, in Luther's judgment, by earlier "foolish exegetes" of the Latin Bible was less one of over-venerating Mary than it was one of undervaluing Jesus Christ. "Let the Blessed Virgin keep her place of honor. Among all the women of the world she has this privilege from God, that as a virgin she gave birth to the Son of God. But this must not be permitted to deprive her Son of the glory of our redemption and deliverance."

The scope of the promised victory over Satan promised in Genesis 3:15 should not be underestimated. "This statement," Luther wrote, "includes the redemption from the Law, from sin, and from death; and it points out the clear hope of a certain resurrection and of renewal in the other life after this life." He explained: "If the serpent's head is to be crushed, death certainly must be done away with. If death is done away with, that, too, which deserved death is done away with, that is, sin. If sin is abolished, then also the Law. And not only this, but at the same time the obedience which was lost is renewed." In short, man's redemption, justification, sanctification, resurrection, and glorification are implied by the promised work of the "Seed."

The victory that Genesis 3:15 ultimately promises Christ in his conflict with Satan, then, is equally a victory for all who place their hope and confidence in Christ. "This victory will also be given to us as a gift, as Christ clearly states (Luke 11:22): 'The spoils are divided after the defeat of the mighty one.'" Thus, Luther ultimately sees "the Seed of the woman" as a reference both to Christ and to those who by faith are joined to Christ and share in his blessings. "By faith the Christian is made victor over sin, over the Law, and over death, so that not even the gates of hell can prevail against him." Indeed, God's promise of One who would ultimately crush Satan's head was proclaimed for the very purpose of engendering that faith which makes one, with Christ, a "victor over sin, over the Law, and over death."

The faith engendered by this "fountainhead of all promises" was first discernable in Adam and Eve. "This, therefore, is the text that made Adam and Eve alive and brought them back from death into the life which they had lost through sin." All who respond to the promise of Genesis 3:15 (and subsequent passages) in faith ultimately share in Adam and Eve's hope of eternal life, even in the midst of suffering and death. "Thus we also live in the same hope. And, because of Christ, when we die, we keep this hope, which the Word sets before us by directing us to put our trust in the merits of Christ."

Luther's examination of Genesis 3:14–15, and the promise of Christ and Christ's saving work he discerned therein, led him ultimately to doxology. He concluded his comments on the text by exhorting his readers to acknowledge God—on the basis of His promise and its fulfillment—as the "God of salvation," to cite the psalmist (cf. Ps. 68:20). "Let us," he wrote, "give this title to God, not only because He grants aid in this temporal life . . . but because . . . He frees those who are overwhelmed by death, and transports them into eternal life. This He does, as Moses teaches here, by crushing the head of the serpent."

Conclusion

"For some years now I have read through the Bible twice every year." So remarked Luther to friends and students gathered around his dinner table in 1532. "If you picture," he continued, "the Bible to be a mighty tree and every word a little branch, I have shaken every one of these branches because I wanted to know what it was and what it meant."[44] The picture Luther thus painted of his own efforts to understand Scripture is appropriate, because it

---

44 *LW*, 54:165.

positions him *under* God's Word. Luther exercised the greatest care throughout his entire life not to impose his own understanding of God and God's
ways onto Scripture—not, that is, to stand *above* Scripture—but to submit to
God's Word, and to let his understanding of God and God's ways be determined by the same.

And Luther was, by any fair reckoning, successful in his efforts to discover
the Bible's meaning. Protestant believers today owe Luther an immeasur-
able debt in precisely this regard. Luther recovered biblical truths—not least
the truth that salvation is God's pure gift to sinners on the basis of Christ's
atoning work appropriated by faith alone—that were largely obscured in the
centuries before the Reformation. But it was never Luther's intention to stand
alone beneath the "mighty tree" of Scripture. His translation of the Bible into
the language of the people was an invitation to others to join him in the shade
of those branches. His lectures and commentaries on the Bible provided
instructions on how to grasp those branches and shake them effectively—that
is, in such a way that they might yield their fruits. The greatest honor, therefore, that we can pay Luther in our day is not to rest content in knowing what
he believed "every word" of Scripture meant, but to accept his invitation and
follow his lead in grasping ourselves, again and again, "every one of [Scrip-
ture's] branches" and shaking them, confident that God will repeatedly bless
our efforts and reveal to us "wonderful things from [his] Law" (Ps. 119:18).

Chapter Eleven

THE MAN IN THE MIDDLE: LUTHER AMONG THE REFORMERS

SCOTT M. MANETSCH

In the waning years of the seventeenth century, a Dutch artist named Carel Allard produced a copper engraving depicting sixteen forerunners and leaders of the Protestant Reformation gathered around a large table. The Reformers Martin Luther and John Calvin command the center of the scene, with Bibles set before them; they are surrounded by a company of other illustrious churchmen, including John Wycliffe, Jan Hus, Huldrych Zwingli, Johannes Oecolampadius, Martin Bucer, Philip Melanchthon, John Knox, Heinrich Bullinger, Theodore Beza, and William Perkins, all of whom are illuminated by a candle set in the center of the table that shines forth the light of the Christian gospel. In the foreground, with their backs to the viewer, are crouching a Roman Catholic cardinal, a demon, a pope, and a monk, who strain unsuccessfully to extinguish the light of the candle. The Dutch inscription reads, "The light placed on the candlestick"—a phrase reminiscent of Jesus' command in Mark 4:21 that God's gospel light must be placed on a stand for everyone to see.[1]

---

1 For discussions of Allard's work, see Émile Doumergue, *Iconographie Calvinienne* (Lausanne, Switzerland: Georges Bridel, 1909), 197–99; and Karla Apperloo-Boersma and Herman J. Selderhuis, eds., *Power of Faith. 450 Years of the Heidelberg Catechism* (Göttingen, Germany: Vandenhoek & Ruprecht, 2013), 239. The Dutch phrase is *'t Licht is op den kandelaer gestalt.*

Allard's engraving is both revealing and misleading. In one sense, Allard's depiction of the Reformers as a company of church leaders committed to God's Word and the Christian gospel communicates the important insight that the Protestants of the sixteenth century shared common theological convictions that animated their protest against the medieval Roman Catholic Church. So too, the engraving illustrates the fact that the Protestant Reformation was never the work of a single individual, nor was it restricted to one region of Europe or to a single language group. On the other hand, Allard's engraving misrepresents the nature of early modern Protestantism in that it suggests a unity and collaboration between the German, Swiss, French, and English Reformers that frequently did not exist in practice. Although Protestant leaders in the sixteenth century were quick to acknowledge Martin Luther's special—even God-ordained—role in the renewal of the Christian church, many of them crossed swords with Luther and his successors in Wittenberg over differences in theology and religious practice. Martin Luther's life and legacy served both as a light that inspired admiration and emulation and as a lightning rod that attracted religious division and controversy.

This chapter will briefly explore the nature of Luther's relationships with and his influence among other evangelical leaders both within and outside of the German empire. After describing Luther's network of allies and friends in and around Wittenberg itself, we will turn our attention to his relationships with other magisterial Reformers[2] such as Martin Bucer and Wolfgang Musculus in southern Germany; Huldrych Zwingli and Heinrich Bullinger in Zurich; John Calvin and Theodore Beza in Geneva; and Thomas Cranmer in England.

Luther and the Wittenberg Theologians

By the time Luther returned to Wittenberg from his temporary exile at Wartburg Castle in the spring of 1522, he had become a household name in the German-speaking lands and the recognized leader of the evangelical reform movement.[3] Luther's strong character, stolid courage, and dynamic theological leadership—to say nothing of his clear exposition of the Christian

---

2 The term *magisterial Reformers* denotes those church leaders whose reform efforts were established and supported by magistrates and territorial princes.

3 The term *evangelical*, drawn from the Greek word *euangelion* (good news), was the self-designation of early proponents of the Reformation in the sixteenth century, before such terms as Lutheran, Calvinist, or Zwinglian came into vogue.

Scriptures—attracted a company of capable and loyal supporters who proved to be instrumental in promoting the evangelical cause in Electoral Saxony and throughout the Holy Roman Empire.[4] Many of Luther's first allies were men under thirty who had been trained in humanistic studies and were committed to the reform of the Christian church through the recovery of the biblical languages, the careful exegesis of Scripture, and regular (rather than occasional) Christian preaching. The institutional center of this reform program was the University of Wittenberg, where, in 1517, Luther and his faculty colleagues instituted curricular reforms that replaced scholastic theology with biblical studies and established faculty chairs in Greek and Hebrew.[5] Thanks to these curricular reforms, as well as Luther's public fame, the University of Wittenberg quickly grew to become one of the largest universities in the German empire.

The Wittenberg circle produced many of the most notable pastors and intellectual leaders of sixteenth-century Lutheranism. Luther's faculty colleague and friend Nicolaus von Amsdorf (1483–1565) left Wittenberg in 1524 to become the pastor of the evangelical church in Magdeburg; thereafter, he served as bishop of Naumburg-Zeitz and then general inspector over the church of Eisenach.[6] A similar career path was followed by the Erfurt humanist Justus Jonas (1493–1555), who arrived in Wittenberg just in time to accompany Luther to the Diet of Worms in April 1521. In the years that followed, Jonas served as provost of Wittenberg's Castle Church and as dean of the faculty of theology; in the final decades of his life, he helped introduce reform in Ducal Saxony and served as preacher and superintendent of the Lutheran church in Halle.[7]

Another humanist who came under the spell of Luther and his gospel-centered theology was the Pomeranian churchman Johannes Bugenhagen (1485–1558).[8] When Bugenhagen first read Luther's treatise *On the Babylonian Captivity of the Church* in 1520, he was mesmerized: "The entire world

---

4   Lewis Spitz, *The Protestant Reformation, 1517–1559* (New York: Harper & Row, 1985), 94. See also Scott H. Hendrix, *Recultivating the Vineyard: The Reformation Agendas of Christianization* (Louisville, Ky.: Westminster John Knox, 2004), 53–56.

5   Carter Lindberg, *The European Reformations* (Oxford, England: Blackwell, 1996), 66.

6   *Oxford Encyclopedia of the Reformation*, ed. Hans Hillerbrand (New York: Oxford University Press, 1996), 1:27–28; David Steinmetz, *Reformers in the Wings: From Geiler von Kaysersberg to Theodore Beza*, 2nd ed. (New York: Oxford University Press, 2001), 100–108.

7   *Oxford Encyclopedia of the Reformation*, 2:352–53.

8   Steinmetz, *Reformers in the Wings*, 58–63; *Oxford Encyclopedia of the Reformation*, 1:226–27.

is blind—this man alone sees the truth!"[9] Moving to Wittenberg, Bugenhagen quickly won the admiration of Luther and was soon appointed minister of the city church. Over the next three decades, Bugenhagen played a strategic role in promoting the evangelical cause: he was Luther's pastor and spiritual advisor; he occupied a professor's post at the university; he published a Low German translation of the Bible and wrote several commentaries on Scripture; and he helped draft Lutheran church ordinances for no fewer than eight cities in northern Germany and Denmark.[10] As did his colleagues Amsdorf and Jonas, Bugenhagen remained to the very end a loyal disciple and defender of Luther and his evangelical theology. Preaching at Luther's funeral in 1546, Bugenhagen eulogized his deceased friend as a "great teacher and prophet, a reformer sent by God to the church," and "this holy apostle and prophet of Christ, our preacher and evangelist in the German lands."[11]

Of all Luther's colleagues in Wittenberg, the brilliant theologian Philip Melanchthon (1497–1560) emerged as the Reformer's closest confidant and most talented disciple.[12] Melanchthon first arrived in Wittenberg in 1518 to assume the professor's chair of Greek at the university when he was only twenty-one years of age. His early lectures, which covered such subjects as Latin and Greek grammar, rhetoric, physics, philosophy, and (a little later) theology, attracted hundreds of auditors and earned him Luther's highest esteem. "No one living is gifted with such talents," Luther effused.[13] Although it was humanist pedagogy—not Luther's reputation—that had initially attracted Melanchthon to Wittenberg, the young professor quickly became a partisan of Luther and a champion of his "new" theology. Like Luther, Melanchthon came to believe that the gospel—the fact that God accepts sinners by grace alone on account of Christ—was the heart of the Christian message.

Between 1518 and 1521, Melanchthon followed Luther's lead in affirming the supreme authority of Scripture (*sola Scriptura*) and justification by

9 Spitz, *The Protestant Reformation*, 94.

10 Spitz, *The Protestant Reformation*, 94; Lindberg, *The European Reformations*, 122–23.

11 Robert Kolb, *Martin Luther as Prophet, Teacher & Hero: Images of the Reformer, 1520–1620* (Grand Rapids, Mich.: Baker, 1999), 35.

12 Manschreck, *Melanchthon*; Steinmetz, *Reformers in the Wings*, 49–57; Carter Lindberg, ed., *The Reformation Theologians* (Oxford, England: Blackwell, 2002), 67–82. See also the work of Timothy Wengert, including *Human Freedom, Christian Righteousness: Philip Melanchthon's Exegetical Dispute with Erasmus of Rotterdam* (New York: Oxford University Press, 1998), and *Law and Gospel: Philip Melanchthon's Debate with John Agricola of Eisleben over Poenitentia* (Grand Rapids, Mich.: Baker Academic, 1997).

13 Manschreck, *Melanchthon*, 44–45.

grace through faith alone (*sola gratia, sola fide*), while rejecting Catholic teaching on transubstantiation and papal authority. Melanchthon articulated the fundamental doctrines of evangelical theology in his *Loci Communes* (first edition, 1521), the first systematic presentation of Reformation theology, which became the primary textbook of Lutheran dogmatics in the following century. Luther said of this work: "You cannot find anywhere a book which treats the whole of theology so adequately as the *Loci Communes* do. . . . Next to Holy Scripture, there is no better book."[14] Alongside the *Loci Communes*, Melanchthon's authorship of the Augsburg Confession and his defense of it in the presence of the emperor at the Diet of Augsburg (1530) were of central importance in the history and doctrinal development of early modern Lutheranism.

Luther and Melanchthon remained close friends and companions-in-arms in gospel work until Luther's death in 1546. Nevertheless, significant differences existed between the two men, both in temperament and in religious outlook.[15] Luther was bold, brash, and quick to defend gospel truths; Melanchthon was timid, calculating, and more irenic. Luther was more the theological genius, Melanchthon the systematizer and pedagogue. Luther described their differences this way: "I am rough, boisterous, stormy, and altogether warlike. I am born to fight against innumerable monsters and devils. I must remove stumps and stones . . . and clear the wild forests; but Master Philip comes along softly and gently sowing and watering with joy, according to the gifts which God has abundantly bestowed upon him."[16]

There were theological differences between the two men as well. Luther was suspicious of philosophy and Aristotle, while Melanchthon praised Aristotle and saw philosophy as a tool to organize and clarify Christian theology. Melanchthon softened the sharp distinction that Luther drew between law and gospel, placing greater weight on Christians' ethical responsibilities. So too, in later editions of his *Loci Communes*, Melanchthon rejected Luther's doctrine of predestination, defending instead the notion that the human will worked concurrently with the Word of God and the Holy Spirit as agents in conversion. One additional difference that became especially significant was Melanchthon's departure from Luther's doctrine of Christ's real presence in the Lord's Supper. In 1540, Melanchthon produced a revised edition of

---

14 Wilhelm Pauck, ed., *Melanchthon and Bucer* (Philadelphia: Westminster, 1969), 17.
15 Steinmetz, *Reformers in the Wings*, 51–57.
16 Manschreck, *Melanchthon*, 54.

the Augsburg Confession (known as the *Variata* edition) intended to reflect more closely the theology of the Wittenberg Concord (1536), an agreement forged between Wittenberg and south German cities on the thorny subject of Christ's presence in the Lord's Supper. Article 10 of the *Variata* stated that the body and blood of Christ are "truly exhibited"—rather than "truly present and . . . distributed," as the Augsburg Confession originally read—to those who partake of the bread and wine. For many conservative Lutherans, this revised statement smacked of Zwingli's so-called "sacramentarian" error in that it stripped the consecrated elements of their true divine substance and called into doubt Luther's teaching that Christ in His human nature is everywhere present (a doctrine known as ubiquity).[17]

These subtle theological differences between Melanchthon and Luther became amplified after Luther's death. After the disastrous defeat of the Protestant princes during the Schmalkaldic War of 1546–47, Melanchthon agreed to sign the Leipzig Interim (1548), which mandated the forcible reintroduction of certain Catholic practices and doctrines (viewed by Melanchthon as "indifferent") into the Protestant churches in the empire. For Lutheran stalwarts such as Amsdorf and Matthias Flacius Illyricus, Melanchthon's actions were nothing less than a betrayal of Luther and the Reformation. Similarly, more conservative Lutherans (known as Gnesio-Lutherans) attacked Melanchthon and his followers (known as "Philippists") for their defense of human cooperation in salvation and their more spiritualist view of Christ's presence in the Lord's Supper. In spite of the invective thrown his way, Melanchthon saw himself as a defender of Luther and his legacy to the end of his life. He ranked Luther among the greatest leaders of the Christian church, in the company of John the Baptist, Paul, and Augustine. In an oration delivered at Luther's funeral, Melanchthon noted: "Some have complained that Luther displayed too much severity. I will not deny this. But I answer in the language of Erasmus: 'Because of the magnitude of the disorders, God gave this age a violent physician.'"[18]

Luther and the Southern German Theologians

The progress of evangelical reform in the cities and towns of Germany was more complex and variegated than in the territory of Electoral Saxony.

---

17 Lindberg, *The European Reformations*, 259; Manschreck, *Melanchthon*, 240–42.
18 Manschreck, *Melanchthon*, 275.

Invariably, Luther's reform message and influence were refracted through a complex matrix of local and regional politics, anti-clericalism, popular dissatisfaction, humanist idealism, and local religious leadership to produce dramatically different results. Whereas cities such as Strasbourg, Ulm, Augsburg, and Constance abolished the Catholic Mass and embraced Protestantism during the 1520s and early 1530s, other cities such as Cologne and Freiburg-im-Breisgau remained committed to the traditional Catholic faith.[19] In southern Germany, the nucleus of first-generation evangelical leaders was drawn primarily from the ranks of urban humanists and Catholic priests and monks. Though these leaders acknowledged their debt to Luther, most felt free to depart from aspects of his theology and religious program. For south German Reformers such as Martin Bucer and Wolfgang Musculus, Luther inspired respect, but not unflinching loyalty.

Next to Luther and Melanchthon, the Strasbourg minister Martin Bucer (1491–1551) was the most important Protestant Reformer in the German empire.[20] Born the son of a poor cobbler in Schlettstadt (Alsace), Bucer was placed in a Dominican monastery at age fifteen and was thereafter introduced to the scholastic theology of Thomas Aquinas. When he was in his mid-twenties, Bucer's superiors sent him to pursue his doctorate in theology at the University of Heidelberg, where he became a devotee of humanistic studies—it was also there, in April 1518, that Bucer attended the Heidelberg Disputation and first heard Luther articulate his evangelical doctrine. This marked a turning point in Bucer's life. Over the next five years, he left the monastery, took a wife in marriage, and migrated to Strasbourg, where he was installed as priest and preacher in the city. In his first published writing, titled *That No One Should Live for Himself but Others* (1523), Bucer defended Luther and his theology while giving special emphasis to the ethical dimension of new life in Christ. Through the efforts of Bucer and his clerical colleagues Matthew Zell (1477–1548), Wolfgang Capito (1478–1541), and Caspar Hedio (1494–1552), the city of Strasbourg moved steadily into

---

19 For an introduction to the extensive literature on the "City Reformation," see Bernd Moeller, *Imperial Cities and the Reformation*, eds. H.C. Erik Midelfort and Mark U. Edwards Jr. (Durham, N.C.: Labyrinth, 1982); Steven Ozment, *The Reformation in the Cities: The Appeal of Protestantism to 16th Century Germany and Switzerland* (New Haven, Conn.: Yale University Press, 1975); Euan Cameron, *The European Reformation* (Oxford, England: Clarendon, 1991), 210–66.

20 Martin Greschat, *Martin Bucer: A Reformer and His Times*, trans. Stephen E. Buckwalter (Louisville, Ky.: Westminster John Knox, 2004); Steinmetz, *Reformers in the Wings*, 85–92.

the evangelical camp, a process completed in 1529, when the city magistrates outlawed the Catholic Mass and closed the city's monasteries.[21]

For the remainder of his career in Strasbourg, Bucer worked tirelessly to establish a Christian social order in the city, one constructed upon the biblical principles central to the Reformation. His literary corpus was expansive, including ponderous biblical commentaries (which Luther deemed as "too long and nothing but eyewash"[22]), catechisms, polemical writings, and works devoted to church polity and discipline. At the same time, the Strasbourg Reformer became an important actor on the European stage of religious politics, as he attempted to breach the divide between Lutheran and Reformed Protestants on the contentious subject of Christ's presence in the Lord's Supper. As a member of the Swiss delegation to the Marburg Colloquy in 1529, Bucer encountered Luther, but found the German Reformer suspicious and critical of his position. "Your spirit and our spirit do not coincide," Luther stated. "On the contrary, it is obvious that we do not have one and the same spirit."[23] Luther's attempt to discredit Bucer by associating his eucharistic theology with Zwingli's memorialist position missed the mark; for Bucer, Christ *does* impart Himself to believers in the Lord's Supper, though He is not *in* the elements of bread and wine. Undeterred by Luther's hostility, Bucer worked tirelessly over the next decade to achieve union between the Wittenberg theologians and Reformed Protestants of southern Germany and Switzerland. The crowning success of this effort came in 1536 when Bucer and a group of south German theologians journeyed to Wittenberg and reached consensus with Melanchthon and Luther on the Lord's Supper. This agreement, known as the Wittenberg Concord, affirmed that unworthy communicants receive Christ in the Lord's Supper (*manducatio indignorum*), and that the body and blood of Christ are truly and substantially present, offered, and received *with* (rather than *in*) the sacramental bread and wine.[24] This doctrinal consensus based on the sacramental union of Christ with the physical elements reduced tensions between Wittenberg and the cities of southern Germany, but it did not unify the Protestant world, nor did it completely allay Luther's suspicions of Bucer and other Reformed churchmen in southern Germany.

---

21 Cameron, *The European Reformation*, 216–18.
22 Greschat, *Martin Bucer*, 190.
23 Ibid., 93.
24 Ibid., 136–38; *Oxford Encyclopedia of the Reformation*, 4:286–87.

Bucer was forced to leave Strasbourg in 1549 by the terms of the Augsburg Interim. At the invitation of Archbishop Thomas Cranmer, he immigrated to England, where he spent the last years of his life as regius professor at Cambridge University. All the while, Bucer never lost his admiration for Luther, even as he recognized his faults. Upon learning of Luther's death in 1546, Bucer wrote this tribute to a friend: "I know how many people hate Luther. And yet the fact remains: God loves him very much and never gave us a holier and more effective instrument of the gospel. Luther had his shortcomings, in fact, serious ones. But God bore them and put up with them, never granting another mortal a mightier spirit and such divine power to proclaim his Son and strike down the Antichrist."[25]

Another south German Reformer who attempted to find middle ground between Luther's doctrine of real presence and Zwingli's memorialism was Wolfgang Musculus (1497–1563).[26] Musculus was a Benedictine monk and priest when he first encountered the controversial writings of Martin Luther in 1518. He soon began to share Luther's evangelical message with his monastic brothers and proclaim this teaching in his parish sermons, earning him the nickname "the Lutheran monk."[27] Even so, it took nearly a decade for Musculus finally to disentangle himself from his monastic vows and relocate to Strasbourg to serve the cause of church reform under the tutelage of the Reformers Bucer, Zell, and Capito.

From 1527 to 1531, Musculus served as a pastoral assistant in Strasbourg as he attended theology lectures, studied humane letters, including Greek and Hebrew, and became an enthusiastic partisan of Bucer's brand of Reformed Protestantism. In 1531, Musculus departed for Augsburg, where he distinguished himself for the next seventeen years as the city's chief preacher, lecturer on Scripture, and theological guide, committed to steering the city's official theology between Lutheranism and Zwinglianism. Musculus' attitude toward Luther appears to have shifted during this period. In one letter to his mentor and friend Bucer, he voiced criticism of the Augsburg Confession and confessed his annoyance at Luther's attacks on Bucer and the Strasbourg church. Elsewhere, he was critical of Luther's wrath, intransigence, and lack of Christian charity toward his theological opponents—even as he praised

---

25 Greschat, *Martin Bucer*, 207–8.
26 Reinhard Bodenmann, *Wolfgang Musculus (1497–1563): Destin d'un autodidacte lorrain au siècles des Réformes* (Geneva: Droz, 2000); *Oxford Encyclopedia of the Reformation*, 3:103–4.
27 Bodenmann, *Wolfgang Musculus*, 133–35.

the German Reformer's resolute courage.[28] Musculus was part of the south German delegation that met with Melanchthon and Luther and signed the Wittenberg Concord in 1536. He also interacted with Melanchthon at conferences held with Catholic theologians at Worms (1540) and Regensburg (1541). Thanks to these face-to-face meetings, Musculus established friendly ties with Melanchthon, but he remained wary of (what he saw as) Luther's pride and explosive temper, particularly as it was expressed toward theologians who disagreed with him.

When Augsburg's magistrates signed the interim in 1548, Musculus was forced to find a new home. He and his family ultimately settled in the Reformed city of Bern, where Musculus taught theology and biblical studies at the municipal secondary school and produced half a dozen substantial biblical commentaries. In this final phase of his career, Musculus remained committed to a Bucerian doctrine of the Lord's Supper: the supper is a sacramental feast in which believers enjoy spiritual communion with the true flesh and blood of Jesus Christ.[29] At the same time, Musculus called for moderation and insisted that such theological subtleties must not divide faithful Christians. Writing to Heinrich Bullinger, Musculus summarized his commitment to doctrinal concord with this memorable statement: "May God give to his ministers a spirit of moderation and modesty, and enable them to serve the good of the Church more than their own party interests! 'He is the great Luther!' 'He is the great Zwingli!' Yes, but the Church of Christ is greater than either one of them! May God, through his Spirit of peace, put an end to this quarrel!"[30] Sadly, Musculus' prayer for unity was never realized in the sixteenth century.

Luther and the Zurich Theologians

Zurich's Reformation in the early 1520s was more than a tributary flowing from Luther's Wittenberg. Though not altogether divorced from Luther's influence, the Zurich Reformation was an urban event that owed more to communal identity, local agitation, and Huldrych Zwingli's formidable

---

28 Ibid., 321–27.

29 Craig Farmer, "Eucharistic Exhibition and Sacramental Presence in the New Testament Commentaries of Wolfgang Musculus," in Rudolf Dellsperger, Rudolf Freudenberger, and Wolfgang Weber, eds., *Wolfgang Musculus (1497–1563) und die oberdeutsche Reformation* (Berlin: Akademie Verlag, 1997), 299–310.

30 Bodenmann, *Wolfgang Musculus*, 531.

biblical and theological leadership.[31] Born of hearty Alpine stock, Zwingli (1484–1521) entered the priesthood in his early twenties and spent the next decade serving parishes in Glarus and Einsiedeln, while also taking academic degrees at the universities of Vienna and Basel.[32] It was at university that Zwingli first discovered humanistic studies and the writings of Erasmus, which spurred him to read classical and early Christian authors, immerse himself in the Greek New Testament, and pursue a Christ-centered piety. Zwingli's humanism was combined with an ardent love for his native Switzerland that made him an outspoken critic of the Swiss mercenary system. He was "a Swiss professing Christ among the Swiss."[33]

Thanks to his reputation as a powerful preacher and Swiss patriot, Zwingli was appointed to the prestigious office of preacher at the Grossmünster church in Zurich in January 1519. The next several years were crucial in Zwingli's spiritual development—and Zurich's religious reformation—as he preached consecutively through the biblical text, discovering important ways in which the message of Scripture conflicted with the teaching and practice of the medieval church. In 1520, Zwingli renounced his papal pension; two years later, he preached a sermon in defense of those who ate meat during Lent. At a public disputation in January 1523, Zwingli published his Sixty-Seven Articles, in which he defended the supreme authority of Scripture and argued that salvation is through Christ alone. In two subsequent public disputations, Zwingli convinced Zurich's magistrates that the Catholic Mass and religious images are incompatible with the teachings of Scripture. Consequently, on Easter Sunday 1525, Zurich's political authorities abandoned the Mass and mandated that Zwingli's evangelical theology would henceforth be the city's confession.

Scholars have long debated the degree to which Zwingli's theology was informed by Luther's Reformation discoveries. In the aftermath of the Leipzig Disputation (July 1519) between Luther and Eck, Zwingli is known to have recommended Luther's books to members of his congregation and praised the German Reformer as a courageous "Elijah."[34] In the turbulent years that followed, Zwingli sometimes compared Luther to David, fighting

---

31 See Cameron, *The European Reformation*, 219–23, 245–50; Lindberg, *The European Reformations*, 169–98.

32 W.P. Stephens, *Zwingli: An Introduction to His Thought* (Oxford, England: Clarendon, 2001); George, *Theology of the Reformers*; Lindberg, ed., *The Reformation Theologians*, 157–69.

33 George, *Theology of the Reformers*, 110.

34 Ibid., 111–12.

Goliath, or to Hercules, who slew the Roman boar; he was "one of the first champions of the gospel."[35] Notwithstanding this positive appraisal, Zwingli refused to identify himself as a "Lutheran," and denied direct dependence on Luther: "I did not learn my doctrine from Luther, but from God's Word itself," he insisted.[36]

This statement appears to be on the whole correct, for although both Reformers shared common evangelical commitments to the supreme authority of Scripture, justification by faith alone, and Christ's unique role as mediator in salvation, at key points Zwingli's and Luther's theologies and reform programs took different trajectories. Indebted to Erasmian humanism and classic Platonism, Zwingli's theology drew sharp distinctions between spirit and flesh, between inward and outward piety, between the Creator and His creation. Consequently, Zwingli's critique of Catholic religious devotion was sharper and more uncompromising than Luther's, as he required that Catholic worship and churches be purified of all "idolatrous" ceremonies and material "props" (such as crucifixes and religious images) not mandated in Scripture.[37] Whereas Luther believed the great failure of the traditional church had been works-righteousness, Zwingli identified the central evil of medieval Catholicism as idolatry.

Another difference between the two Reformers was in their understanding of the communication of attributes between Christ's divine and human natures—a difference that would prove especially significant in their contentious debate over Christ's presence in the Lord's Supper. Luther emphasized the unity of Christ's person (while also affirming the distinctiveness of His natures), and thus believed that the properties of Christ's divine nature (e.g. omniscience, omnipresence) could legitimately be ascribed to His human nature. On this basis, Luther argued that Christ's human nature was ubiquitous and, thus, truly present in, with, and under the consecrated sacramental elements. By contrast, Zwingli's Christology placed a stronger accent on the two distinct natures of the one person, Jesus Christ, and he rejected the idea that the properties of Christ's divine nature could be directly ascribed to His human nature.[38]

---

35 Stephens, *Zwingli*, 109.

36 George, *Theology of the Reformers*, 113.

37 Carlos Eire, *War against the Idols: The Reformation of Worship from Erasmus to Calvin* (Cambridge, England: Cambridge University Press, 1986), 73–86.

38 George, *Theology of the Reformers*, 153; Stephens, *Zwingli*, 58–59.

Another important difference between the Reformers emerged from their unique social locations. As the Reformer of a city, Zwingli was more concerned than Luther was with the social and political entailments of reform. He believed that the church and city government should be interdependent and cooperate closely with one another to establish a Christian city. "The Christian man is nothing else but a faithful and good citizen," Zwingli once opined, "and the Christian city nothing other than the Christian church."[39]

In their sacramental theology, Luther and Zwingli had much in common: they both emphasized the centrality of the Word in the celebration of the sacraments; they both affirmed infant baptism; they both rejected the sacrificial character of the Catholic Mass and insisted that laypeople be given the cup as well as the bread in the Lord's Supper. What eventually divided Zwingli from Luther—and the Swiss Reformed from German Lutherans—was their disagreement over Christ's corporeal presence in the Lord's Supper. No later than the summer of 1524, Zwingli adopted a symbolic view of Christ's presence in the sacrament, believing that the word "is" in Jesus' statement "this is my body" (Matt. 26:26) was a trope or figure of speech, best understood to mean "signifies." For Zwingli, believers do not feed upon the actual body of Christ in the sacrament—the ascended body of Christ, he believed, is now with the Father in heaven. Nor do the physical elements of bread and wine convey spiritual benefit to the recipient. Instead, the Lord's Supper should be understood as a memorial service in which Christ's death is proclaimed and believers make public testimony of their faith.

From 1526 to 1529, Zwingli and his allies published a steady stream of treatises defending this symbolic understanding of the supper and attacking Luther's doctrine of Christ's real presence.[40] Luther and the Wittenberg theologians responded in force, accusing the Zwinglians of having proud, unbelieving hearts, unwilling to submit to the clear teaching of Scripture. From Luther's perspective, Zwingli was now "seven times more dangerous than when he was a papist."[41]

As the two sides blasted each other, hope for unity among German-speaking evangelicals appeared lost. In an effort to heal this dangerous breach, the Landgrave Philip I of Hesse summoned Luther and Melanchthon to his castle

---

39 George, *Theology of the Reformers*, 134.

40 Amy Nelson Burnett, *Karlstadt and the Origins of the Eucharistic Controversy: A Study in the Circulation of Ideas* (New York: Oxford University Press, 2011), 91–141.

41 George, *Theology of the Reformers*, 149.

at Marburg in October 1529 to meet with a delegation from Switzerland and southern Germany that included Zwingli, Bucer, and Oecolampadius in order to forge consensus. Over the course of four days, the church leaders debated core theological points, achieving agreement on fourteen of fifteen major articles. On the fifteenth point, related to Christ's corporeal presence in the Lord's Supper, however, the parties could not reach agreement. The Colloquy of Marburg broke up with Luther resolute and uncompromising, refusing to extend the right hand of Christian fellowship to Zwingli and the south German theologians. In response to Luther's rebuff, Zwingli is reported to have cried out: "There are no people on earth with whom I would rather be at one than the Wittenbergers!"[42] In the months after the colloquy, Zwingli appears to have moved away from a "mere" memorialist perspective to affirm that the body of Christ, when contemplated by faith, is *sacramentally* present in the Lord's Supper.[43] Despite this shift, however, Zwingli remained estranged from Luther when the Zurich Reformer died in battle during the Second Kappel War (1531).

The rupture between the German Lutherans and the Swiss Reformed proved to be irreparable. Heinrich Bullinger (1504–74), who succeeded Zwingli as chief preacher at the Grossmünster, was deeply wounded by Luther's harsh attacks against Zwingli and the Zurich church.[44] At the same time, Bullinger and his colleagues did not entirely trust Bucer and the south Germans, nor were they willing to sign the Wittenberg Concord in 1536. Consequently, Zurich and her Swiss allies became increasingly isolated from the larger Protestant world. The hostile confessional climate only worsened when Luther published the *Short Confession of the Holy Sacrament* (1544), which denounced Zwingli, Karlstadt, Oecolampadius, and Caspar Schwenck-feld as heretics and fanatics. "Luther has damned us as heretics," Bullinger complained, "and has insulted the faith and honor of our faithful ancestors, who were honorable Christian men, and our churches."[45]

In response to such attacks, Bullinger and other Swiss theologians attempted to create a common theological and political front against the

---

42 Ibid., 150.

43 Stephens, *Zwingli*, 105–6.

44 Bruce Gordon and Emidio Campi, eds., *Architect of Reformation: An Introduction to Heinrich Bullinger, 1504–1575* (Grand Rapids, Mich.: Baker Academic, 2004); Steinmetz, *Reformers in the Wings*, 93–99; Lindberg, ed., *The Reformation Theologians*, 170–83.

45 Andreas Mühling, "Heinrich Bullinger as Church Politician," in Gordon and Campi, eds., *Architect of Reformation*, 245.

Lutherans and Catholics. In 1549, Bullinger and Calvin and their respective cities signed the *Consensus Tigurinus*, which contained a compromise statement on the Lord's Supper.[46] In a similar fashion, Bullinger's magisterial summary of Reformed doctrine known as the Second Helvetic Confession (1566) became the confessional standard for Reformed churches in Switzerland, France, Hungary, Poland, and Scotland.[47] While rejecting the Lutheran doctrines of ubiquity, the sacramental eating of the unworthy (*manducatio indignorum*), and Christ's corporeal presence in the supper, Bullinger's confession affirms that the Lord's Supper is both a remembrance of Christ's redemption and a spiritual feast in which Christ provides spiritual nourishment to believers through His own flesh and blood to eternal life.[48] Bullinger remained an outspoken critic of Luther and his theological disciples to the very end. In a letter written a few months before his death, Bullinger pinned the blame for Protestant disunity squarely on Luther's shoulders: all hope for concord and unity were "cut to pieces and vanished in smoke" due to the German Reformer's moodiness, rudeness, stubbornness, and irrational attacks on his opponents.[49]

Luther and the Genevan Theologians

Unlike most of the magisterial Reformers examined thus far, the Genevan churchman John Calvin (1509–64) belonged to a younger generation than Martin Luther and never had direct contact with the German Reformer.[50] Raised in the home of an episcopal clerk in Noyon, France, Calvin received the arts degree at the University of Paris in 1528 and then pursued the license in civil law at the universities of Orléans and Bourges. During his legal studies, Calvin was introduced to French humanism and became an avid student of classical literature and the biblical languages. In 1531, with his law degree in hand, Calvin returned to Paris and rubbed shoulders with a group of reform-minded church leaders who were reading and discussing the writings

---

46 *Oxford Encyclopedia of the Reformation,* 1:414–15.

47 Ibid., 2:219–22. The Reformed city of Basel signed the Second Helvetic Confession much later.

48 Joel R. Beeke and Sinclair B. Ferguson, eds. *Reformed Confessions Harmonized* (Grand Rapids, Mich.: Baker, 1999), 220–30. See also *Oxford Encyclopedia of the Reformation,* 2:219–22.

49 Bullinger to Beza, 1575, in *Correspondance de Théodore de Bèze,* vol. 16, eds. Alain Dufour, Béatrice Nicollier, and Reinhard Bodenmann (Geneva: Droz, 1993), 25–26.

50 Bruce Gordon, *Calvin* (New Haven, Conn.: Yale University Press, 2009); B.A. Gerrish, *The Old Protestantism and the New: Essays on the Reformation Heritage* (Chicago: University of Chicago Press, 1982), 27–48. Calvin sent one letter to Luther via Melanchthon in 1544. Fearing that Calvin's letter would annoy Luther, Melanchthon never delivered the letter to its intended recipient.

of Erasmus and Luther. Calvin later reported that he was reading Luther's writings at the time he began to extricate himself from the "darkness of the papacy."[51] Though the precise moment of Calvin's "sudden conversion" to evangelical faith is not known, by the end of 1534 he had become a sharp critic of the Catholic Church and was committed to the cause of religious reform. Two years later, Calvin published the first edition of his famous *Institutes of the Christian Religion*, a succinct summary and defense of Protestant doctrine, which drew extensively from the theological insights of Luther, Melanchthon, Bucer, and (to a lesser extent) Zwingli.[52]

In the summer of 1536, during a brief stopover in Geneva, Calvin was confronted by the fiery preacher William Farel, who convinced him to remain in the city and help construct the new Protestant church order. Consequently, over the next twenty-eight years—aside from a three-year "exile" in Strasbourg (1538–41)—Calvin served as the chief preacher, pastor, and theologian of the Genevan church, making the city the epicenter of French Protestantism and a safe haven for Reformed Christians fleeing from persecution elsewhere in Europe. Calvin's theological vision and practical plan for religious reformation were spelled out in successive editions of the *Institutes,* in several dozen polemical treatises, in his learned biblical commentaries, and in the *Ecclesiastical Ordinances* (1541) and Genevan Catechism (1542). In these expansive works, one finds the signature doctrines of Calvin's Reformed theology, including the supreme authority of Scripture, justification by grace through faith alone, the Holy Spirit's role in the Christian life, God's providence and predestination, ecclesiastical discipline, the so-called third use of the law, and unadorned Word-centered worship.

During his years in Geneva, Calvin established friendly ties with other Protestant leaders, including Bucer in Strasbourg, Bullinger in Zurich, Melanchthon in Wittenberg, and Musculus in Bern. Calvin's attitude toward Luther, however, was more ambivalent due to the German Reformer's repeated attacks against the Swiss theologians after the Marburg Colloquy. In a letter to Bucer in 1538, Calvin acknowledged that Luther was a godly man, but criticized him for being too obstinate and abusive in defending his theological viewpoints. Moreover, Calvin believed that Luther was guilty of

---

51 John Calvin, *Ioannis Calvini opera omnia quae supersunt*, eds. G. Baum, E. Cunitz, and E. Reuss (Braunschweig, Germany: C.A. Schwetschke, 1863–1900), 9:51.

52 Alexandre Ganoczy, *The Young Calvin*, trans. David Foxgrover and Wade Provo (Philadelphia: Westminster, 1987), 137–68.

ignorance and gross delusion on several debated doctrines.[53] Three years later, Calvin's opinion of Luther softened somewhat when he received word from Wittenberg that Luther had read and approved his treatise against the Catholic cardinal Jacob Sadoleto. Calvin also gained a more favorable opinion of Luther and the Wittenberg Reformers as he interacted face-to-face with Melanchthon and other Lutheran theologians at religious colloquies held in the early 1540s. Calvin even signed the Augsburg Confession (*Variata* edition) while a delegate to the Colloquy of Ratisbon (1541). Consequently, over time, Calvin presented a more positive assessment of Luther in his private correspondence, calling him a "gifted man," an "illustrious servant of God," a "faithful doctor of the church," and his "most respected father."[54] On one occasion, Calvin even described Luther as "a remarkable apostle of Christ, through whose work and ministry . . . the purity of the gospel has been restored in our time."[55] Though Calvin recognized Luther's failings, he was not as critical in his assessment of the Reformer as Bullinger and the Zurich theologians were.

That is not to say that church leaders in Wittenberg entirely trusted Calvin. For Luther and his more conservative disciples, Calvin's doctrine of "real spiritual presence"—that in the Lord's Supper, the Holy Spirit enables believers to feed on the real substance of Christ's body, which is in heaven—appeared dangerously close to Zwingli's view. In the years after Luther's death, Calvin's relationship with Gnesio-Lutherans rapidly deteriorated. His role in drafting the *Consensus Tigurinus* all but confirmed Lutheran suspicions of his sacramental theology. Beginning in 1552, the conservative Lutheran minister Joachim Westphal initiated a furious pamphlet war against Calvin and the *Consensus* that not only reignited smoldering hostility between Lutherans and the Swiss Reformed but also sharpened the divide between Melanchthon's allies and more conservative Lutherans back in Germany. In his sharp responses to Westphal, Calvin expressed his strong aversion to Gnesio-Lutheran views regarding the ubiquity of Christ and sacramental eating by the unworthy (*manducatio indignorum*). From Calvin's perspective, Westphal and other Lutheran "monkeys" were eager to mimic Luther's vehemence but had abandoned Luther's more moderate theological

---

53 *Ioannis Calvini opera omnia quae supersunt*, 10.2:138–39.
54 Ibid., 10.2:432; 11:774–75; 15:212–13; 12:8.
55 Ibid., 6:250.

positions. In the heat of this controversy, Calvin complained: "Oh, if only Luther was still alive!"[56]

After Calvin's death in 1564, it was left to Theodore Beza (1519–1605) to navigate the Genevan church through these perilous confessional waters.[57] Overall, Beza held Luther in high esteem. The Wittenberg Reformer was an "excellent instrument of God" and a Christian champion whom God had sent to rescue the church from papal superstition.[58] In his *Icones* (1580), Beza wrote a poem celebrating the courage, piety, and zeal with which Luther defended the Christian religion against his Roman opponents. Even so, Luther's sound theological instincts were sometimes blinded by his natural sinfulness and the "turbulent spirit" of his disciples.[59] While praising the memory of Luther, Beza found his more conservative disciples insufferable. For much of his long career, Beza engaged in acrimonious battles of books with Lutheran "ubiquitarians" such as Joachim Westphal, Tilemann Hesshus, Nikolas Selnecker, and Jacob Andreae over the nature of Christ's presence in the Lord's Supper, religious images, predestination, and the communication of Christ's two natures. In his correspondence, Beza expressed horror at reports that effigies of Calvin were being burned in Lutheran cities, and that Melanchthon's disciples (accused of being "crypto-Calvinists") were being imprisoned or exiled from Lutheran territories. When the Lutheran princes approved the Formula of Concord in 1577—an agreement that decisively condemned the Reformed churches—Beza likened it to Pandora's box that unleashed misery on the Protestant world. Writing to the Landgrave of Hesse in 1580, Beza described the Lutherans as the "first-born" sons of the Reformation, but with this ironic twist: just as God had rejected the firstborn sons of Abraham, Isaac, and Jacob on account of their wickedness, so now God was rejecting the Lutherans and giving His blessing to Reformed Christians—the "younger sons" of the Reformation.[60]

---

56 Ibid., 15:501–2.

57 Paul-F. Geisendorf, *Théodore de Bèze* (Geneva: Alexandre Jullien, 1949); Lindberg, ed., *The Reformation Theologians*, 213–24; Robert Linder, "The Early Calvinists and Martin Luther: A Study in Evangelical Solidarity," in *Regnum, Religio, et Ratio*, ed. Jerome Friedman (Kirksville, Mo.: Sixteenth Century Journal Publishers, 1987).

58 *Correspondance de Théodore de Bèze*, 8:239; ibid., 16:93.

59 Theodore Beza, *Les Vrais Portraits des Hommes Illustrés* [Latin: *Icones*] (Geneva: Slatkine Reprints, 1986), 26–27.

60 *Correspondance de Théodore de Bèze*, 21:184–85. Scott M. Manetsch, *Theodore Beza and the Quest for Peace in France, 1572–1598* (Leiden, Netherlands: Brill, 2000), 134–38, 178.

Luther and the English Theologians

Historians disagree as to whether the English Reformation was initiated primarily from above or below—that is, whether the reform of the English church during the 1530s and 1540s was chiefly enacted by royal fiat or owed more to various historical factors such as anti-clericalism, biblical humanism, Lutheran literature, popular unrest, and a tradition of Lollard dissent.[61] Though royal policy was no doubt decisive, social and religious conditions were also significant in creating a climate that favored church reform. As early as 1519, merchants and travelers were smuggling Luther's writings and other evangelical books into England, where they were eagerly read by scholars and churchmen at Cambridge, Oxford, and London. In response, on May 12, 1520, Cardinal Thomas Wolsey and an assembly of English bishops condemned Luther's teachings, anathematized his writings, and burned his books in a public ceremony.[62] The following year, King Henry VIII received the title "Defender of the Faith" from Pope Leo X for his pamphlet against Luther titled *Assertion of the Seven Sacraments*.[63]

During the 1520s, Cambridge emerged as a center for evangelical ferment as reform-minded scholars and humanists such as Robert Barnes, Thomas Bilney, and Hugh Latimer met at the White Horse Tavern to study Scripture, discuss Luther's writings, and voice criticism of the ecclesiastical establishment. During this same period, a graduate of Oxford named William Tyndale (c. 1494–1536) left England to study with Luther in Wittenberg before settling in Antwerp, where he translated the Greek New Testament into English (completed in 1525) and produced a stream of religious literature in support of reform. Though Catholic authorities were not able to prevent the wide distribution of Tyndale's famous New Testament, they did finally succeed in tracking him down and arresting him near Brussels in May 1535. Sixteen months later, Tyndale was convicted of heresy, strangled, and his body burned at the stake. His final words reportedly were, "Lord, open the king of England's eyes."[64]

Henry's eyes, however, were focused more on his marriage difficulties than on evangelical reform. In hopes of procuring a male heir, Henry began intense negotiations with the papacy in 1527 to secure the annulment of his

---

61 Lindberg, *The European Reformations*, 309–10.
62 Ibid., 311; Spitz, *The Protestant Reformation*, 245–46.
63 Lindberg, *The European Reformations*, 316.
64 *Oxford Encyclopedia of the Reformation*, 4:189–90; Spitz, *The Protestant Reformation*, 247–48.

marriage to Catherine of Aragon and permission to remarry. The pope's refusal triggered a protracted political and religious crisis in England that culminated in Henry's divorce from Catherine and subsequent marriage to Anne Boleyn in 1533; the rupture of ties between the English church and the Church of Rome; and the promulgation of the Act of Supremacy in 1534, which recognized Henry and his successors as "the only Supreme Head on earth of the Church of England."[65] This crisis also brought to power a new generation of church leaders who, though supporters of the Catholic king and his policies, played a central role in moving the English church toward the Protestant fold.

One of the chief actors in this high-stakes drama was Thomas Cranmer (1489–1556).[66] Educated at Cambridge, Cranmer was ordained to the Catholic priesthood and then served as a theological instructor at his alma mater in the early 1520s. Though Cranmer was influenced by humanist ideals, he never belonged to the White Horse Tavern group, nor was he a supporter of Luther, whom he once accused of misleading Christian souls and mocking the people of God. "O the arrogance of this most wicked man!" he commented.[67] In 1527, Cardinal Wolsey recruited Cranmer to serve as a diplomat responsible for securing support for the king's annulment throughout the German empire and in Rome. In Nuremberg, Cranmer found a ready ally in the person of the Lutheran minister Andreas Osiander, with whom he enjoyed long and earnest conversations "concerning Christian faith and true religion."[68] In 1532, Cranmer secretly married Osiander's niece, Margaret—a blatant violation of canon law. During this period, Cranmer also studied Scripture and the early church fathers, seeking to build a case against papal supremacy. Cranmer's tireless efforts on behalf of the king were rewarded when Henry appointed him archbishop of Canterbury in 1533.

Despite his secret marriage and strong opposition to papal authority, Archbishop Cranmer was not a Protestant—at least not in the early 1530s. His viewpoint subtly shifted during the next decade as he scoured the writings of Protestant Reformers, including Zwingli and Oecolampadius. In a letter from 1537, Cranmer stated his approval of the Reformers' attacks on

---

65 Lindberg, *The European Reformations*, 316–17.
66 Diarmaid MacCulloch, *Thomas Cranmer* (New Haven, Conn.: Yale University Press, 1996); Lindberg, ed., *The Reformation Theologians*, 239–52.
67 MacCulloch, *Thomas Cranmer*, 27–29.
68 Lindberg, ed., *The Reformation Theologians*, 242.

the papacy and scholastic theology, including the doctrine of transubstantia-tion, but he rejected Zwingli's sacramental theology. The doctrine of Christ's real presence in the Lord's Supper was "well rooted and supported" by the Apostles and the early church, he believed.[69] Three years later, Cranmer joined his reform-minded colleague, the king's chief minister, Thomas Cromwell (c. 1485–1540), in securing the publication of the Great Bible. In his preface to this Bible, Cranmer wrote that "this book . . . is the word of God, the most precious jewel, and most holy relic that remains upon the earth."[70] Despite this gradual turn toward Protestant conviction, Cranmer continued to provide unwavering public support for Henry's religious policy; he thus published without protest the king's Statute of Six Articles (1539), which mandated adherence to traditional Catholic doctrines such as transubstantiation, clerical celibacy, and auricular confession, under penalty of execution by burning.[71] When Cromwell was arrested and charged with treason and heresy in 1540, there was nothing that Cranmer could do to save his friend from the executioner.

With the decease of Henry VIII and the accession of the "boy king" Edward VI in 1547, Cranmer became the chief architect of religious reform in the kingdom. He oversaw the confiscation and destruction of religious images and artifacts in his archdiocese. He welcomed Protestant refugees from the Continent, including Martin Bucer and Peter Martyr Vermigli, who were given professorships at Cambridge and Oxford, respectively. In the early 1550s, Cranmer even established contact with Calvin, Bullinger, and Melanchthon in hopes of convening an ecumenical council in England as an evangelical response to the Council of Trent.[72] Cranmer's doctrine of the Lord's Supper also changed. The Book of Common Prayer (second edition), which Cranmer published in 1552, states that Christ is spiritually present in the Eucharist and available only to those who partake by faith. Clearly, the archbishop's theological position had moved away from Luther's doctrine of real corporeal presence toward the south German understanding of the Lord's Supper as spiritual communion with the true flesh and blood of Christ.

Cranmer's efforts to reform the English church came to an abrupt end

---

69 MacCulloch, *Thomas Cranmer*, 180.
70 Lindberg, ed., *The Reformation Theologians*, 245.
71 Lindberg, *The European Reformations*, 317–19.
72 MacCulloch, *Thomas Cranmer*, 501–2.

with the death of Edward VI in 1553. Before the year was out, the Catholic Queen Mary ordered that Cranmer be arrested for treason. During the next two years, the archbishop's religious views were investigated and, under duress, he recanted the Protestant faith. Cranmer was condemned to death by burning on March 21, 1556. Minutes before the execution, the prisoner retracted his recantation, shouting that the pope was the enemy of Christ and a teacher of false doctrine. As the flames sprang up, Cranmer extended the "unworthy right hand" that had signed his original recantation into the fire so that it might be immolated first; in his final moments, he cried out the words of Saint Stephen, "Lord Jesus, receive my spirit . . . I see the heavens open and Jesus standing at the right hand of God."[73]

Conclusion

The figure of Martin Luther looms large in the history of the Protestant Reformation. It was with good reason, therefore, that Carel Allard's engraving placed Luther toward the center of the company of Reformers gathered around the candlestick. But from another perspective, the central figure in Allard's portrait is not a man at all, but a message—the message that God's gospel alone can bring the light of salvation to the darkness of the human heart. The magisterial Reformers we have studied—located in Wittenberg, southern Germany, Zurich, Geneva, and England—understood this well, and they devoted their lives to announcing this gospel of grace and forgiveness from their pulpits, in private conversations, and in print media. Although religious unity was frequently elusive, these church leaders shared a commitment to the recovery of biblical Christianity and the renewal of Christ's church in their day. The Reformation was ultimately God's work—not theirs. Martin Luther articulated this viewpoint in one of his final sermons, delivered in 1545: "Do not say on the Last Day, 'Dr. Martin taught me that.' Instead [say], 'Jesus Christ taught me this through the mouth of my pastor's mouth. I do not believe in Dr. Martin, but in the Father, Son, and Holy Spirit who speaks through apostles and preachers.'"[74]

---

73 MacCulloch, *Thomas Cranmer*, 603–4.

74 From Luther's sermon on the Second Sunday after Epiphany, *WA*, 49:684. I'm grateful to Mr. Todd Hains for bringing this quotation to my attention.

Chapter Twelve

THE FURY OF THEOLOGIANS: LUTHERAN THEOLOGY AFTER LUTHER

SEAN MICHAEL LUCAS

When Philip Melanchthon was on his deathbed, he asked to be taken to his study so that he might look at his books one last time. As he lay on a bed in his study, with his friends and former students gathered around him, he asked for a piece of paper. On one side of the paper, he listed the reasons why he would be glad to die: "You shall be done with sin. You shall be free from trouble and vexations and from the fury of the theologians." After reflecting on what he would leave, Philip turned the paper over and wrote about what he would gain: "You shall come into the light. You shall see God. You shall behold the Son of God. You shall learn secret mysteries which in this life you cannot understand." Two days later, on April 19, 1560, Philip Melanchthon was free and in the presence of God.[1]

Well might Melanchthon have longed to be free from the fury of theologians. Even before Luther's death in 1546, the developing evangelical church movement in Germany used the teaching of Luther as the standard by which all other theological formulations were judged. To be sure, the Augsburg Confession was the doctrinal standard for the Protestant city-states, and

---

1   E. Gordon Rupp, "Philip Melanchthon and Martin Bucer," in Hubert Cunliffe-Jones and Benjamin Drewery, eds., *A History of Christian Doctrine* (Philadelphia: Fortress, 1978), 378.

Melanchthon was the key author of that document. And yet, Augsburg drew its authority from its consonance with Luther's own theology. Even more, from 1530 on, Augsburg would be interpreted through the lens of Luther's thought.

As Melanchthon developed Luther's insights, and sometimes disagreed with his older Wittenberg colleague, a fissure developed within Lutheran theology. Those who sought to preserve Luther's theological formulations came to be known as the "Gnesio-Lutherans" (the "true" or "genuine" Lutherans). Those who followed Melanchthon's moves away from certain of Luther's statements were called the "Philippists" or, pejoratively, "the crypto-Calvinists." This fissure began early in Lutheran theology—shortly after the Augsburg Confession in 1530—and lasted until the adoption of the Formula of Concord in 1577.[2]

All of this meant that Philip's life, and Lutheran theology, would be dominated by controversy. Though Melanchthon desired to make positive theological contributions and to bridge the gaps between Lutheran and Reformed theological formulations in the turbulent period of the mid-sixteenth century, he found himself constantly defending his work, especially in his *Loci Communes*, the systematic theology that he produced in four editions between 1521 and 1550. Melanchthon's thought, along with all other German evangelical theologians, would be tested on these grounds: What did Luther say, and how close were these new theological propositions to Luther?

The Preceptor of Germany

Philip Melanchthon was born in southwest Germany in the town of Bretten in 1497. The nephew of the German humanist Johannes Reuchlin, he inherited the family's brilliance with languages. As he studied at Heidelberg, he embraced humanist ideals, evidenced in his translating his family name, Schwartzerdt (black earth), into Greek as Melanchthon. By 1512, he was at Tübingen, where he received his master's degree. There he read some theology, but focused mainly on classics; eventually, he began to lecture on Virgil and Cicero.[3]

At age 21, Melanchthon accepted a call to become professor of Greek at the University of Wittenberg. It was 1518, just months after Luther had

---

2 Robert Kolb, *Confessing the Faith: Reformers Define the Church, 1530–1580* (St. Louis: Concordia, 1991), 60.
3 A convenient biographical summary can be found in Steinmetz, *Reformers in the Wings*, 49–57. A standard biography is Manschreck, *Melanchthon*.

sought disputations on scholastic theology and indulgences in Wittenberg and on the theology of the cross in Heidelberg. And yet, Melanchthon did not go there as a result of a prior familiarity with Luther. No matter—shortly after arriving, he came under the Reformer's influence as Luther urged him to study theology and to set aside his planned studies on Aristotle. Melanchthon did earn a theological degree and started to lecture on the Bible.

In the 1520s, Melanchthon served as Luther's most important lieutenant. He participated in the Leipzig Disputation with Luther against Johann Eck in 1519 and led the Reformation movement in Wittenberg when Luther was squirreled away in Wartburg Castle in 1521–22. More importantly, he arranged Luther's wide-ranging insights into a single, synthetic whole.

That synthesis was called the *Loci Communes*, published in 1521. Merging his own interest in rhetoric with Luther's theological insights, Melanchthon came to see that the central proposition in Romans, and in all Pauline theology, was the righteousness that comes by faith. From there, Melanchthon combed Romans for "topics" (or *loci*) that developed this central proposition. These topics served as "basic concepts" that were necessary to know for salvation in and through Christ. This first edition led with justification by faith alone and a general suspicion of philosophy's impact on theology. Above all, Melanchthon focused on Christ: "I do not see how I can call that man a Christian who is ignorant of the remaining topics such as the power of sin, the law and grace. For by them is Christ properly known, if indeed this is to know Christ, to wit, to know his benefits."[4]

Not only would Melanchthon's *Loci Communes* serve as the main theology textbook for ministerial students in the days ahead, but he and Luther were profoundly interested in general education throughout Germany. In 1527, the two men participated in ecclesiastical visitations throughout the country. They were especially appalled by the lack of knowledge among the priests and people. Melanchthon returned with a determination to redouble his efforts in education. His consistent attention to these issues led him to be called "the Preceptor of Germany."

---

4   For the importance of rhetorical studies for Melanchthon's theological development in the *Loci*, see John R. Schneider, "Melanchthon's Rhetoric as a Context for Understanding His Theology," in *Melanchthon in Europe: His Work and Influence beyond Wittenberg*, ed. Karin Maag (Grand Rapids, Mich.: Baker, 1999), 153–54; Steinmetz, *Reformers in the Wings*, 51.

The Antinomian Controversy

Even as he was seeking to teach German priests and peoples the rudiments of the gospel, Melanchthon had to deal with someone who should have known better. In 1527, Johannes Agricola, an erstwhile Luther ally, former faculty member at Wittenberg, and pastor at Eisleben, began publishing his views, which denied any role for works or the law in a believer's life. He further denied any continuing use of the law in producing repentance. Instead, as historian Timothy Wengert noted, Agricola suggested that repentance occurred only in response to gospel promise, not in response to law's conviction: "One does not move from an anxious conscience to absolution, but from the promise of God to sorrow over sin and, better still, to refraining from sin completely." Likewise, the law does not serve to guide the Christian life; rather, the Christian life is a response to the free promise of gospel forgiveness.[5]

Melanchthon responded forcefully to this developing antinomianism within the Wittenberg movement. First, he argued that the law had important roles both at the beginning of and throughout the Christian life. "The beginning of the Christian life is hearty and earnest terror of God's wrath for our sins," Melanchthon argued. However, the law also played a role in the continuing Christian life, for it teaches "the righteousness of the heart." That was why several of the commandments were repeated in Jesus' Sermon on the Mount: "Lest we imagine that that part of the law has been abrogated," Jesus repeated this law to guide those who belong to His kingdom.[6]

Second, Melanchthon also stressed that repentance as well as faith must be preached and that the law is as necessary for repentance as the gospel. "Pastors ought to follow the example of Christ" in preaching both repentance and faith for the remission of sins, he argued. To preach faith without repentance, "without teaching the fear of God, without teaching the law," would simply produce a false faith and a carnal security. "Those who neglect to teach *poenitentia* [repentance] take away one of the principal parts from the Gospel."[7]

Finally, the law must be taught as a guide to the Christian life, Melanchthon noted, if holiness is to be pursued. "May those who teach in the churches diligently teach the doctrine of the law," he wrote. "Otherwise, where the doctrine of faith is taught without the law, infinite scandals arise, the common

---

5   Wengert, *Law and Gospel*, 45.
6   Melanchthon quotations in Wengert, *Law and Gospel*, 78, 93.
7   Ibid., 97.

folk become secure, and they imagine that they possess the righteousness of faith because they do not know that this faith is possible only in those who have contrite hearts through the law." As Melanchthon continued to grope toward a "third use" of the law—the law as a guide to the Christian life—he was able to deal with this burgeoning antinomian controversy at this point.[8]

However, even without a fully articulated third use of the law, Melanchthon was keen to continue to debunk both nomistic Catholic and antinomian Lutheran claims that the evangelical faith was law-free and works-free. In the 1530 Augsburg Confession, Melanchthon complained, "Our people are falsely accused of prohibiting good works." Far from prohibiting good works, Lutheran preachers have "given useful instruction concerning all kinds and walks of life: what manner of life and which activities in every calling please God." They also taught that genuine faith "is bound to yield good fruits and that it ought to do good works commanded by God on account of God's will." What Lutherans have stood against are "childish and needless works"—feast and fast days, brotherhoods, pilgrimages, rosaries, monasticism, and the cult of saints. In addition, the Lutheran movement also sought to clarify the proper basis for works: faith in Christ's promise of salvation and power from the indwelling Holy Spirit.[9]

Moreover, repentance was to be preached to all as the pathway to faith and good works. "True repentance is nothing else than to have contrition and sorrow, or terror about sin," the Augsburg Confession taught, "and yet at the same time to believe in the gospel and absolution that sin is forgiven and grace is obtained through Christ." Once the heart is thus assured, "improvement [good works] should also follow, and a person should refrain from sins." Clearly, the Lutheran tradition was not going to tolerate a licentious abuse of the gospel.[10]

Confessing the Faith

Of course, the entire process of confessionalization that led to the Augsburg Confession was not tied directly to the antinomian controversy, but to larger political issues that battered the nascent Lutheran movement. In 1529, Holy

---

8 Ibid., 102. Wengert suggests that the "third use" of the law developed by Melanchthon would date from 1534: see *Law and Gospel*, 177–210.

9 Augsburg Confession, Articles VI and XX, in *The Book of Concord* (2000), 41, 53.

10 Augsburg Confession, Article XII, in *The Book of Concord* (2000), 44. I quote here from the German version; the bracketed insert comes from the Latin version of the same article.

Roman Emperor Charles V sent his brother, Ferdinand, to be his regent at the Second Diet of Speyer. Ferdinand commanded the German princes to work against the Lutheran Reformation. Six rulers and fourteen imperial cities protested against this direction. Their formal appeal—or *protestatio*—was the first time that Luther's followers would be called "Protestants."

However, Charles was frustrated with his brother's heavy-handed approach with the Germans. He needed the princes' support for a war against Turkish imperial forces, which had laid siege to Vienna. In order to secure their support, he wanted to settle "the religious question." And so, he called for another imperial diet to be held in Augsburg in January 1530. When the princes and their theologians arrived at the diet—without Luther, who was banned from the empire, even though he continued to live in safety at Wittenberg—they were confronted by a publication from Johann Eck that lumped the Wittenberg theology with less-orthodox positions. Unanswered, this document would scuttle any chance for religious freedom for the Lutherans.

In response, Melanchthon determined to write a confession that would show that the Wittenberg theology stayed true to the catholic tradition. This confession would defend biblical truth as articulated by Luther and his followers while also condemning a range of false teachings also rejected by Roman Catholics. In order to prepare this document, Melanchthon drew upon articles written the previous year, called the Schwabach Articles, as well as working papers that he and Luther had developed in advance of the meeting, now called the Torgau Articles.[11]

After several weeks of negotiation with the Roman Catholic representatives in an attempt to secure freedom for the Lutheran faith, seven Lutheran princes and two municipal governments subscribed to Melanchthon's confession and presented it to the emperor on June 25, 1530. Chancellor Christian Beyer, representing the government of Elector John of Saxony, read the German version of the confession to the diet; his voice was so loud that it carried down into the street below. In response, Charles' representatives tried to negotiate further, but when those talks broke down, they produced a "Confutation," which they presented to the emperor. Charles gave the Lutheran princes until April 15, 1531, to return to the Roman Catholic Church or face suppression.[12]

---

11 Both the Schwabach Articles and the Torgau Articles can be found translated in Robert Kolb and James A. Nestingen, eds., *Sources and Contexts of the Book of Concord*, (Minneapolis: Fortress, 2001), 83–87, 93–104.

12 "Editors' Introduction to the Augsburg Confession," in *The Book of Concord* (2000), 28.

The German princes and their theologians were already acting in response to these decisions. By September, Melanchthon had prepared a reply to the Confutation; however, while his response was being typeset in October, he was forced to redraft several sections once he actually received a copy of the Catholic document. The final *Apology of the Augsburg Confession* appeared in late April or early May 1531. A second version of the *Apology* was produced several months later as Melanchthon continued to work on his statement of justification. This version, published in September 1531, became the official Latin version of the *Apology* until a later German version was approved for use in the Book of Concord in 1580. In addition, in February 1531, the German princes formed the Schmalkaldic League, which would serve the causes of both religious liberty and military combination should they be attacked by imperial forces. At its height, thirty-five states belonged to the league, representing Zwinglian and Lutheran theological commitments.[13]

In order to provide some sort of theological unity for the league, Elector John Frederick of Saxony asked Luther to set forward his theological position for potential negotiation with Roman Catholic opponents as well as a statement of Luther's own final theological position. The resulting document, the Smalcald Articles, would serve as a final summary of Luther's teaching. While John Frederick would not use it for his negotiations with the pope's representatives, the Schmalkaldic League would subscribe to the document in 1537.[14]

The Smalcald Articles would join with the Augsburg Confession and Luther's Small and Large Catechisms as the definitive confessional documents for Lutheran theology. After Luther's death in 1546, Melanchthon continued to work out his own theological trajectory. As he did so, both he and his followers would be judged against these definitive Lutheran summaries. At stake was not only theological precision, but also personal loyalty and religious identity: How close would the Philippists remain to Luther? What did it mean to be genuinely or truly "Lutheran" (or, in their terms, "evangelical")? How could the Reformation continue to advance in Germany without some measure of theological agreement?

---

13 Charles P. Arand, Robert Kolb, and James A. Nestingen, *The Lutheran Confessions: History and Theology of the Book of Concord* (Minneapolis: Fortress, 2012), 107–38.

14 Ibid., 139–58.

The Adiaphoristic Controversy

As Lutherans sought to work out their theological identity, they often used the polemical skills that were part of late medieval university life: "For a generation they hammered out their definition of [Luther's] doctrine as they hammered at each other in the polemical style of seeking the truth common in the period." The upshot would be that, for the thirty years prior to the Formula of Concord, the Philippists and Gnesio-Lutherans would work out their differences and the definition of the Lutheran faith in painful controversies that often sapped the energies of the movement.[15]

There were three major controversies—and several minor ones—that would shape Lutheran thought in the thirty years after Luther's death. The first was the adiaphoristic controversy. From the beginning, the Lutheran movement had viewed most forms in worship as *adiaphora*, or "things indifferent." While some parts of the Mass and other worship forms were viewed as idolatrous or superstitious, Luther himself wanted to give space for pastors to lead their congregations gently toward a service that was shaped by God's Word. Even in the Augsburg Confession, the Lutheran circle could note that "no noticeable changes have been made in the public celebration of the Mass, except that in certain places German hymns are sung alongside the Latin responses for the instruction and exercise of the people. For after all, all ceremonies should serve the purpose of teaching the people what they need to know about Christ." While the Reformed tradition would view the Mass differently, Luther was content to reform it more slowly as a way of caring for the consciences of his people.[16]

This general approbation of the adiaphoristic principle held until Luther's death. After that, however, the ground began to shift for political, instead of theological, reasons. Charles V had finally consolidated power in his empire to the degree that he was ready to deal with the Schmalkaldic League. He was also able to secure the support of Duke Mortiz, the Lutheran son-in-law of Landgrave Philip I of Hesse and cousin of Elector John Frederick of Saxony, both leaders of the league. In less than a year, Charles was able to smash the league, capture both John Frederick and Philip, and establish a measure of control over the German lands.

---

15 Ibid., 161.

16 See, for example, *LW*, 53:20, 31, 37; Augsburg Confession, Article XXIV, *The Book of Concord* (2000), 68.

As a result, Charles decided to launch his own reform of the church. Composed at the imperial diet in Augsburg in early 1548 and published on May 15, 1548, his reforming document has come to be known as the Augsburg Interim. It was an "interim" policy because the Council of Trent was meeting at this time; Charles expected that whatever reforms came from Trent would replace those that he enacted at Augsburg. But the Tridentine reforms were simply a return to Roman Catholicism, albeit of a gentler, Erasmian kind. The Augsburg Interim defended the authority of the pope and his hierarchy and argued that only this magisterium could interpret Scripture authoritatively. It also saw the Roman Mass as having a sacrificial nature because the body and blood of Jesus are present in a corporeal manner, as the doctrine of transubstantiation teaches. Further, the Augsburg Interim upheld seven sacraments and restored a range of medieval practices in clothing, ritual, festivals, and other practices.[17]

The Augsburg Interim was anathema to most German evangelicals. While it led to the exile of many Lutherans, especially in the southern portions of the German states, it also produced anxious opposition from Mortiz and others in the northern territories. As part of his responsibility to advise Mortiz, his new sovereign over the ducal lands of Saxony and the University of Wittenberg, Melanchthon wrote a document that "urged rejection of the Interim, noting the many points at which it deviated from biblical truth, as understood by the Wittenberg theology."[18]

However, Mortiz was torn. He owed his current lands and titles to Charles; and yet, his own Lutheran commitments led him to reject the interim document as unacceptable. Was there a way to find a middle ground between Luther's teaching and the Augsburg Interim? Mortiz asked Melanchthon to prepare a document that could be used as such a middle-ground proposal. Melanchthon agreed to do so, both because he felt it was his duty in obedience to his direct ruler and because he sought to protect the university from falling into Catholic hands.

The resulting proposal came to be known as the Leipzig Interim. In the document, Melanchthon gave ground on what he considered to be "nonessential matters," or *adiaphora*. As he would put it in the Leipzig document, "Our first consideration is that everything that the ancient teachers regarded

---

17 Arand et al., *Lutheran Confessions*, 176. A translation of the Augsburg Interim can be found in *Sources and Contexts of the Book of Concord*, 146–82.

18 Arand et al., *Lutheran Confessions*, 177.

as *adiaphora*, that is, things that are neither commanded nor forbidden by God, may still be regarded as *adiaphora* without compromising Scripture." And so, when it came to the Mass, Melanchthon provided for "bells, lights, vessels, chanting, vestments, and ceremonies." He also suggested that it be performed entirely in Latin, except for the reading of the epistle and gospel, which would be done in both Latin and German.[19]

While the document was never officially published—having been rejected by the other Saxon leaders and Lutheran princes—as it circulated around Germany, Melanchthon's former students "found it an appalling betrayal of God, Luther, and their Preceptor's own integrity." For those, especially in the south, who had lost their livelihood as a result of the Augsburg Interim, the Melanchthon proposal was a bitter compromise on those very issues that had sent them into exile. Others, especially Nicolaus von Amsdorf, criticized Melanchthon's Catholic-friendly allowances on the Mass. While Amsdorf agreed that these forms were generally indifferent, they were no longer indifferent if they were being forced upon the church. At that point, indifferent things are not indifferent. The times demanded confession, not compromise.[20]

The adiaphoristic controversy was more important for the distrust sown by the Leipzig Interim than for the actual theological issues raised. Those who saw themselves as true or genuine Lutherans never forgave Melanchthon and his colleagues for being prepared "to betray the gospel and compromise away their Lutheran heritage." On the other side, Melanchthon and his supporters became "embittered by what he saw as bad faith and purposeful misunderstanding of his efforts to save the church and Lutheran teaching." Without a Luther-like figure present to smooth over the tensions, the 1550s and 1560s would bring other controversies that caused great division in the Lutheran movement.[21]

The Synergistic Controversy

The second controversy that divided the Philippists and Gnesio-Lutherans was over the role of the will in salvation. In his *On the Bondage of the Will*, Luther had taken a strong stand regarding the will's utter inability to turn to

---

19 Leipzig Interim, in Kolb and Nestingen, eds., *Sources and Contexts of the Book of Concord*, 184, 194.

20 Arand et al., *Lutheran Confessions*, 179–81, 183; Timothy J. Wengert, *A Formula for Parish Practice: Using the Formula of Concord in Congregations* (Grand Rapids, Mich.: Eerdmans, 2006), 165–79.

21 Arand et al., *Lutheran Confessions*, 182.

God on its own. Not only were human beings contingent upon God as Creator, but also, because of original sin, they were dependent upon His working within them for salvation. Those human beings whom God saved were those whom He graciously chose to save, predestinating them before the foundation of the world and acting in time through the Spirit's use of God's Word to move their wills to respond to Him. Such a high view of God's sovereignty in relation to human agency was necessary to preserve the Reformational principle of salvation by grace alone.[22]

In his initial version of the *Loci Communes* in 1521, Melanchthon agreed with Luther's views in *On the Bondage of the Will*, published four years later. He argued that the will is not free because God the Creator is sovereignly responsible for all that happens in His world and because human sin vitiated humans' ability to choose the good. Likewise, in the Augsburg Confession, Melanchthon affirmed that "without the grace, help, and operation of the Holy Spirit a human being cannot become pleasing to God, fear or believe in God with the whole heart, or expel innate evil lusts from the heart. Instead, this happens through the Holy Spirit, who is given through the Word of God." Again, God's sovereign grace alone turned the will to believe and so become pleasing to God. The two factors in one's conversion were the Holy Spirit and the Word of God.[23]

As Melanchthon continued to wrestle with these things, however, he began to worry about two aspects of Luther's teaching. One was the psychological side of human experience. The individual in the pew cannot sense the Holy Spirit's work in her heart; rather, she simply believes the good news that Jesus died for sinners. It would not do to suggest that human beings are simply as passive as stones or blocks of wood; their wills act in conversion. That belief as an exercise of the will had to be accounted for in some fashion. The second concern was whether strong statements of divine sovereignty and absolute necessity might make God responsible for evil as its author. Even though Luther had repeatedly denied that this is the case in *On the Bondage of the Will*, still Melanchthon feared that some stricter Luther followers were not as careful as their master.[24]

---

22 See the excellent summary in Robert Kolb, *Bound Choice, Election, and Wittenberg Theological Method: From Martin Luther to the Formula of Concord* (Grand Rapids, Mich.: Eerdmans, 2005), 30–66.

23 Kolb, *Bound Choice*, 76–78; Augsburg Confession, Article XVIII, in *The Book of Concord* (2000), 50.

24 Arand et al., *Lutheran Confessions*, 201; Kolb, *Bound Choice*, 87–95.

And so, as he revised his *Loci Communes*, Melanchthon suggested that "we meet three causes of good works, namely, the Word of God, the Holy Spirit, and the human will which assents to and does not contend against the Word of God. For the will could disregard the Word of God, as Saul did of his own free will." He also further agreed with some early church fathers that "the free choice in man is the ability to apply oneself toward grace, that is, our free choice hears the promise, tries to assent to it and rejects the sins which are contrary to conscience." While, at the time, few engaged Melanchthon on these points, they would be read and heard differently after the Leipzig Interim.[25]

That was the result of moves that Melanchthon made in the Leipzig proposal that appeared to accommodate a semi-Pelagian perspective. He brought two statements from the detested Augsburg Interim into his own proposal: "They do not receive Christ's benefits if the will and the heart are not moved by prevenient grace, so that they stand in fear of God's wrath and detest sin" and "For this reason to say it briefly, it is easy to understand that good works are necessary [for salvation] for God has commanded them." The first statement seemed to echo Melanchthon's claim in the *Loci* that the will coordinates with prevenient grace as an independent factor in salvation; the second appeared to bring works back into justification through the back door.[26]

As the 1550s progressed, Melanchthon's followers continued to affirm that it was the individual's own willing or choice that made the difference in his or her salvation or damnation; that is, the will is a factor in conversion. Johann Pfeffinger, theologian at the University of Leipzig, argued that "all people have received God's promise of forgiveness and offer of salvation through it. God is no respecter of persons. The difference [therefore] between the elect and the damned must lie in themselves." And this difference that was within the individual was the personal necessity to assent to the gospel as it "lies in us and not to resist the Holy Spirit as he moves."[27]

Nicolaus von Amsdorf opposed Pfeffinger's position again. He argued that the Holy Spirit must renew and engage the individual's will before anyone can turn in faith to God. Further, this work of the Holy Spirit has its prior motivation in God's own sovereign, undetermined will. God's electing

---

25 Philip Melanchthon, *Loci Communes 1543*, trans. J.A.O. Preus (St. Louis: Concordia, 1992), 43, 44.
26 Compare the Augsburg Interim and the Leipzig Interim in Kolb and Nestingen, eds., *Sources and Contexts of the Book of Concord*, 152, 185, 190.
27 Arand et al., *Lutheran Confessions*, 201–2.

will and the Spirit's renewing work are irresistible; while sinners resist until they are converted, no sinner can return to God without God's working in him. While Amsdorf was content to deal directly with Pfeffinger, his allies, such as Nicolaus Gallus, knew that the source of the synergistic teaching was Melanchthon himself.[28]

The Sacramentarian Controversy

A third controversy centered on the Lord's Supper. Luther had held that the sacrament is "the true body and blood of the Lord Christ, in and under the bread and wine, which we Christians are commanded by Christ's word to eat and drink. . . . It is bread and wine set within God's Word and bound to it." It is not the believer's faith that makes the sacrament, but rather God's Word joined with the elements that make the sacrament. Hence, whether someone is a worthy receptor or unworthy does not invalidate the sacrament: "Even though a scoundrel receives or administers the sacrament, it is the true sacrament (that is, Christ's body and blood), just as truly as when one uses it most worthily." Further, it was necessary to ensure that only genuine believers took the Lord's Supper, because unbelievers who ate and drank the elements were taking Jesus' body unworthily and so brought judgment upon themselves.[29]

When Melanchthon wrote the Augsburg Confession, he was content simply to replicate Luther's teaching that "the true body and blood of Christ are truly present under the form of bread and wine in the Lord's Supper and are distributed and received there." However, Melanchthon never stopped tweaking or revising the confession; over time, this article came to say that "on the Lord's Supper they teach that with the bread and wine the body and blood of Christ are truly exhibited to those who eat the Lord's Supper." On the whole, Melanchthon was uncomfortable with explaining how the presence of Christ is connected to the elements; he often referred to 1 Corinthians 10:16 and suggested that the supper offered a "participation" in the body and blood of Christ. He was more concerned to explain how the elements serve as a sign of Christ's presence and so assure believers of the forgiveness of sins.[30]

Even before Luther's death, Melanchthon also distanced himself from

---

28 Arand et al., *Lutheran Confessions*, 203, 204.
29 The Large Catechism in *The Book of Concord* (2000), 467, 468.
30 Augsburg Confession in *The Book of Concord* (2000), 44; Arand et al., *Lutheran Confessions*, 175, 229.

Luther's teaching that the attributes of Christ's divine nature were communicated to His human nature, so that Christ's body and blood became ubiquitous. He also hedged on Luther's insistence that the sacrament was Christ's body and blood even for unbelievers and that the sacrament remained Christ's body and blood even after the ritual action was over. On the whole, Melanchthon and his followers tried to avoid "metaphysical speculation" and emphasized a more "functional" approach to the Lord's Supper.[31]

Because he had been present at the 1529 Marburg Colloquy, Melanchthon saw how divisive this issue of Christ's presence in the supper was for the Reformation movement. He dedicated himself to trying to broker some measure of peace on the issue. In 1536, he and Martin Bucer crafted the Wittenberg Concord. The document affirmed that the body and blood of Christ are "truly and essentially present" and "distributed and received" in the Lord's Supper. This is because there is a sacramental union between the elements themselves and Christ's body and blood. The concord further affirmed that the unworthy do receive Christ's body and blood and so misuse the sacrament and bring judgment upon themselves. However, the Wittenberg Concord did not emphasize the more metaphysical aspects of Luther's sacramental teaching.[32]

Melanchthon's willingness to moderate aspects of Luther's teaching on the sacrament led some to accuse him and his followers of being "crafty sacramentarians." And his slide toward aspects of John Calvin's teaching on the Lord's Supper—especially Calvin's criticism of Luther on the communication of Christ's divine attributes to His human nature—would cause others to accuse Melanchthon of being a "crypto-Calvinist." The fact was that Melanchthon's own position was closer to Bucer's than Calvin's; not only this, but he would not defend Calvin publicly when Calvin was engaged in an ongoing dispute over the Lord's Supper with the Gnesio-Lutheran Joachim Westphal. Still, this would be another ongoing controversy for the Lutheran movement.[33]

Finding Concord

The so-called Thirty Years' War among Lutheran theologians left them and their churches weakened, divided, and distracted. It was necessary to work

---

31 Arand et al., *Lutheran Confessions*, 229–30.

32 Ibid., 230–31; The Marburg Articles, in Kolb and Nestingen, eds., *Sources and Contexts of the Book of Concord*, 88–92.

33 Arand et al., *Lutheran Confessions*, 232–34; Timothy J. Wengert, "'We Will Feast Together in Heaven Forever': The Epistolary Friendship of John Calvin and Philip Melanchthon," in Maag, ed., *Melanchthon in Europe*, esp. 36–42.

toward a consensus, or concord, that would bring peace to the warring Philippist and Gnesio-Lutheran factions. However, in order to forge a lasting peace, there needed to be honest brokers whom both sides could trust to speak to those issues. The two key figures in this process were Martin Chemnitz and Jakob Andreae.

Chemnitz was one who could bridge the divide. Undoubtedly, this was the result of his time on the faculty at the University of Wittenberg, where he expounded Melanchthon's *Loci Communes*. He would later write theological lectures, the *Loci Theologici*, that were generally Philippist in orientation. Yet on one of the major controversies of the day, he sided with the Gnesio-Lutherans: he defended Luther's claim that Christ's body and blood are ubiquitous and so united to the elements in the Lord's Supper. Andreae, professor of theology and chancellor of the University of Tübingen, was a Gnesio-Lutheran who was generally moderate in tone and who was tasked by his prince, Duke Christopher of Württemberg, with trying to find a way forward for the splintering Lutheran movement.

Andreae and Chemnitz worked with David Chytraeus and Nikolaus Selnecker as a committee of theologians in seeking to craft a consensus document that would put an end to the controversies of the day. In 1576–77, this committee, along with Andreas Musculus and Christopher Korner, worked through a process that would eventually produce what would be called the Solid Declaration. Because of its length, some German princes desired a condensed version or an "epitome." These two documents, the Solid Declaration and the Epitome, together would become the Formula of Concord. Eventually, through the political skills of Andreae especially, two-thirds of the German theologians signed the document, and it gained a sort of confessional status when it was included in the Book of Concord in 1580.[34]

The Formula of Concord dealt with the significant controversies and generally sided with the Gnesio-Lutherans while admitting key points that the Philippists got right. For example, in article II on free will, the document clearly states that "the unregenerated human will . . . has become God's enemy [and] it has only the desire and will to do evil and whatever is opposed to God." As a result, the document rejects Melanchthon's claims that the will applies itself to grace or in any way prepares itself for grace and that individuals could

---

34 Arand et al., *Lutheran Confessions*, 265–76; Wengert, *Formula for Parish Practice*, 5–6. A good entry point to Chemnitz's life is J.A.O. Preus, *The Second Martin: The Life and Theology of Martin Chemnitz* (St. Louis: Concordia, 1994).

resist or reject the work of the Holy Spirit. In the end, Formula of Concord holds plainly that "before the conversion of the human being there are only two efficient causes, the Holy Spirit and God's Word as the instrument of the Holy Spirit, through which he effects conversion."[35]

In dealing with the adiaphoristic controversy, the Concordists agreed that religious forms belong to things indifferent: "the community of God in every place and at every time has the authority to alter such ceremonies according to its own situation." That said, they sided with Amsdorf over against Melanchthon in the controversy itself, pointing out that "in a time of persecution, when an unequivocal confession of the faith is demanded of us, we dare not yield to the opponents in such indifferent matters. . . . For in such a situation it is no longer indifferent matters that are at stake. The truth of the gospel and Christian freedom are at stake." Melanchthon and the Philippist approach in the Leipzig Interim were wrong.[36]

Finally, in the sacramentarian controversy, the authors of the formula sided with Luther's position. Before unpacking their affirmations and denials, they noted that there were two kinds of sacramentarians: "crude sacramentarians," a position that largely coheres with John Calvin's, and "cunning sacramentarians," by whom they meant the Philippists. In the affirmations, the formula affirmed that "in the Holy Supper the body and blood of Christ are truly and essentially present, truly distributed and received with the bread and wine." The authors also explicitly affirmed Luther's understanding of the communication of divine attributes to Jesus' human nature, quoting Luther in the document itself. Finally, they held that unworthy receivers of the supper actually eat and drink Christ's body and blood and so bring judgment upon themselves. Luther's position was upheld in strong fashion. In the negative theses, the crude and cunning sacramentarian positions were rejected along with those of the Zwinglians, Anabaptists, and Roman Catholics.[37]

In the end, through the Formula of Concord, Lutheran theology would answer its major question about theological identity by standing fairly close to Luther's own teaching. While the confessional documents in the Book of Concord would serve a regulating function, they stood alongside

---

35 Epitome, Article II, in *The Book of Concord* (2000), 492–94.

36 Epitome, Article X, in *The Book of Concord* (2000), 515–16.

37 Epitome, Article VII, in *The Book of Concord* (2000), 504–8. Also, Article VIII continued to deal with the christological questions raised by Luther's teaching on ubiquity; see *The Book of Concord* (2000), 508–14.

the continued authority of Luther's own words in adjudicating various disputes within the movement. In this regard, a major difference between the Lutheran and Reformed traditions emerged. While Lutheranism emphasized the importance of the Luther's own prophetic teaching for deciding the meaning of God's Word, the Reformed tradition has contained multiple streams under its umbrella. This is the result, in part, of the multiple starting points and theologians in the Reformed tradition—Bucer in Strasbourg, Zwingli and Bullinger in Zurich, and Calvin in Geneva all were contributors to and representatives of the Reformed tradition in the sixteenth century. While this reality did not lessen theological controversy in the Reformed tradition, it did give it a different shape. By contrast, as we have seen, Lutheran theological conflict centered on what Luther said and one's fidelity to his teaching. For Lutherans, and especially for Philip Melanchthon, it made the sixteenth century a period of theological fury—a period that Melanchthon was glad to be done with when he went to his reward.[38]

---

38 For some of the differences between the Lutheran and Reformed tradition in this regard, see Phillip Benedict, *Christ's Churches Purely Reformed: A Social History of Calvinism* (New Haven, Conn.: Yale University Press, 2004).

Chapter Thirteen

A NEW SONG BEGUN: LUTHER AND MUSIC

TERRY YOUNT

We in the twenty-first century speak of the Protestant Reformers in somewhat hushed tones—those fabled heroes who carved out a safe path for future generations to follow. Certainly, John Calvin, Huldrych Zwingli, Heinrich Bullinger, Martin Bucer, and John Knox were heroes of the faith. But only one of them was able to establish a healthy relationship with the arts that has lasted for five hundred years, and that is Luther. Although he was a theologian, he did not put forward what would amount to a systematic theology of music. Instead, he developed a paradigm for musical practice through letters and commentary, through informal communication with colleagues, and through a brilliant strategy for musical formation in the new Lutheran church.

Luther's thoughts on music for Christian worship were varied and sometimes fluid, but his ability to winsomely articulate those developing thoughts helped to nurture the young Lutheran movement. He wrote on music and its effects in several of his published works, including the preface to Georg Rhau's *Symphoniae Iucundae*, where he penned what may be the closest he came to a system of theology of music:

Here it must suffice to discuss the benefit of this great art. But even that transcends the greatest eloquence of the most eloquent, because of the infinite variety of its forms and benefits. We can mention only one point (which experience confirms), namely, that next to the word of God, music deserves the highest praise.[1]

In studying Martin Luther the musician and Reformer, we can read his own words, and we can gain further insight from scholars who have studied music's profound influence on his life. As we explore Luther's thoughts on music, we will look into the significance of Luther's musical training in his role as Reformer. Living when he did, Luther inherited medieval ideas about music theory; we will examine how these ideas show up in his writings. We will also look at the common accusation that Luther advocated the use of "bar tunes" in Christian worship, and we will conclude by considering the influence of Luther's ideas on later generations.

The heritage of Lutheranism in its first 150 years is one of a growing church music held in esteem by musicians of the era. Among those influenced by Luther were Louis Senfl, Johann Walter, and Georg Rhau, who composed, performed, or published into the next generation. Local German composers and *Kappellmeisters* approached with delighted seriousness the job of providing the newly established church with music for its congregational singing. Instrumental music grew, flourished, and expanded to include organ chorales and choral settings (with instruments) of the great texts of the church: *Magnificat*, German Mass, passion, and cantata. The German tradition was becoming the busiest in Europe, and it spawned new musicians through choir schools whose training provided competent singers and organists for the next generation.

The German musical tradition reached its pinnacle in the eighteenth century in Johann Sebastian Bach. The great composer hailed from Eisenach in Thuringia, near where Luther started his career. As Luther faced trials after posting his Ninety-Five Theses, Bach suffered criticism of the music he created. He stood his ground despite loss of income and prestige, demonstrating a Luther-like refusal to compromise beauty and truth for expediency.

Luther's rather straightforward thoughts about music continued through Bach and beyond—into the next three hundred years. By the late twentieth

---

1 "Preface to Georg Rhau's *Symphoniae Iucundae*" (1538), in *LW,* 53:323.

century, composer/writer Carl Schalk confirmed Luther's view of church music as "proclamation and ministry."[2]

Luther's Musical Training

Luther's greatest contribution is arguably his rediscovery of the glorious gospel of salvation by faith alone in Christ alone. So much did Luther exult in this truth that he proclaimed it throughout his ministry, including in doctrinally rich chorales of praise. Through music, the Reformer led thousands of followers toward a deeper understanding of God and His Word.[3] Given the role of music in his career as a theologian and Reformer, it is good for us to ask how Luther developed his musical sensibilities.

Little is known about Luther's exposure to music at home. During his student years, he studied music in the *Ratsschule* at Mansfeld, where he learned music theory, sang Psalms as a choir boy, served in Catholic processions, and learned the changing responses of the liturgical year.[4] He became an accomplished singer and lutenist, and he even transcribed "polyphonic vocal compositions for the lute."[5]

At the Augustinian monastery at Erfurt, Luther was the most musically accomplished of the monks. He was among the few who took time to write in notation what he improvised, leaving tangible proof of his skills, and he chanted for the appointed daily services or "offices." His love of music was not limited to spiritual songs, and he became a devotee of certain popular (i.e., familiar to the common people) songs improvised by the *Meistersingers* (like troubadors). He also appreciated art songs by renowned Renaissance composers, among them Josquin des Prez and Ludwig Senfl.

These varied experiences begat in Luther a hearty appreciation of music that informed his work in the early years of the German Reformation. As he labored to establish a new, biblical form of worship in Reformation churches, Luther composed, collected, or commissioned songs that married congregational usefulness with his own sense of their doctrinal suitability. As a performer and composer, Luther encouraged music at every level.

---

2 Carl F. Schalk, *Luther on Music: Paradigms of Praise* (St. Louis: Concordia, 1988), 51.

3 Jeremy S. Begbie, *Resounding Truth: Christian Wisdom in the World of Music* (Grand Rapids, Mich.: Baker Academic, 2007), 104.

4 Schalk, *Luther on Music*, 13.

5 Ibid., 20.

Luther's Musical Ideals

As Europe emerged from the medieval period, its culture was ripe for change. Musicians and artists in the sixteenth century began to create a new synthesis of the humanities and arts. Sixteenth-century Europeans grew more sophisticated in their preferences for poetry, painting, and music that celebrated man and his ideas.

Despite these changes, Martin Luther remained a medieval man when it came to music. While his contemporaries were questioning music's place in the classical quadrivium—the classical curriculum that also included arithmetic, geometry, and astronomy—Luther was not so quick to do so. This curriculum had enjoyed wide acceptance: "arithmetic, geometry, music, and astronomy—four sciences that were studied alongside the trivium of grammar, logic, and rhetoric. Together, the quadrivial and trivial arts formed the corpus of learning in the arts faculty of the medieval university." [6] Luther was a staunch advocate for what has been called the "Great Tradition."

Though Luther could argue his love of Jesus (and music) with any humanist, his musical ideals were moored in the previous 1,100 years of tradition, going back to Augustine and Boethius. The Great Tradition of medieval theologians and philosophers provided Luther with a framework out of which to define but also to practice music. Luther no doubt had to study Boethius, especially book one of his five-part treatise *De Institutione Musica*. And, like any good student, he absorbed the sixth-century Roman philosopher's musical views.

Boethius distinguished between three kinds of music: "The first is music of the spheres [*mundana*]; the second is music of the body [*humana*]; and the third [is] that which is made by certain instruments [*instrumentalis*], for example, the *kithara* or the *aulos* and others which assist with songs." [7] The "music of the spheres" is a kind of unheard music that expresses celestial harmony; the "music of the body" is a harmony that unites body and soul; and music by instruments is that which we typically think of as music.

Luther's debt to this tradition can be seen in his distinction between "natural" and "artificial" music. However, he slightly adjusted his fidelity to

---

6   Andreas Loewe, *"Musica est optimum": Martin Luther's Theory of Music* (dissertation, Melbourne College of Divinity, Australia 2013), 6, http://ml.oxfordjournals.org/content/early/2013/12/19/ml.gct133.

7   Translated from the original Latin found online: *Thesaurus Musicarum Latinarum* http://www.chmtl.indiana.edu/tml/start.html.

Boethius, according to Jeremy Begbie. He refused to elevate the theoretical above the practical and emphasized the goodness of the created realm (and the creative acts that men do in the midst of it):

> His main interest is not in music as a vehicle through which we rise to mathematical comprehension (although he may have believed this). The stress is on music as full and glorious, a *good gift*, with little sense that its physical, material, and sensual nature is a potential hindrance to union with God. Moreover, Luther does not treat practical music making as secondary and inferior to the theoretical discipline of music; hence . . . his massive investment in music as practiced.[8]

For Luther, music was a primary force for all things emotional. He saw music as serving the purposes of the church to "turn the hearts" of all within earshot of the true gospel:

> Experience testifies that, after the Word of God, music alone deserves to be celebrated as mistress and queen of the emotions of the human heart (of animals nothing is to be said at present). And by these emotions men are controlled and often swept away as by their lords. A greater praise of music than this we cannot conceive. For if you want to revive the sad, startle the jovial, encourage the despairing, humble the conceited, pacify the raving, mollify the hate-filled—and who is able to enumerate all the lords of the human heart, I mean the emotions of the heart and the urges which incite a man to all virtues and vices?—what can you find that is more efficacious than music?[9]

The enthusiasm Luther felt for music was not without sobriety. In fact, he ends his introduction to Georg Rhau's collection of contrapuntal motets[10] with a sense of caution:

> Take special care to shun perverted minds who prostitute this lovely gift of nature and of art with their erotic rantings; and be quite assured that none but the devil goads them on to defy their very nature which

---

8 Begbie, *Resounding Truth*, 100. Emphasis original.
9 *WA*, 50:371f; *What Luther Says*, 2:982–83.
10 Jeremy S. Begbie, *Music, Modernity, and God* (London: Oxford University Press, 2013), 30.

would and should praise God its Maker with this gift, so that these bastards purloin the gift of God and use it to worship the foe of God, the enemy of nature and of this lovely art.[11]

Augustine had warned about the pernicious influence of erotic, sensuous music. Luther had read Augustine, but unlike the great bishop of Hippo, he was no enemy of music's powers. In fact, it was the power of music to effect joy that gave Luther reason to praise it. Luther further saw the power present in musical performance as a catalyst for the growth of the church. In keeping with his general liberality toward culture as a gift of God, Luther included music within his paradigm to awaken all believers:

I firmly believe, nor am I ashamed to assert, that next to theology no art is equal to music; for it is the only one, except theology, which is able to give a quiet and happy mind. This is manifestly proved by the fact that the devil, the author of depressing care and distressing disturbances, almost flees from the sound of music as he does from the word of theology. This is the reason why the prophets practiced music more than any art and did not put their theology into geometry, into arithmetic, or into astronomy, but into music, intimately uniting theology and music, telling the truth in psalms and songs.[12]

Unlike his younger contemporary John Calvin, Luther was not driven primarily to protect parishioners from music's potential power. Calvin famously retained a profound suspicion for music:

But when they [believers] frequent their sacred assemblies, musical instruments in celebrating the praises of God would be no more suitable than the burning of incense, the lighting up of lamps, and the restoration of the other shadows of the law. The Papists, therefore, have foolishly borrowed this, as well as many other things, from the Jews . . . but we should always take care that no corruption creep in which might both defile the pure worship of God and involve men in superstition.[13]

---

11 *LW,* 53:324.
12 Letters of 1528–1530, *WABr,* 5:639; *What Luther Says,* 2:983; cf. *LW,* 49:428.
13 John Calvin, *Commentary on Psalms,* 5:320.

Luther maintained that in creation, music and the arts are manifestations of God's image in man. In fact, he evaluated those who lacked proper appreciation for music: "I am not satisfied with him who despises music, as all fanatics do; for music is an endowment and a gift of God, not a gift of men. It also drives away the devil and makes people cheerful; one forgets all anger, unchasteness, pride, and other vices. I place music next to theology and give it the highest praise."[14]

In his speaking and writing, then, Luther carved out a fresh musical paradigm. Though he inherited the medieval understanding of music, he did not adopt it uncritically. Instead, he built upon the medieval paradigm, resulting in a fresh and novel approach. Indeed, music was Luther's apparent inspiration, his resource, as he resisted, fled from, and eventually overcame the civil and ecclesiastical authorities who opposed his Ninety-Five Theses in 1517 and beyond.[15]

Luther's Tunes

Luther asserted that by praising God in music, humans were enabled to "to taste with wonder (but not to comprehend fully) the absolute and perfect wisdom of God in his wonderful work of Music."[16] Worship in the earliest Lutheran parishes included rudimentary instruction in the gospel, in sound doctrine, and in the practice of godly singing. Largely due to a growing unrest among the populace, Luther's ideas were welcomed with open arms. The newly allowed congregational practice of singing rustic chorales was a boon to the early Reformation. In keeping with the spirit of the age, community singing was a breath of fresh air to the poor, often downtrodden, working-class folk who resented church officials' keeping company with the sometimes oppressive nobility. But were there sinister, clandestine sources

---

14 *WATR*, 6:7034; *What Luther Says*, 2:980.

15 Luther was of the opinion that "music enabled people to endure the very *Anfechtungen* that led him to challenge the late-medieval doctrine of justification in the first place is theologically significant. Like the scholastic supernatural habit of grace, music also was a free gift [*Gabe, donum*] created by God. Like the habit of grace, music was in itself grace-filled [*gnadenreich*]. Like the habit of grace, music had a profound effect on the human soul, encouraging and enabling other habits of goodness and grace. In this way, while it was not in itself an agent of justification, music contributed to the formation of a character or *habitus* that closely resembled the late-scholastic supernatural habit of grace [*gratia creata*]. As Luther made clear in his *Marginalia to Peter Lombard's Sentences* (1509–12), rejecting the scholastic distinction between created and uncreated grace as artificial, "that habit is the Holy Spirit." Loewe, "*Musica est optimum.*"

16 *WA*, 50:372, 12–13.

for these chorales? Did Martin Luther endorse "bar tunes" for use in Christian worship?

Luther was careful with his sources, but he rarely denied the value of a good tune. His chorales were derived from community songs, Gregorian chants, and *Meistersinger* melodies performed at courts and community fairs. In one of his chorale books, *Geistliche Gesangbuch* (Spiritual songbook), published in 1524, Luther included artful part songs written in sophisticated counterpoint. Later on, his friend and composer Johann Walter wrote complex motets for worship. By mid-century, it was clear that the new Lutheran chorale tradition, at first known for simple melodies and strong rhythmic patterns, had inspired a measure of quality and artfulness. This further distanced the Reformers in Germany from the church in Rome.

Luther himself was a composer, and it is well known he wrote texts and tunes for a number of German chorales, including *"Wir glauben all an einen Gott"* (We all believe in one God), *"Ein' feste Burg ist unser Gott"* (A mighty fortress is our God), and the *Sanctus* from the German Mass. In keeping with *Meistersinger* tradition, Luther set his own texts to music and played them for gathered crowds.[17] It was his careful fusing of lyrical beauty with good theology, then, that gave his hymns a particular effect. By 1545, this version of *"Ein' feste Burg"* was published, still with its isorhythms (repeating patterns) from the *Meistersinger* tradition.

Since the musical form of this and many other chorales was known as "bar tunes" or held to a "bar form," some have accused Luther of appropriating musical forms from taverns. The implication is that it would be inappropriate to import such licentious tunes into the sanctuary (others, more approvingly, use such a practice to justify the use of popular forms of music in church today).

However, such tunes are called "bar tunes" not because of their origin, but because of their structure. The term refers to a musical notation, the bar, indicating that the melody of the first line is to be repeated.[18] Over the last five

---

17 Schalk, *Luther on Music*, 26.

18 Bar form, in music, the structural pattern *aab* as used by the medieval German *Minnesingers* and *Meistersingers*, who were poet-composers of secular monophonic songs (i.e., those having a single line of melody). The modern term *bar form* derives from a medieval verse form, the *bar*, consisting of three stanzas, each having the form *aab*. The musical term thus refers to the melody of a single stanza, the *a* sections (called *Stollen*) having the same melody, and the *b* section (*Abgesang*) having a different melody. *Encyclopaedia Britannica Online*, s.v. "Bar form," accessed 1-5-15, http://www.britannica.com/EBchecked/topic/52460/Bar-form.

hundred years, this form has been in use commonly, and has no connection to consuming ale in a tavern.

Although these hymns were perhaps rhythmically more driving, Lutheran musicians eventually began to refine the rustic simplicity inherent to the German chorales. Only a generation or two later, organists and choral composers such as Heinrich Schütz and Samuel Scheidt set about creating ornamented and elaborate versions of the once-simple chorales. By the middle of the seventeenth century, early Baroque chorale cantatas and passions, with their elaborate choral settings, bypassed the simple chorale tune tradition and soon became weekly fare at the larger urban churches.

Luther loved to gather his family and sing songs, play the lute, and enjoy music for its own sake. His newly formed churches in central Germany were now in need of a repertoire of sung praise in the German language. Two publications of 1524 met the need. The first was the *Achtliderbuch* (Eight-song book), originally titled *Etlich Cristlich lider Lobgesang . . . in der Kirchen zu singen* (Some Christian songs to sing in the church). The other was *Enchiridion oder eyn Handbüchlein* (An enchiridion or a little handbook); it contained twenty-five poems to sixteen melodies, in two volumes. These books contained only melodies for unison singing.[19]

Chief among some of the newer forms employed in Lutheran churches in the seventeenth century are the chorale cantata and the chorale-based passion. In both cases, as composers became familiar enough with the newly applied tradition of chorale tunes, they were able to base entire multimovement works on one or more chorales. An example would be *Passion according to St. Luke* by Heinrich Schütz. During a period of study in Venice, the young composer learned Italian vocal style. He returned to Germany to write remarkably dramatic settings of the texts from the week before Easter.

As the now-century-old Lutheran movement progressed, more chorales, including elaborate motets based on them, along with vocal part songs that could only have been sung by a trained choir, were performed in many urban churches. There was money to support concert performances, such as Buxtehude's *Abendmusiken* (Evening music) series at Marienkirchen in Lübeck, furthering the developing musical life of central and northern Germany.

---

19 Willi Apel, ed., *Harvard Dictionary of Music,* 2nd ed. (Cambridge, Mass.: The Belknap Press of Harvard University Press, 1969), 158.

Luther's Influence

It had been Luther's practice to establish schools for children of the new Lutheran faith, to ground them in grammar and the rhetorical arts, including music. Over the years, this method of inculcating the ecclesiastical solidarity of Lutherans nationally was more than effective. Indeed, there was a virtual explosion in singing, composing, and commissioning music and in concert performances. The chorale-based cantatas with their Italian forms opened a well of rich musical activity in Germany. They and the passion settings, based on accounts in John and Luke, paved the long road to the eventual masterpieces of the next generation.

By the late 1600s, a young Saxon organist began as a chorister and eventually set about creating even larger and more elaborate vocal and instrumental music for the Saxon cities where he served. His name was Johann Sebastian Bach.

Dietrich Buxtehude (1637–1707) in Lübeck to the north, Johann Pachelbel (1653–1706) in the south, and Georg Böhm (1661–1733) in Thuringia (where Bach spent his early years) wrote organ chorale settings that were often used to introduce the Sunday tunes to the congregations they served. These masters of organ and choral composition heavily influenced the young Eisenach-born organist. Their advocacy of the maturing chorale tradition— chorale preludes, fantasias, and fugues—resulted in the direct transmission of tunes that had been sung by sixteenth-century Lutherans, to the sophisticated choirs and organist/cantors of Lübeck, Lüneberg, and Hamburg. And in an era of largely improvised hymn and chorale introductions, these organists took the time to write their works out for future players and churches. These works are now not only still used in liturgies throughout the Western church, but they also have become the best training ground for young organists learning the delicate intricacies of pedal and hand coordination.

Bach, who by 1723 had assumed the post of cantor in the university city of Lübeck, was well versed in these traditions, with one important caveat. Bach, who was noted for his ability to soak up the various traditions around him, was not satisfied to limit his study to the chorale and cantata forms of his mentors. He also copied scores by French composers such as Nicolas De Grigny and the Italian composers Corelli and Vivaldi, and he imbibed other styles and forms including dance suites, secular operatic works, and more.[20]

---

20 Peter Washington, *Bach, Everyman's Library—EMI Classics Music Companions* (New York: Alfred A. Knopf, 1997), 30.

All these influences began to show themselves in Bach's compositions for organ, harpsichord, choir, orchestra, and solo voice. The result was a truly Lutheran musician, a man after Luther's own heart, who agreed with his two-centuries-removed mentor that next to theology, music, in all its magnificent forms, is the greatest art. We may estimate the depth of Bach's admiration for the Erfurt theologian from his library, which, at his death, contained more than eighty volumes of Luther's collected writings.

We also know there was a genuine affection in Bach for the chorale texts and tunes that the mighty Luther penned as he (and the people's rebellion) gradually pushed back against the Roman Catholic Church authorities. Bach's Luther was the progenitor, the rebel with a cause, the catalyst for all that was lasting in theology and music. One might expect this great liturgical tradition to continue into the next generation. Tragically, that was rarely the case.

After the towering Bach, very little can be said of his successors. Music scholars generally agree that the second half of the eighteenth century experienced a decline in its liturgical practice and in the overall output of church composers. As the center of compositional and performing activity moved farther away from the church and toward the concert hall and opera house, compositional output in the churches diminished. In Lutheranism, a parallel movement away from orthodoxy and toward an emotion-based pietism focused the church inward. Worship and its music became enmeshed in a sentimentalism based in human experience and moved away from the objective gospel of the Bible and the Reformers.

While the buildings and grand traditions were usually maintained in Germany's larger urban churches, rural churches often experienced a definite decline in their music. Training schools for choirs, once the center of education for Lutheran children who were headed toward vocations in the church, were closed in some cities.

Even Bach suffered a period of underappreciation. Though he was remembered mainly for his legendary organ playing, he composed more than three hundred cantatas, passions, and concerti that were tucked away in storage in Leipzig and the other cities where he worked. Eventually, most of Bach's music was gathered and safely deposited in manuscript libraries, where students and scholars have studied it. Though Bach was extremely influential, disinterest in his church music continued, despite the best efforts of Bach scholars.

Then, young Felix Mendelssohn dusted off Bach's *St Matthew Passion* for its return to public consumption in a Leipzig performance in the 1820s. Bach was back, eighty years after he dictated some of his final notes to his assistant.

Thankfully, today there is a resurgence of interest in fine church music, both historical and current. One of the centers for a Lutheran musical revival, the Japan Bach Collegium, has recorded under its director, Masaaki Suzuki, almost the entire corpus of Bach's works for chorus and orchestra. As European and American university and conservatory students rediscover some of the greatest music of the period from Luther to Bach, it is being replayed. Music from that period (and more recent music as well) is hailed for its beauty. Remarkably, some of Bach's scores are still being uncovered.

Luther's Musical Legacy

Luther's warm enthusiasm for music in all its powerful forms is best found in his own words, which still resonate from concert hall to church nave to classroom:

> I, Doctor Martin Luther, wish all lovers of the unshackled art of music grace and peace from God the Father and from our Lord Jesus Christ! I truly desire that all Christians would love and regard as worthy the lovely gift of music, which is a precious, worthy, and costly treasure given to mankind by God. The riches of music are so excellent and so precious that words fail me whenever I attempt to discuss and describe them. . . . In summa, next to the Word of God, the noble art of music is the greatest treasure in the world. It controls our thoughts, minds, hearts, and spirits. . . . Our dear fathers and prophets did not desire without reason that music be always used in the churches. Hence, we have so many songs and psalms. This precious gift has been given to man alone that he might thereby remind himself that God has created man for the express purpose of praising and extolling God. However, when man's natural musical ability is whetted and polished to the extent that it becomes an art, then do we note with great surprise the great and perfect wisdom of God in music, which is, after all, His product and His gift; we marvel when we hear music in which one voice sings a simple melody, while three, four, or five other voices play and trip lustily around the voice that sings its simple melody and adorn this simple melody wonderfully with artistic musical effects, thus reminding us of a heavenly dance,

where all meet in a spirit of friendliness, caress and embrace. A person who gives this some thought and yet does not regard music as a marvelous creation of God, must be a clodhopper indeed and does not deserve to be called a human being; he should be permitted to hear nothing but the braying of asses and the grunting of hogs.[21]

Luther's legacy is best measured in the categories where he expressed himself. First, he was a scholar who believed in the value of the written word, including letters, sermons, and his thirty-six hymns.[22] Through his vast writings, he blazed trails for other Reformers who would follow him.

Second, he was able to articulate his position in underscoring music's power and unquestioned influence on the human heart while remaining convinced that its power could be abused and should be curbed when necessary.

Third, his musical tastes ranged from the vocal polyphony of art music composers such as Josquin des Prez to tunes such as "*O Welt, ich muss dich lassen*" (O world, I now must leave thee), which he borrowed and transformed from Heinrich Isaac's beautiful "Innsbruck, I Now Must Leave Thee."[23]

Fourth, Luther's understanding of musical style proved useful in a growing Lutheran church where vestiges of old Roman rites remained, but in which singing chorales such as "*Ein' feste Burg ist unser Gott*" was a unifying element. His chorales combined vital biblical theology and freshly derived music.

Fifth, Luther embraced all the arts, including painting, stained glass, organ, architecture, and poetry. He affirmed their value even as others in the quickly moving Reformation were condemning them: "Nor am I at all of the opinion that all the arts are to be overthrown and cast aside by the Gospel, as some super spiritual people protest; but I would gladly see all the arts, especially music, in the service of Him who has given and created them."[24]

In all the crosscurrents of the modern worship discussion, few have this enlarged view of the arts. Indeed, lack of appreciation for the arts, even with a clear declaration of the gospel, is a truncated approach to evangelism. One of the hallmarks of Luther's spiritual and aesthetic maturity was that the *adiaphora* benefit the proclamation of the gospel, when properly managed and

---

21 "Preface to Georg Rhau's *Symphoniae Iucundae*," in *LW*, 53:323. Quoted in John Barber, "Luther and Calvin on Music and Worship," *Reformed Perspectives Magazine* 8, no. 26 (2006): 1–16.
22 Barber, "Luther and Calvin," 1.
23 Ibid., 4.
24 Ibid., 6.

sensitively encouraged throughout the church's life. Perhaps, then, if Luther were allowed a glimpse into the modern evangelical church, he would scratch his head at much that he saw.

The five-hundred-year legacy of Luther's life and work, from a musical perspective, is considerable. God used Luther to enrich the true church of Jesus Christ with music. Since the first days of the Reformation heroes, he alone among his contemporaries held out this hope: that in using choirs, bells, stringed and brass instruments, and richly derived polyphony, not all was rejected as the property of the Roman Catholic Church. Though these things were connected in many people's minds to the pope and his minions, the things themselves were in fact just things, and could be used again, in another age, with a different spirit, for the greater glory of God who created all things.

Luther innovated in the use of music in the education of children as they learned catechism, pastors as they learned theology, and a fledgling church as it experienced congregational singing anew. Luther never let the devil turn him away from supporting and advocating the truths of the Bible, and he used music to cheer his soul in the process. Luther, in his ecstatic support of God's gift of music, used it as a weapon against "all anger, unchasteness, pride, and other vices." As a student of the Word of God and an amateur musician himself, he wrote, "Reason sees the world as extremely ungodly, and therefore it murmurs. The spirit sees nothing but God's benefits in the world and therefore begins to sing."[25]

All the volumes of words written to describe Luther's impact on the West for the last five hundred years pale in comparison to Luther's own sense of gratitude to God for the precious gift of music. We can be likewise thankful that God allowed this German monk the years he worked, in order that the world might be a more truthful, good, and beautiful place.

---

25 Quoted in Begbie, *Resounding Truth*, 100.

Chapter Fourteen

SPARE EVERYTHING BUT THE WORD: LUTHER AS PREACHER

DEREK W.H. THOMAS

"The Protestant Reformation would not have been possible without the sermon," the historian Harold Grimm wrote. Reflecting on the importance of sermons during the Reformation period, Grimm continued: "Regardless of how the reformers gained their new theological insights, they used the sermon to bring their doctrines directly to their followers in the vernacular and to apply those doctrines to the immediate and practical religious needs of the people. Since the pulpit was one of the most important means of communicating information in the sixteenth century, the role of the sermon in making the Reformation a mass movement can scarcely be overestimated."[1]

By any standard, Martin Luther had a high view of sermons and preaching. "When the preacher speaks, God speaks," he once wrote.[2] Reflecting Swiss views expressed in the 1560s by Heinrich Bullinger and others in the

---

1 Harold J. Grimm, "The Human Element in Luther's Sermons," in *Archiv fur Reformationsgeschichte*, 49 (1958), 50.
2 *WA*, 51:517. Cited by Fred W. Meuser, "Luther as Preacher of the Word of God," in McKim, ed., *The Cambridge Companion to Martin Luther*, 136. See also Meuser's definitive volume *Luther the Preacher*, 11.

Second Helvetic Confession,[3] Luther had something to say to those who did not share this view of preaching: "So the pastor must be sure that God speaks through his mouth. Otherwise it is time for him to be quiet."[4] Elsewhere, Luther put it this way: "The apostles wrote very little, but they spoke a lot. . . . Notice: it says let their voices be heard, not let their books be read. The ministry of the New Testament is not engraved on dead tablets of stone; rather it sounds in a living voice. . . . Through a living Word God accomplishes and fulfills his gospel."[5]

Luther's high view of preaching must, of course, be set in the context of the Reformation as a movement of reform, or change—change both in the content and manner of preaching. In his massive seven-volume analysis of the history of preaching, Hughes Oliphant Old comments: "The classical Protestant Reformation produced a distinct school of preaching. It was a preaching of reform, to be sure, but it was also a reform of preaching."[6] Old points out that the Reformation did not reintroduce preaching. The medieval church had a great deal of preaching, but "it was a bit like the churches in which it took place: flamboyant and gothic." Old summarizes, "What happened was that with the Reformation came a refocusing of preaching, a rethinking of its purpose and reevaluation of its relation to the worship of the Church."[7]

Perhaps we do not think of Luther, first of all, as a preacher but as a stalwart teacher and defender of the doctrine of justification by faith alone. However, statistics concerning his lifelong preaching ministry reveal a very different perspective. Upon receiving his doctorate in 1512, Luther's life was that of an academic. He was professor of biblical studies at the University of

---

3 See chapter 1 of the Second Helvetic Confession's statement, "The preaching of the Word of God is the Word of God." Scholars have made much of this insistence that preaching *is* the Word of God. Heiko Oberman views it in connection with the Eucharistic "real presence" in Luther's view of the supper, and David Steinmetz viewed preaching as Luther's "third sacrament." See Heiko A. Oberman, "The Preaching of the Word of God in the Reformation," *Harvard Divinity Bulletin* 25 (October 1960): 16; David C. Steinmetz, *Luther in Context*, 2nd ed. (Grand Rapids, Mich.: Baker Academic, 2002), 134.

4 Bruno Jordan, "Die Auferstehung Christi von den Toten in Luthers Osterpredigten," *Luther: Mitteilungen der Luthergesellschaft* 1995:13. Cited by Meuser, *Luther the Preacher*, 12.

5 *WA*, 5:537, as quoted in Arthur Skevington Wood, *Captive to the Word: Martin Luther, Doctor of Sacred Scripture* (Grand Rapids, Mich.: Eerdmans, 1969), 90.

6 Hughes Oliphant Old, *The Reading and Preaching of the Scriptures in the Worship of the Christian Church, Vol. 4: The Age of the Reformation* (Grand Rapids, Mich.: Eerdmans, 2002), 1.

7 Ibid.

Wittenberg. As Garry Williams points out, "Luther was never a minister."[8] It is therefore somewhat surprising that Luther preached as much as he did.

From the moment Johann von Staupitz assigned him to preach in the monastery in 1511, Luther preached about four thousand sermons (approximately 2,300 have survived) during the course of his life, most of them in the town church (*Stadtkirche*) in Wittenberg. Allowing for a two-year gap in preaching, Luther preached on average 120 sermons a year, or one sermon every three days. In 1528, he preached two hundred sermons. There were three preaching services in Wittenberg every Sunday, the first one starting at 5 a.m. In addition, there were sermons on weekdays and Saturdays. During the Passiontide of 1529, for example, Luther preached eighteen times in eleven days.

The Weimar edition of Luther's works, also known as the *Weimarer Ausgabe*, contains 122 volumes, of which twenty-two consist of Luther's sermons translated into English (and in some cases, Latin). They are not in German—the language in which Luther preached all his sermons. The process of recording the sermons (shorthand taken down by a variety of scribes) and the translation process means that some of the rhetoric and flow of the spoken word has been lost. The sermons may read much more formally than they were delivered. Something of the passion of their delivery is perhaps absent.

In addition to his own sermons, Luther was also realistic concerning the needs of churches without trained preachers of the caliber he desired. To make up for this, he wrote several books (postils) for other preachers to preach or even read—"expository sermonettes for clergy who could not write sermons of their own."[9]

Reading these sermons (Luther's own and the postils) may convey entirely the wrong impression. The Reformers, generally, did not write out their sermons and read them. Luther entered the pulpit with a *Konzept* (a short outline containing the "heads" of the sermon) that elaborated on the lectionary text for the day. Since there was little by way of precedent, his students referred to it as "the heroic method."[10] They were studied and thought

---

8   Garry J. Williams, *Silent Witnesses: Lessons on Theology, Life, and the Church from Christians of the Past* (Edinburgh, Scotland: Banner of Truth, 2013), 190. See especially the chapter "Preaching the Word: Martin Luther (1483–1546)," 189–203.

9   "Martin Luther," in *The Collected Shorter Writings of J.I. Packer, Vol. 4: Honouring the People of God* (Carlisle, Pa.: Paternoster, 1999), 12. See also *The Complete Sermons of Martin Luther*.

10 Richard Lischer, preface to *Faith and Freedom: An Invitation to the Writings of Martin Luther*, eds. John F. Thornton and Susan B. Varenne (New York: Random House, 2002), xxiv.

out beforehand for sure, but their delivery was extemporary and immediate, spoken in the common vernacular. Unlike Calvin's Geneva, where one stenographer, Denis Raguenier, took down word-for-word what Calvin said in French (employing a shorthand system), Luther's sermons were taken down by several stenographers. The number of stenographers probably varied. The notes, partly in German and partly in Latin, were then collated and written up in Latin only later to be retranslated into German. Getting a feel for the flow of words is therefore a difficult task. But some things are very clear, not least of which is Luther's absolute commitment to the authority of Scripture.

Commitment to the Authority of Scripture

The theological commitments that Luther grasped in the turbulent years between 1512 and 1517, and maintained steadfastly thereafter, included a commitment to the authority of Scripture. For Luther, this meant denying the role given to ecclesiastical tradition, papal pronouncements, canon law, and allegorical interpretations of Scripture.[11] This was, in effect, a commitment to the "literal" interpretation of Scripture. This meant interpreting Scripture according to the rules of literature—history as history, law as law, parable as parable, etc. Since all of Scripture is the Word of God—without contradiction, since Scripture is of divine origin—Luther viewed preaching as subject to Scripture's authority. What right, after all, did any human being have to declare to another that he must conform to this or that, apart from divine authority? The only justification to exercise such control over the consciences of men and women is a divine authority based on the nature of Scripture as the Word of God.

Luther would have agreed with the English Calvinist theologian-preacher William Perkins, who, a half-century after Luther's death, wrote in what might be the very first book on preaching, *The Arte of Prophecying* (1607): "The Word of God alone is to be preached, in its perfection, and inner consistency. Scripture is the exclusive subject of preaching, the only field in which the preacher is to labour."[12]

The preacher's principal task, then, is to explain and apply the Scriptures.

---

11 Gary Williams somewhat controversially draws positive attention to Luther's christological reading of Psalm 69, suggesting that it should give us pause to consider what he thinks of as the overemphasis given to grammatical-historical exegesis, or the plain reading of Scripture in our time. Williams, *Silent Witnesses*, 190f.

12 William Perkins, *The Art of Prophesying* (Edinburgh, Scotland: Banner of Truth, 1996), 9.

Not all Scripture is equally clear, and Luther told his students that the exegete/ preacher should treat a difficult passage no differently than Moses did the rock in the desert, which he smote with his rod until water gushed out for his thirsty people.[13]

Keeping Things Simple

By far, the most extensive analysis of Luther's preaching is by Fred Meuser in his marvelous summary *Luther the Preacher* (1983). According to Meuser, Luther was well liked as a preacher. He "spoke slowly but with great vigor and often had a moving effect upon the hearers."[14] Given what we know about his convictions, it would be hard to imagine that Luther's preaching was dull and devoid of rhetorical passion. It is equally hard to fathom, then, that Luther felt the need to chastise some who did not listen well, saying that some fell asleep and some even snored during the sermon, adding that they sometimes coughed whenever he preached on justification, only to wake up again whenever he told a story.[15] Times do not seem to have changed. All the more reason, then, for the Reformer to keep his sermons relatively simple and straightforward.

Those who have studied Luther's theological works find themselves in deep waters. Luther's theology is complex at best.[16] Concepts such as his theology of the cross (*theologia crucis*), the doctrine of consubstantiation, and the exact distinction between law and gospel (did Luther advance in his understanding of the so-called third use of the law, as some have suggested?) continue to occupy scholars of Luther to this day. Is it surprising, then, that Luther's preaching was essentially simple and plain? Not really. According to Hughes Oliphant Old, Luther "made no attempt to be a great orator." Old expands, "[Luther] had none of the rhetorical culture that Basil, Chrysostom, or Augustine had. Luther was a popular preacher with a natural mastery of language. He taught preachers of the Reformation to preach in the language

---

13 Oberman, *Luther: Man between God and the Devil,* 224.

14 Meuser, "Luther as Preacher of the Word of God," 144.

15 Ibid.

16 For Crisp summaries of Luther's central thought, see Carl R. Trueman, *Luther's Legacy: Salvation and English Reformers 1525-1556* (Oxford, England: Clarendon, 1994), 54–80; Steven Paulson, *Luther for Armchair Theologians* (Louisville, Ky.: Westminster John Knox, 2004); Markus Wriedt, "Luther's Theology," trans. Katarina Gustavs, in McKim, ed., *The Cambridge Companion to Martin Luther,* 86–119.

of the people."[17] Garry Williams cites a similar statement that Luther makes in his *Table Talk*:

> In the pulpit we are to lay bare the breasts and nourish the people with milk. . . . Complicated thoughts and issues we should discuss in private with the eggheads [*Klueglinge*]. I don't think of Dr. Pomeraneus, Jonas, or Philip [Melanchthon] in my sermon. They know more about it than I do. So I don't preach to them. I just preach to Hansie and Betsy.[18]

Although Luther had been schooled in classical rhetoric as part of the awakening of the Renaissance movement in late-medieval Europe, the Reformer seemed deliberately to avoid its more elaborate affectations, employing in its place a more conversational style.[19] He was, for example, particularly scornful of the use of Hebrew in the pulpit. Though able to converse in both Greek and Hebrew with the best of Renaissance scholarship—scholarship that had triumphed in returning to the sources for meaning (*ad fontes*)—Luther did not employ Greek and Hebrew terms in his sermons. Williams cites Luther's acerbic comment about Zwingli: "How I do hate people who lug in so many languages as Zwingli does; he spoke Greek and Hebrew in the pulpit at Marburg."[20]

Despite these warnings, Luther was firmly committed to the study of the original languages and urged that all preachers have the same passion:

> Though the faith and the Gospel may be proclaimed by simple preachers without the languages, such preaching is flat and tame, men grow at last wearied and disgusted and it falls to the ground. But when the preacher is versed in the languages, his discourse has freshness and force, the whole of Scripture is treated, and faith finds itself constantly renewed by a continual variety of words and works.[21]

---

17 Old, *The Reading and Preaching of the Scriptures*, 4:5–6.

18 *WABr*, 3:3421. Cited by Meuser, "Luther as Preacher of the Word of God," 144–45. A slightly different rendition of this quotation is cited by Williams, *Silent Witnesses*, 194.

19 Old suggests that he avoided Aristotle and even Augustine in favor of Quintilian. *The Reading and Preaching of the Scriptures*, 6.

20 Williams, *Silent Witnesses*, 195.

21 Hugh T. Kerr, *A Compend of Luther's Theology* (Whitefish, Mont.: Kessinger, 2010), 148.

On another occasion, Luther is even stronger in urging the use of the original languages:

> It is a sin and shame not to know our own book or to understand the speech and words of our God; it is a still greater sin and loss that we do not study languages, especially in these days when God is offering and giving us men and books and every facility and inducement to this study, and desires his Bible to be an open book. O how happy the dear fathers would have been if they had our opportunity to study the languages and come thus prepared to the Holy Scriptures! What great toil and effort it cost them to gather up a few crumbs, while we with half the labor—yes, almost without any labor at all—can acquire the whole loaf! O how their effort puts our indolence to shame.[22]

Commenting on these statements of Luther, John Piper makes the following deduction:

> Now that is a discouraging overstatement for many pastors who have lost their Greek and Hebrew. What I would say is that knowing the languages can make any devoted preacher a better preacher—more fresh, more faithful, more confident, more penetrating. But it is possible to preach faithfully without them—at least for a season. . . . The test of our faithfulness to the Word, if we cannot read the languages, is this: Do we have a large enough concern for the church of Christ to promote their preservation and widespread teaching and use in the churches? Or do we, out of self-protection, minimize their importance because to do otherwise stings too badly?[23]

Luther's insistence upon simplicity of language is, in part at least, a byproduct of the free delivery of his sermons; his sermons were extemporaneous rather than read from a manuscript. This fact alone almost guarantees that the language employed is simpler, ensuring that if a complex thought is uttered, sufficient explanation is given to elucidate it, drawn from (among other things) eye contact with one's listeners that often reveals understanding

---

22 Meuser, *Luther the Preacher*, 43.

23 John Piper, *The Legacy of Sovereign Joy: God's Triumphant Grace in the Lives of Augustine, Luther, and Calvin* (Wheaton, Ill.: Crossway, 2006), 99.

or perplexity. One puzzled look from a listener, or clear signs that no one is actually listening, will urge simplicity of language—repeating a thought in different language until the point is made clear.

Perhaps one way to get a grasp of Luther's sermonic style is to attempt an outline of one of his sermons. A sermon on Luke 21:25–36,[24] delivered on the lectionary text for the second Sunday of Advent, 1522, reveals the following outline:

I. The signs of the day of judgment
   A. In general
      1. Although manifold and great, the world pays no attention to these signs
      2. Whether some will recognize these signs when they come
   B. In detail
      1. The first class of these signs
         a. In the secular world, everything has reached its climax
         b. In spiritual things, everything has reached its climax, especially the abominations of the papacy
      2. The second class of these signs
         a. The darkening of the sun
         b. The moon shall not give its light
         c. The fall of the stars
         d. The people on earth will be in distress and perplexity (further subdivided)
         e. The roaring of the sea (further subdivided)
         f. Men fainting for fear (further subdivided)
         g. The shaking of the powers of the heavens (further subdivided)
      3. The third class of these signs

II. The comfort Christians have when these signs appear
   A. How and why this comfort will be given to all true Christians
      1. Why believers pray God for the coming of the day of judgment
      2. What we are to think of those who fear before the day of judgment

---

24 The sermon can be viewed online at http://www.martinluthersermons.com/sermons2.html.

3. The day of judgment will be welcome in the highest degree to believers, but to the godless it will be terrifying in the highest degree

4. What we are to answer those who fear the day of judgment, because they still have sin

5. Who are the best armed for the day of judgment

B. The nature of this comfort

C. What moved Christ to impart this comfort

D. How the visionary preachers withhold their comfort from poor souls

   1. Few people pray the Lord's prayer aright

   2. The right and the wrong use of the fear of the day of judgment

In the printed form, the sermon was divided into sixty-eight numbered paragraphs for simplicity of reading. The outline looks cumbersome, but in fact the structure is entirely an expositional commentary on the text, similar in many respects to Calvin's preaching in Geneva. Like so many of Calvin's sermons, Luther's sermons were rarely delivered with obvious transitions from one point to another or the annunciation of a typical three-point form. Indeed, the outline above is not present in any apparent way in the text of the sermon. The distinction of "points" is an editorial imposition on the sermon. This is, possibly, the genius of an outline. Too often, its props and supports, looking and sounding as much out of place as an unfinished building that reveals its steel girders and masonry pillars, artificially distort the flow and sense of directness of a sermon. That such supports are necessary is all too clear. Sermons that have none do not go anywhere and achieve little. But perhaps, also, traditional sermons can be too dependent upon such devices. Three-point sermons with clever (but often artificial) alliteration, for example, can all too easily appeal to the architectural mind-set at the expense of the deeper level of the conscience and affections.

Expository Preaching

One central aspect of the Renaissance was a commitment to the study of the original text. To that end, the Renaissance commitment to *ad fontes* proved a marvelously providential encouragement for the Reformers to study the actual text of Scripture rather than engage in moral and ultimately legalistic outbursts. Preaching the Bible on its own terms as the inerrant Word of God meant that the Reformers refused to engage in sermons that consisted simply in the opinions of learned men; rather, preaching became an exercise in declaring the meaning and application of Scripture. This was, for Luther, the glory of preaching, for thereby God's Word was declared. The commitment to expository preaching—opening up what the text of Scripture says according to a series of hermeneutical rules, chiefly that Scripture is self-interpreting and cannot contradict itself—was a necessary corollary of their understanding of what the Bible is and what the Bible is for.

If today's preacher, having succumbed to postmodernity's skepticism, can be caricatured as "one without authority," Luther as preacher signified the opposite. Today's preacher has all too often lost confidence in the authority of the Bible as the Word of God and is left with little to say and no authority for saying it apart from prejudice and personal conviction. Western society no longer recognizes the authority of a clergyman, or even the authority of a preacher. Still less does our society acknowledge the authority of Scripture. In a world of moral relativism, today's preacher questions the right of any individual to deliver a monological address that requires repentance and points the way to an exclusive Savior who alone can save. Luther knew no such restrictions. The freedom and conviction he knew as a preacher lay in an unquestioned commitment to the binding nature of Scripture's authority. Meuser cites Luther to this effect:

> Some pastors and preachers are lazy and no good. They do not pray; they do not study; they do not read; they do not search the Scripture. . . . The call is: watch, study, attend to reading. . . . You cannot read too much in Scripture, what you read you cannot read too carefully, what you read carefully you cannot understand too well . . . what you understand well you cannot teach too well, what you teach well you cannot live too well. . . . Therefore dear . . . . pastors and preachers, pray, read, study, be diligent. . . . This evil, shameful time is no reason for being lazy, for sleeping, and snoring.[25]

Expository preaching—allowing the text to govern the content and shape of the sermon—need not necessarily be a commitment to *lectio continua* preaching. Luther did undertake the latter, preaching almost two hundred

---

25 *WABr*, 53, 218. Cited by Meuser, "Luther as Preacher of the Word of God," 141.

sermons on the gospel of John on Saturdays while the Wittenberg minister, Johannes Bugenhagen of Pomerania (Dr. Pomeranus, as Luther called him), was away in Denmark. These are verse-by-verse expositions of the text of the gospel, sometimes taking only a few verses at a time.

However, Luther also preached catechetical and textual sermons, the former covering essential points of doctrine (particularly the Apostles' Creed) and the latter committed to the lectionary reading for the day at hand.

Catechetical preaching was reintroduced at the Reformation in keeping with a similar practice in the fourth century, largely as a way of instructing those who were about to make a solemn commitment of public profession before the church.[26] Luther's catechetical sermons of 1528, for example, are the first such series recorded for us from the Reformation period and include ten expositions on weekdays over a two-week period. These sermons provided the basis for Luther's Shorter and Larger Catechisms of 1529. The sermons included expositions of the Ten Commandments, the Lord's Prayer, and the Apostles' Creed and explanations of baptism and the Lord's Supper. Five sermons were devoted to the Ten Commandments while only one was given to the Apostles' Creed.[27] Given the (false) accusations of antinomianism sometimes made about Luther's understanding of the place of the moral law in the Christian life, this sermonic ratio seems to suggest the very opposite. The fact is, however, that these sermons were given in a very specific context and (perhaps of greater importance) not during the Sunday services, when it was deemed more appropriate to expound Scripture rather than heads of doctrine.

Discouragement in Preaching

With the standards that Luther imposed upon preaching, his own as much as others', it is not surprising that he was prone to discouragement. In 1530, in particular, he was disconsolate because of what he deemed as insufficient response by the congregation. In 1528, he warned the congregation at the Castle Church that he would stop preaching unless he saw more fruit of the gospel. In 1530, from January to September, Luther preached only three times, and two of those were at the express command of the prince. Employing some hyperbole, he declared that had he known in advance what a miserable call-

---

26 What we tend to call "communicant membership" today.
27 Old, *The Reading and Preaching of the Scriptures*, 18–19.

ing preaching was, twenty-four horses would not have been enough to draw him into it. Preaching, he said, was hard work, "a rotten office, whose misery is such that a person would rather be a swineherd!"[28] In his New Year sermon in 1530, he complained bitterly of the congregation's selfishness. A short time later, he said he would rather preach to raving dogs than to them and that from then on, he would confine himself to the classroom. This gloomy Luther revived after a stay at Coburg and suddenly, without any apology or explanation, he resumed preaching in September 1530. The following year, he was back to his average of 180 sermons a year.

Luther believed that preaching was an essential part of his calling as a Reformer, and apart from this sense of calling, "I would not want to preach another sermon to the end of my days."[29] Despite misgivings he often felt and expressed about the effectiveness of preaching, Luther continued to preach. In the same sermon, Luther expressed himself this way:

> God says, "You must do this regardless of the consequences to you, you must remain in your office." If you are in the ministry and see that you have rascals and knaves, fornicators and adulterers, and robbers in your parish, you must say, "Since this is my duty, I will point sins to peasants, burghers, and noblemen, and rebuke them for these without paying attention to their complaints when they say: 'Look here, you are defaming me!'" For if I held back, I would make myself guilty of your sin. And why should I go to hell for you? They might retort, "Well, I am not asking you to do this; I am not forcing you." Yes, this may be true. . . . If I see adultery or other sins in people and neglect to take the sinners to task, God will visit their sins on me. . . . Do you consider it a good evangelical sermon if I keep silence and let you do as you please?[30]

Luther was a direct preacher, engaging in a battery of rhetorical questioning that engaged his listeners motivationally as much as they did cerebrally. But most of all, it was the gospel of Jesus Christ that engaged him and his sermons. It is impossible to read his sermons today without hearing a man who

---

28 Cited by Meuser in "Luther the Preacher of the Word of God," 146.
29 In the thirty-second sermon on John, preached September 7, 1538. *WA*, 22:372.
30 Ibid., 372–73.

loved Christ and understood the truth of the gospel and its relevance for his listeners. He paved the way for the importance of preaching as a distinctive mark of the Reformation.

If we are to see another reformation in our own time, we will need to preach with the conviction and zeal of Martin Luther. We will need to trust the Bible by the power of the Holy Spirit to do what we cannot—awaken dead hearts and transform lives.

Reflection

LUTHER AND THE LIFE
OF THE PASTOR-THEOLOGIAN

R.C. SPROUL

ugustine . . . Anselm . . . Athanasius . . . Martin Luther . . . John Calvin . . . Jonathan Edwards. These are some of the titans, the veritable giants of church history. Each had his own personality, his own emphasis, his own vocation. They differed in personality, style, and even in points of doctrine. Yet there is one point of similarity that they shared. They were all scholars and pastors. All were world-class academicians who, at the same time, served the church as pastors.

There is no disgrace in being a full-time scholar working exclusively in the academy. Such labor can be an enormous benefit to the church. Sound research adds vital knowledge to our understanding of Scripture and the things of God. For most scholars, however, it is an either/or situation. Either we keep exclusively to the ivory tower or we devote our labors full time to the pastoral work of the church. Rare are those who can be both scholars and pastors.

As a young seminary student, I pondered the ghastly situation of the church in the United States. The influence of liberalism had an iron grip on the mainline churches. It seemed a hopeless task to see any recovery from this malaise. As I studied the writings and the work of the great teachers mentioned above, I saw a pattern emerge, especially from the ministries of Luther, Calvin, and Edwards. I saw that these men were "battlefield theologians." They not only engaged with their scholar-opponents as Luther versus Rome and Erasmus of Rotterdam, or Calvin versus Pigius et al., or Edwards versus the Unitarian and Arminian opponents of his day, but they all took their case to the people. In this regard, they were following in the footsteps of the two greatest theologians who ever walked the earth: the Apostle Paul and the Lord Jesus Christ Himself.

This I saw as a strategy that God in His providence has used over the ages to nurture, protect, and defend His church. It was the strategy I longed to adopt as my own. John Piper has said that it is necessary for the Christian not only to believe the truth, but to defend the truth, and finally to contend for the truth. For Paul, the battlefield started in the public square and then extended to the ends of the earth.

When we recall the issues that developed into the greatest theological conflict in the history of Christendom, the debates that culminated in the sixteenth century, we see that initially these matters grew out of a profoundly pastoral concern. To be sure, the Ninety-Five Theses posted on the church door at Wittenberg were penned in Latin as a request for theological discussion among the faculty members of the university. But what provoked Luther to request such a discussion? Simply put, it was pastoral concern.

Luther had received word of the indulgences that were being sold by Johann Tetzel, who was laboring both for Rome and for the interests of the Fugger banking clan. Tetzel's traveling indulgence show had the markings of a circus and drew thousands of people. Flush with commissions and bonuses, Tetzel claimed that he had saved more souls through indulgences than St. Peter had through the gospel.[1]

Tetzel's work was carried on outside of Wittenberg. The sale of indulgences became so popular that throngs of people from Wittenberg (including many from Luther's own congregation) joined the multitude that crossed the Elbe River to avail themselves of the newly available indulgences. Impenitent members of his congregation boldly displayed their letters of indulgence to their neighbors and even to their pastor.

This travesty of false forgiveness forced Luther not only to question the

---

1 Ernest G. Schwiebert, *Luther and His Times: The Reformation from a New Perspective* (St. Louis: Concordia, 1950), 309. .

matter of indulgences but the whole salvific system of the church, including the treasury of merit itself. Hence, the Ninety-Five Theses were intended for a handful of scholars. Students, however, without Luther's knowledge or permission, took it upon themselves to translate the theses into German, and they distributed them to every city and hamlet in Germany within two weeks. The Reformation was now afoot.

One of the deepest ongoing concerns Luther had as a pastor was to liberate his congregation from the chains of superstition. As people began to leave the Roman Catholic system, they did not expunge from their lives all of their former convictions. This was particularly evident with respect to relics.

The town of Wittenberg boasted one of the largest reliquaries in Germany, amassed by Luther's protector, Frederick the Wise, elector of Saxony. Frederick had spent a fortune to gather precious relics from around the world in the hopes that it would make Wittenberg a mecca for Christian pilgrims, thus enhancing the town as a spiritual and commercial center in Germany. From 1509 to 1518, Frederick's collection of relics had grown to 17,443 pieces with an indulgence value of 127,799 years and 116 days' release from purgatory.[2]

Luther risked the wrath of Frederick by challenging the validity of the use of relics. In the last sermon Luther preached before he died, he stressed the impotence of relics in contrast to the potency of the gospel:

> After all, there is preaching every day, often many times every day, so that we grow weary of it. . . . Alright, go ahead, dear brother, if you don't want God to speak to you every day at home and in your parish church, then be wise and look for something else: in Trier is our Lord God's coat, in Aachen are Joseph's pants and our blessed Lady's chemise; go there and squander your money, buy indulgences and the pope's secondhand junk.[3]

Luther wanted his flock to be fed by the gospel, not the pope's secondhand junk.

As a pastor, Luther was concerned to minister to the souls of his people. He ministered to their grief in this world. He understood the pain of the loss of loved ones as his own soul was wounded by the death of his young

---

2 E. Gordon Rupp, *Luther's Progress to the Diet of Worms* (New York: Harper & Row, 1964), 52.
3 *LW*, 51:390–91.

daughter. He bore the physical pains of a host of maladies in his own body and thus exuded empathy for the physical suffering of others.

But Luther's chief pastoral concern was that his people would know Christ and His gospel. To this end, Luther carried on a profoundly deep practice of intercessory prayer. He said:

> Open your eyes and look into your life and the life of all Christians, particularly the spiritual estate, and you will find that faith, hope, love . . . are languishing. . . . Then you will see that there is need to pray throughout the world, every hour, without ceasing, with tears of blood.[4]

Luther's pastoral heart is seen not only in his prayers but most notably in his preaching. He was a doctor of the church, a professor, and an academic. In his role as a professor, his primary task was to teach. There is a clear difference between teaching and preaching. The teacher instructs; he imparts information to his students. But a theologian/preacher can never sever the two roles of teacher and preacher. The great teacher/preachers of history never taught as mere isolated spectators of the past. They combined exhortation with instruction—inspiration with education. In a word, at times their teaching turned to preaching. In like manner, the scholar/pastor mixes teaching with his preaching.

Luther mirrored this method in his preaching. He was concerned to inform his congregation as well as to exhort it. He insisted that his messages should be clear and simple enough that the unlearned could understand them. He said:

> Infinite and unutterable is the majesty of the Word of God. . . . These words of God are not words of Plato or Aristotle, but God himself is speaking. And those preachers are the most suitable who very simply and plainly, without any airs or subtlety, teach the common people and youth, just as Christ taught the people with homespun parables.[5]

The gospel, the gospel . . . all for the gospel. This is the love, the task, the vocation of all who wear the robes of the theologian and all who wear the gowns of the preacher. Luther was equally comfortable attired in either.

---

4 *What Luther Says*, 1084.
5 Ibid., 1118.

Appendix

THE NINETY-FIVE THESES

Disputation on the Power and Efficacy of Indulgences

October 31, 1517

Out of love for the truth and the desire to bring it to light, the following propositions will be discussed at Wittenberg, under the oversight of the Reverend Father Martin Luther, Master of Arts and Sacred Theology, & Lecturer on these subjects at Wittenberg.

Wherefore he requests that those who are unable to be present and debate orally with us, may do so by letter.

In the Name of Our Lord Jesus Christ. Amen.

1. When our Lord and Master Jesus Christ said "Repent," he intended that the entire life of believers should be repentance.
2. This word *repentance* cannot be understood to mean the sacrament of penance, or the act of confession and satisfaction administered by the priests.
3. Yet it does not mean inward repentance only, as there is no inward repentance that does not manifest itself outwardly through various mortifications of the flesh.
4. The penalty of sin, therefore, continues so long as hatred of self, or true inward repentance, continues, and it continues until our entrance into the kingdom of heaven.

---

6 This text is taken from *Martin Luther's Ninety-Five Theses*, ed. Stephen J. Nichols (Phillipsburg, N.J.: P&R, 2002).

5. The pope does not intend to remit, and cannot remit, any penalties except those that he has imposed either by his own authority or by the authority of the canons.

6. The pope cannot remit any guilt, except by declaring that it has been remitted by God and by assenting to God's work of remission. To be sure, however, the pope may grant remission in cases reserved to his judgment. If his right to grant remission in such cases was disregarded, the guilt would remain entirely unforgiven.

7. God remits guilt to no one whom he does not at the same time humble in all things and also bring him into subjection to his vicar, the priest.

8. The penitential canons are imposed only on the living, and according to them nothing should be imposed on the dying.

9. Therefore the Holy Spirit through the pope is kind to us, because in his decrees he always makes exception of the article of death and of necessity.

10. Ignorant and wicked are the acts of those priests who, in the case of the dying, reserve canonical penances for purgatory.

11. This changing of the canonical penalty to the penalty of purgatory is quite evidently one of the tares that were sown while the bishops slept.

12. In former times the canonical penalties were imposed not after but before absolution, as tests of true contrition.

13. The dying are freed by death from all penalties. They are already dead to canonical laws and have a right to be released from them.

14. The imperfect spiritual health, or the imperfect love, of the dying person necessarily brings with it great fear; and the smaller the love, the greater is the fear.

15. This fear and horror is sufficient in itself alone, to say nothing of other things, to constitute the penalty of purgatory, since it is very near to the horror of despair.

16. Hell, purgatory, and heaven seem to differ as do despair, near despair, and the assurance of safety.

17. Concerning souls in purgatory, it seems necessary that horror should grow less and love increase.

18. It seems unproved, either by reason or Scripture, that they are outside the state of merit, that is, of increasing love.

19. Again, it seems unproved that souls in purgatory, or at least that all of them, are certain or assured of their own blessedness, though we may be quite certain of it.

20. Therefore by "full remission of all penalties" the pope means not actually "of all," but only of those penalties imposed by himself.

21. Therefore those preachers of indulgences are in error, who say that by the pope's indulgences a man is freed from every penalty and is saved.

22. In fact, the pope remits no penalty for the souls in purgatory that, according to the canons, they would have had to pay in this life.

23. If it is at all possible to grant to anyone the remission of all penalties whatsoever, it is certain that this remission can be granted only to the most perfect, that is, to the very few.

24. Therefore, the greater part of the people are necessarily deceived by that indiscriminate and high-sounding promise of release from penalty.

25. The power that the pope has in a general way over purgatory is just like the power that any bishop or curate has in a particular way over his own diocese or parish.

26. The pope does well when he grants remission to souls in purgatory, not by the power of the keys, which in this case he does not possess, but by way of intercession.

27. They preach man-made doctrines who say that so soon as the coin jingles into the money-box, the soul flies out of purgatory.

28. It is certain that when the coin jingles into the money-box, greed and avarice can be increased, but the result of the intercession of the church is in the power of God alone.

29. Who knows whether all the souls in purgatory wish to be bought out of it, as in the legend of Sts. Severinus and Paschal?

30. No one is sure that his own contrition is sincere, much less that he can attain full remission.

31. As the man who is truly repentant is rare, so rare also is the man who truly buys indulgences. Indeed, such men are most rare.

32. They will be condemned eternally, together with their teachers, who believe themselves sure of their salvation because they have letters of pardon.

33. Men must be on their guard against those who say that the pope's pardons are that inestimable gift of God by which man is reconciled to him;

34. For these graces of pardon concern only the penalties of sacramental satisfaction, and these are appointed by man.

35. They preach no Christian doctrine who teach that contrition is not necessary in those who intend to buy souls out of purgatory or to buy confessional privileges.

36. Every truly repentant Christian has a right to full remission of penalty and guilt, even without letters of pardon.

37. Every true Christian, whether living or dead, has part in all the benefits of Christ and the church; and this is granted to him by God, even without letters of pardon.

38. Nevertheless, the remission and participation in the benefits of the church, which are granted by the pope, are in no way to be despised, for they are, as I have said, the declaration of divine remission.

39. It is very difficult, even for the most educated theologians, at one and the same time to commend to the people the abundance of pardons and also the need of true contrition.

40. True contrition seeks and loves penalties, but liberal pardons only relax penalties and cause them to be hated, or at least they give a reason for hating them.

41. Papal indulgences are to be preached with caution, so that the people may not falsely think of them as preferable to other good works of love.

42. Christians are to be taught that the pope does not intend the buying of pardons to be compared in any way to works of mercy.

43. Christians are to be taught that he who gives to the poor or lends to the needy does a better work than buying pardons;

44. Because love grows by works of love, man becomes better by doing works of love. By buying pardons, however, man does not grow better, only more free from penalty.

45. Christians are to be taught that he who sees a man in need and passes him by and gives his money for pardons instead, purchases not the indulgences of the pope, but the indignation of God.

46. Christians are to be taught that unless they have more money than they need, they are bound to reserve what is necessary for their own families, and by no means to squander it on pardons.

47. Christians are to be taught that the buying of pardons is a matter of free will, not of commandment.

48. Christians are to be taught that the pope, in granting pardons, needs and therefore desires their devout prayer for him more than their money.

49. Christians are to be taught that the pope's pardons are useful so long as they do not put their trust in them; but altogether harmful if they lose their fear of God because of them.

50. Christians are to be taught that if the pope knew the exactions of the indulgence preachers, he would rather that St. Peter's church should go to ashes than that it should be built up with the skin, flesh, and bones of his sheep.

51. Christians are to be taught that it would be the pope's wish, as it is his duty, to give of his own money to many of those from whom certain hawkers of pardons cajole money, even though the church of St. Peter might have to be sold.

52. The assurance of salvation by letters of pardon is vain, even though the indulgence commissary or the pope himself were to stake his soul upon it.

53. They are enemies of Christ and the pope who bid the Word of God to be silent in some churches in order that pardons may be preached in others.

54. Injury is done to the Word of God when, in the same sermon, an equal or a longer time is spent on pardons than on the Word.

55. It must be the pope's intention that if pardons, which are a very small thing, are celebrated with one bell, single processions, and ceremonies, then the gospel, which is the very greatest thing, should be preached with a hundred bells, a hundred processions, and a hundred ceremonies.

56. The treasures of the church, out of which the pope grants indulgences, are not sufficiently named or known among the people of Christ.

57. That they are not temporal treasures is certainly evident, for many vendors do not pour out such treasures so easily, but only gather them.

58. Nor are they the merits of Christ and the saints, for even without the pope, these always work grace for the inner man, and the cross, death, and hell for the outward man.

59. St. Laurence said that the treasures of the church were the church's poor, but he spoke according to the usage of the word in his own time.

60. Without being rash we say that the keys of the church, given by Christ's merit, are that treasure;

61. For it is clear that the power of the pope is in itself sufficient for the remission of penalties and of cases reserved for his jurisdiction.

62. The true treasure of the church is the most holy gospel of the glory and grace of God.

63. But this treasure is naturally most odious, for it makes the first to be last.

64. On the other hand, the treasure of indulgences is naturally most acceptable, for it makes the last to be first.

65. Therefore the treasures of the gospel are nets with which they would formerly fish for men of riches.

66. The treasures of the indulgences are nets with which they now fish for the riches of men.

67. The indulgences that the preachers cry as the "greatest graces" are known to be truly such, insofar as they promote gain.

68. In truth, however, they are the absolute smallest graces compared with the grace of God and the piety of the cross.

69. Bishops and curates are bound to admit the commissaries of papal pardons with all reverence.

70. But still more are they bound to strain all their eyes and attend with all their ears, lest these men preach their own dreams instead of the pope's commission.

71. Let him who speaks against the truth of papal pardons be anathema and accursed!

72. But let him who guards against the lust and license of the pardon-preachers be blessed!

73. The pope justly thunders against those who, by any means, contrive harm to the traffic of pardons.

74. But much more does he intend to thunder against those who use the pretext of pardons to contrive injury to holy love and truth.

75. To consider the papal pardons so great that they could absolve a man even if he had committed an impossible sin and violated the Mother of God is madness.

76. We say, on the contrary, that the papal pardons are not able to remove the very least of venial sins, so far as its guilt is concerned.

77. It is said that even St. Peter, if he were now pope, could not bestow greater graces. This is blasphemy against St. Peter and against the pope.

78. We say, on the contrary, that even the present pope, and any pope at all, has greater graces at his disposal: namely, the gospel, powers, gifts of healing, etc., as it is written in 1 Corinthians 12.

79. To say that the cross emblazoned with the papal arms, which is set up by the preachers of indulgences, is of equal worth with the cross of Christ, is blasphemy.

80. Bishops, curates, and theologians who allow such talk to be spread among the people will have to account for this.

81. This unbridled preaching of pardons makes it difficult, even for learned men, to rescue the reverence due to the pope from slander, or even from the shrewd questions of the laity.

82. Such questions as the following: "Why does the pope not empty purgatory, for the sake of holy love and for the sake of desperate souls that are there, if he redeems an infinite number of souls for the sake of miserable money with which to build a church? The former reasons would be most just, while the latter is most trivial."

83. Or: "Why are funeral and anniversary masses for the dead continued, and why does he not return or permit the withdrawal of the endowments founded on their behalf, since it is wrong to pray for the redeemed?"

84. Or: "What is this new piety of God and the pope, that for money they allow a man who is impious and their enemy to buy out of purgatory the pious soul of a friend of God, and do not rather, because of that pious and beloved soul's own need, free it for pure love's sake?"

85. Or: "Why are the penitential canons, long since in actual fact and through disuse abrogated and dead, now satisfied by the granting of indulgences, as though they were still alive and in force?"

86. Or: "Why does not the pope, whose wealth today is greater than the riches of the richest, build this one basilica of St. Peter with his own money, rather than with the money of poor believers?"

87. Or: "What does the pope remit, and what participation in the benefits of the church does he grant, to those who, by perfect contrition, have a right to full remission and participation?"

88. Or: "What greater blessing could come to the church than if the pope were to do a hundred times a day what he now does once, and bestow on every believer these remissions and participation?"

89. Or finally: "Since the pope, by his pardons, seeks the salvation of souls rather than money, why does he suspend the indulgences and pardons granted prior to now, since these have equal efficacy?"

90. To repress these convincing arguments of the laity by force alone, and not to resolve them by giving reasonable answers, is to expose the church and the pope to the ridicule of their enemies, and to leave Christians unsatisfied.

91. If, therefore, pardons were preached according to the spirit and mind of the pope, all these doubts would be readily resolved. Indeed, they would not exist.

92. Away, then, with all those prophets who say to the people of Christ, "Peace, peace," and there is no peace.

93. Blessed be all those prophets who say to the people of Christ, "Cross, cross," and there is no cross!

94. Christians are to be exhorted to be diligent in following Christ, their Head, through penalties, death, and hell;

95. And thus be confident of entering into heaven through many tribulations, rather than through the false assurance of peace.

FOR FURTHER READING

Luther's Writings

Annotated Luther, The. 5 vols. Minneapolis: Fortress.

    Vol. 1: The Roots of Reform. Edited by Timothy J. Wengert. 2015.

    Vol. 2: Word and Faith. Edited by Kirsi I. Stjerna. 2015.

    Vol. 3: Church and Sacraments. Edited by Paul W. Robinson. 2016.

    Vol. 4: Pastoral Writings. Edited by Mary Jane Haemig. 2016.

    Vol. 5: Christian Life in the World. Edited by Hans J. Hillerbrand. Forthcoming.

Bondage of the Will, The. Translated by J.I. Packer and O.R. Johnson. Grand Rapids, Mich.: Baker Academic, 2012.

Luther's Works, 55 vols. Edited by Jaroslav Pelikan and Helmut T. Lehman. Philadelphia: Muhlenberg and Fortress; St. Louis: Concordia, 1955–.

Martin Luther's Basic Theological Writings. Edited by Timothy F. Lull. Minneapolis: Fortress, 1989.

Martin Luther: Selections from His Writings. Edited by John Dillenberger. New York: Anchor, 1958.

Martin Luther's Ninety-Five Theses. Edited by Stephen J. Nichols. Phillipsburg, N.J.: P&R, 2002.

Simple Way to Pray, A. Translated by Matthew C. Harrison. St. Louis: Concordia, 2012.

Three Treatises. Minneapolis: Fortress, 1970.

Biography and Analysis

Bainton, Roland. *Here I Stand: A Life of Martin Luther.* New York: Meridian, 1977.

Dowley, Tim. *Atlas of the European Reformations.* Minneapolis: Fortress, 2012.

Godfrey, W. Robert. *Reformation Sketches: Insights into Luther, Calvin, and the Confessions.* Phillipsburg, N.J.: P&R, 2003.

Hendrix, Scott H. *Martin Luther: Visionary Reformer.* New Haven, Conn.: Yale University Press, 2015.

Lawson, Steven J. *The Heroic Boldness of Martin Luther.* Orlando, Fla.: Reformation Trust, 2013.

Lohse, Bernhard. *Martin Luther's Theology: Its Historical and Systematic Development.* Minneapolis: Fortress, 2011.

Nichols, Stephen J. *Martin Luther: A Guided Tour of His Life and Thought.* Wheaton, Ill.: Crossway, 2002.

Oberman, Heiko A. *Luther: Man between God and the Devil.* New York: Doubleday, 1992.

Pettegree, Andrew. *Brand Luther: How an Unheralded Monk Turned His Small Town into a Center of Publishing, Made Himself the Most Famous Man in Europe—and Started the Protestant Reformation.* New York: Penguin, 2015.

Children's Books

Maier, Paul L. *Martin Luther: A Man Who Changed the World.* St. Louis: Concordia, 2004.

Nichols, Stephen J., and Ned Bustard, *Reformation ABCs: The People, Places, and Things of the Reformation—from A to Z.* Wheaton, Ill.: Crossway. Forthcoming.

Sproul, R.C. *The Barber Who Wanted to Pray.* Wheaton, Ill.: Crossway, 2011.

CONTRIBUTORS

Dr. Joel R. Beeke is president of Puritan Reformed Theological Seminary in Grand Rapids, Mich., pastor of Heritage Netherlands Reformed Congregation in Grand Rapids, and editorial director of Reformation Heritage Books. He is also editor of Banner of Sovereign Grace Truth and vice president of the Dutch Reformed Translation Society. He has authored, coauthored, or edited many books, including *A Puritan Theology* (with Mark Jones), *Parenting by God's Promises*, and *The Reformation Heritage KJV Study Bible*.

Dr. David B. Calhoun is professor of church history emeritus at Covenant Theological Seminary in St. Louis. He previously taught at Covenant College and Columbia International University, served as principal of Jamaica Bible College, and was overseas director of Ministries in Action. He is author of *The Glory of the Lord Risen upon It, Our Southern Zion*, and a two-volume history of Princeton Seminary.

Dr. Aaron Clay Denlinger is department chair in Latin at Arma Dei Academy in Highlands Ranch, Colo., adjunct professor of church history at Westminster Theological Seminary in Philadelphia, and a research fellow for the Puritan Studies Program of the University of the Free State, South Africa. He formerly served as a teaching fellow in church history at the University of Aberdeen in Scotland. He is the editor of *Reformed Orthodoxy in Scotland: Essays on Scottish Theology 1560–1775*.

Dr. Sinclair B. Ferguson is distinguished visiting professor of systematic theology at Westminster Theological Seminary in Philadelphia and a Ligonier teaching fellow. He previously served as senior minister of First Presbyterian Church in Columbia, S.C., and as minister at the historic St. George's–Tron Church in Glasgow, Scotland. A popular speaker and teacher, he is author of numerous books, including *The Whole Christ, In Christ Alone, The Holy Spirit,* and *The Sermon on the Mount.*

Dr. W. Robert Godfrey is president and professor of church history at Westminster Seminary California and a Ligonier teaching fellow. He is a minister in the United Reformed Churches in North America and a council member for the Alliance of Confessing Evangelicals. He is author of several books, including *An Unexpected Journey, Reformation Sketches, God's Pattern of Creation,* and *John Calvin: Pilgrim and Pastor.*

Dr. Michael S. Horton is J. Gresham Machen Professor of Systematic Theology and Apologetics at Westminster Seminary California. He is editor-in-chief of *Modern Reformation* magazine and host of the popular radio show *The White Horse Inn.* He also serves as associate pastor of Christ United Reformed Church in Santee, Calif. He is author of many books, including *The Christian Faith, Pilgrim Theology, Covenant and Salvation, Christless Christianity,* and *Core Christianity,* and he has contributed to numerous other books, journals, and magazines.

Dr. Steven J. Lawson is founder and president of OnePassion Ministries. He is also professor of preaching and dean of the doctor of ministry program at The Master's Seminary, executive editor of *Expositor* magazine, and a Ligonier teaching fellow. He previously served as senior pastor of Christ Fellowship Baptist Church in Mobile, Ala. He is author of nearly two dozen books, including *The Passionate Preaching of Martyn Lloyd-Jones, The Kind of Preaching God Blesses,* and *Foundations of Grace.*

Dr. Sean Michael Lucas is senior minister of First Presbyterian Church in Hattiesburg, Miss., and associate professor of church history at Reformed Theological Seminary in Jackson, Miss. He has written or edited several books, including *For a Continuing Church, God's Grand Design: The Theological Vision of Jonathan Edwards, On Being Presbyterian,* and *What Is Grace?* He is also coeditor of the American Reformed Biographies Series.

Dr. John MacArthur is pastor-teacher of Grace Community Church in Sun Valley, Calif., president of The Master's College and Seminary, and featured teacher on the radio program *Grace to You*. He has written numerous books, including *The Gospel according to Jesus, Charismatic Chaos, Faith Works,* and *Ashamed of the Gospel*. He is also editor of the *MacArthur Study Bible*, which is available in multiple English translations and has been translated into numerous other languages.

Dr. Scott M. Manetsch is professor of church history at Trinity Evangelical Divinity School in Deerfield, Ill. He previously served as assistant professor of religion at Northwestern College (Iowa). He is author of *Calvin's Company of Pastors* and editor of the Reformation Commentary on Scripture, and he is ordained in the Reformed Church in America.

Dr. Stephen J. Nichols is president of Reformation Bible College in Sanford, Fla., and chief academic officer and a teaching fellow for Ligonier Ministries. He previously served as research professor of Christianity and culture at Lancaster Bible College. He is author of several books, including *For Us and for Our Salvation, Jesus Made in America, and Heaven on Earth: Capturing Jonathan Edwards's Vision of Living in Between,* and he is coeditor of the Theologians on the Christian Life series.

Dr. R.C. Sproul is founder and chairman of Ligonier Ministries, copastor of Saint Andrew's Chapel in Sanford, Fla., chancellor of Reformation Bible College, and executive editor of *Tabletalk* magazine. He can be heard on the radio program *Renewing Your Mind,* which is broadcast on hundreds of radio outlets in the United States and around the world. Dr. Sproul is author of more than one hundred books, including *The Holiness of God, Faith Alone,* and *Everyone's a Theologian*. He also serves as general editor of the *Reformation Study Bible*.

Dr. Derek W.H. Thomas is senior minister of First Presbyterian Church in Columbia, S.C., and Robert Strong Professor of Systematic and Pastoral Theology at Reformed Theological Seminary in Atlanta. He is also a Ligonier teaching fellow. He previously served at First Presbyterian Church in Jackson, Miss. He is author of many books, including *How the Gospel Brings Us All the Way Home, Calvin's Teaching on Job, Let's Study Galatians,* and *Praying the Saviour's Way*.

Dr. Gene Edward Veith is professor of literature emeritus at Patrick Henry College in Purcellville, Va. He previously served as provost at Patrick Henry College, culture editor at *World* magazine, and as professor of English at Concordia University Wisconsin. He is author of more than twenty books, including *God at Work, Christianity and Literature,* and *Reading between the Lines.*

Dr. Guy Prentiss Waters is James M. Baird Jr. Professor of New Testament at Reformed Theological Seminary in Jackson, Miss. He is also ordained as a teaching elder in the Presbyterian Church in America. He previously taught at Duke Divinity School and Belhaven University. He is author of several books, including *What's in the Bible, A Christian's Pocket Guide to Justification, How Jesus Runs the Church,* and *Acts.*

Dr. Terry Yount serves as organist of Saint Andrew's Chapel in Sanford, Fla., and as dean of Saint Andrew's Conservatory of Music. He earned his doctor of musical arts from the Eastman School of Music at the University of Rochester, N.Y. He has published reviews, editorial pieces, and articles for and about church music for *World* magazine, *Reformation Today, The Hymn, The American Organist,* and *Tabletalk.*

Interior Artwork

1: *Martin Luther's 95 Theses,* Ferdinand Pauwels / Photo: akg-images
2: *Luther Before the Reichstag in Worms,* bpk, Berlin / Staatsgalerie, Stuttgart, Germany // Art Resource, NY
3: *Portrait of Martin Luther as an Augustinian Monk,* c.1523-24 (oil on vellum on panel), Cranach, Lucas, the Elder / Germanisches Nationalmuseum, Nuremberg, Germany / Bridgeman Images
4: *Martin Luther,* Cranach, Lucas, the Elder / © Nationalmuseum, Stockholm, Sweden / Bridgeman Images
5: *Martin Luther Translating the Bible,* Gustav Adolph, Spangenberg, bpk, Berlin / Nationalgalerie, Staatliche Museen, Berlin, Germany / Art Resource, NY
6: *Luther as Professor,* 1529 (oil on panel), Cranach, Lucas, the Elder / Schlossmuseum, Weimar, Germany / Bridgeman Images

SCRIPTURE INDEX

SUBJECT INDEX